Federal Preemption: The Silent Revolution

Federal Preemption
THE SILENT REVOLUTION

Joseph F. Zimmerman

Iowa State University Press / Ames

JOSEPH F. ZIMMERMAN is a professor of political science in the Graduate School of Public Affairs, State University of New York at Albany, and is research director for the State Legislative Commission on Critical Transportation Choices.

© 1991 Iowa State University Press, Ames, Iowa 50010

Manufactured in the United States of America
⊗ Printed on acid-free paper

First edition, 1991

Library of Congress Cataloging-in-Publication Data
Zimmerman, Joseph Francis
    Federal preemption : the silent revolution / Joseph F. Zimmerman. – 1st ed.
    p. cm.
    Includes bibliographical references and index.
    ISBN 0-8138-1933-4
    1. Exclusive and concurrent legislative powers – United States. 2. Federal government – United States. I. Title.
KF4600.Z56   1991
320.473′049 – dc20   90-49105

Contents

Preface

Revolutionary changes in the American federal system since the mid-1960s that make the system considerably more malleable have raised important questions about the future roles of the states. In 1985, for example, the U.S. Supreme Court issued a decision, *Garcia v. San Antonio Metropolitan Transit Authority,* 469 U.S. 528, suggesting that the sovereignty of states exists at the pleasure of the Congress.

By 1965, the Congress concluded that incentives – grants-in-aid and tax credits – were insufficient to stimulate the desired subnational governmental response and that its powers of preemption would have to be exercised more freely if national goals were to be established. In deciding to use its preemptory powers, Congress did not abandon the use of financial incentives to procure the assistance of states and their political subdivisions, although many incentives were reduced or eliminated in the 1980s.

An explosion has occurred in the number of preemptive statutes enacted by Congress based on its latent delegated and implied powers. In certain instances, Congress assumed complete reponsibility for a regulatory function, as illustrated by a decision to assume total responsibility for establishing maximum truck sizes and weights on certain highways. In other instances, Congress prodded the states to take more vigorous regulatory action, particularly in the environmental area, under the threat of total federal assumption of responsibility if a state fails to act.

The pervasiveness of federal preemption in the closing years of the twentieth century has produced a complexity in nation-state-local relations that is baffling to elected officials, bureaucrats, and citizens. This exploratory study is designed to make the system more understandable by examining the mechanisms that Congress has employed to structure nation-state relations in the period since 1965. One product of this study is a small contribution to the theory of American federalism, emphasizing its dynamic metamorphic nature.

This work should generate case studies of each of the approaches employed by Congress to fashion intergovernmental relations and of the costs incurred by subnational governments in complying with federal mandates. Such a series of case studies will prove invaluable in refining the broad outline of a modified federalism theory contained in this volume.

Studies are also needed to determine the effectiveness of each type of federal preemption in achieving policy objectives and promoting intergovernmental cooperation where essential. The results of such analyses can provide guidance to Congress when it considers employment of or changes in the exercise of its preemptive powers in the future.

After an introduction to recent preemptive statutes and theories of federalism in Chapter 1, Chapter 2 examines the Articles of Confederation and Perpetual Union, the drafting of (and campaign for the adoption of) the U.S. Constitution, power distribution under the Constitution, expansion of national powers, and the intent of the framers of the fundamental document.

Informal federal preemption is the subject of Chapter 2—the use of conditional grants-in-aid and tax credits by Congress to induce subnational units to execute national policies. Chapter 3 examines criticisms of categorical grants-in-aid, federal responses to the criticisms, tax credits, block grants, general revenue sharing, the "Reagan Revolution," and the federal-mandate problem.

Chapter 4 examines the employment of total-preemption powers by Congress and the nature of congressional preemption, contains a typology of total federal preemption, and presents two case studies involving total federal preemption.

Imperium in Imperio and partial federal preemption are the focal points of Chapter 5. The nature of an *Imperium in Imperio* is explained, and a typology of *Imperium in Imperio* is presented. In addition, the chapter presents a typology of partial federal preemption, illustrating the manner in which Congress has structured national-state relations in various functional areas.

Chapter 6 examines the role of the judiciary in federal preemption and points out that the courts can nullify laws of subnational units if the those laws conflict with the guarantees of the Constitution. More importantly, the courts play key roles in determining whether Congress intended to preempt in the absence of an explicit preemption provision, the extent of the preemption, and whether Congress has exceeded its constitutional authority in enacting a pre-emptive statute.

The concluding chapter, "The Silent Revolution," focuses on the various types of preemptive statutes enacted by Congress, the accountability-responsibility problem, congressional and administrative responsiveness to the complaints of the states and their subdivisions, a modified theory of federalism incorporating elements of informal and formal preemption, the fiscal note process, the federal-mandate problem, a typology of federal mandates, and suggestions relative to mandate reimbursement.

This volume is the result of many years' study of federal preemption, and its completion was heavily dependent upon the cooperation of numerous academic and government officials who supplied information and answered inquiries. Without their support, the book would not have been possible. I also owe a debt of gratitude to Seung-ho Lee for research assistance, to Margaret B. Zimmerman for her editorial assistance, to Maxine H. Morman for typing the manuscript, and to Robert K. Burdette for copyediting. Any errors of fact or misinterpretation, of course, are solely my responsibility.

Federal Preemption: The Silent Revolution

I

Metamorphic Federalism

he optimal degree of centralization of political power in a federal system is a subject of never-ending controversy as dramatic changes in the means of production, degree of urbanization, and technology produce continuing pressures for readjustments in the respective competencies of the national government and the states. Fortunately, the drafters of the U.S. Constitution decided to formulate a lithe document generally capable of responding effectively to new challenges. Inclusion in the Constitution of general terms and phrases, provision for formal constitutional amendments, and authorization for Congress to employ partial and total preemptive powers relative to several concurrent and reserved powers of the states ensured that the original distribution of political power between the two planes of government would not remain static. *Formal preemption,* the principal focus of this book, is the authority granted to the Congress by the U.S. Constitution to assume partial or total responsibility for a governmental function, thereby delimiting the roles of the states and their political subdivisions.

A genuine *independence* model of nation-state relations never existed in the United States, although the model was approximated at the beginning of the federal system. The original federal model was largely "symbiotic" in terms of nation-state relations, two planes of government coexisting in close proximity with relatively little contact and one plane not encroaching seriously upon the preserve of the other.

By the middle of the twentieth century, the system approximated a *mutuality* model, reflecting the interdependence of the planes and the reliance of one plane upon the others for the performance of certain functions or functional components, standard setting, or financial assistance. Increasing federal preemption of traditional state and local governmental responsibilities since 1965 has produced an intergovernmental revolution of the magnitude of that produced earlier by federal conditional grants-in-aid, yet the impact of the preemption revolution has not been recognized fully in its implications for the governance system in the future.

The focal points of this book are the accretion of national powers, changing roles of various actors in the federal governance system, preemption criteria, structuring of nation-state relations by congressional employment of total and partial preemptive powers, accountability of governments to the citizenry where responsibility for action or inaction is shared by two or three planes of government, federal preemption and goal achievement, congressional and Reagan-administration responsiveness to the concerns of states and their political subdivisions, modification of current federalism theory, and fiscal implications of federal mandates.

Centralized Political Power

In 1788, opponents of the proposed U.S. Constitution feared that the document's redistribution of certain formal powers between Congress and the states without formal constitutional amendments would convert a federal system into a unitary system similar to the existing state-local legal relationships under the ultra vires rule. Elbridge Gerry, a Massachusetts delegate to the Constitutional Convention, expressed the views of many citizens opposed to the proposed fundamental document.

My principal objections to the plan, are, that there is no adequate provision for a representation of the people—that they have no security for the right of election—that some of the powers of the Legislature are ambiguous, and others indefinite and dangerous—that the Executive is blended with and will have an undue influence over the Legislature—that the judicial department will be oppressive—that treaties of the highest importance may be formed by the President with the advice of two thirds of a quorum of the Senate—and that the system is without the security of a bill of rights.[1]

As noted in Chapter 2, the *Federalist Papers* were written by Hamilton, Jay, and Madison to allay these fears of overcentralization of political power, and the Bill of Rights was proposed and ratified in response to these fears.

Although concern over the development of a federal Leviathan continued throughout the nineteenth century, it was not until the Great Depression of the 1930s that predictions were made that the states and the federal system would vanish. Writing in 1933, Luther Gulick, director of the Institute of Public Administration, maintained that "the American State is finished" and added:

The revolution has already taken place. The States have failed; the Federal Government has assumed responsibility for the work. The Constitution and the law must be made to conform to avoid needless complications, judicial squirmings, and great waste of time and money. Without clean-cut constitutional revisions, the States will continue to maintain their futile duplicating organizations at great expenses.

All essential powers affecting economic planning and control must be taken from the States and given to the Nation. . . .

What would the States then become? They would become organs of local government. They would abandon their wasteful and bungling endeavors and pretense of competency in the field of national economics and settle down to perform honestly and successfully their allotted tasks in creating and maintaining the organs of local government and service.[2]

In 1939, Harold J. Laski declared that federalism was obsolete and in 1948 wrote that "the States are provinces of which the sovereignty has never since 1789 been real."[3]

Felix Morley, in 1959, offered an explanation for the drift of power to Washington.

State governments, with a few honorable exceptions, are both ill-designed and ill-equipped to cope with the problems which a dynamic society can not, or will not solve for itself. State constitutions are in many cases unduly restrictive. Their legislatures meet too briefly and have the most meagre technical assistance. . . . Governors generally have inadequate executive control over a pattern of local governments unnecessarily complex and confusing.[4]

To a large extent, Morley was convinced that Hamilton's forecast was correct: Political power would shift to the national government if the states failed to "administer their affairs with uprightness and prudence."[5]

In 1960, an English observer of the American federal system, Professor D. W. Brogan, concluded that the states possess relatively few important powers.

Of the division of powers, probably the least important today is that between the Union and the States. There is, of course, an irreducible minimum of federalism. The States can never be reduced to being mere counties, but in practice, they may be little more than mere counties. The Union may neglect to exercise powers that it has and so leave them to the States (subject to varying Supreme Court doctrines as to whether the States can legislate freely in the mere absence of federal legislation, on matters affecting interstate commerce for instance). But in a great many fields of modern legislation, States' rights are a fiction, because the economic and social integration of the United States has gone too far for them to remain a reality. They are, in fact, usually argued for, not by zealots believing that the States can do better than the Union in certain fields, but by prudent calculators who know that the States can do little or nothing, which is what the defenders of States' rights want them to do.[6]

It is interesting to note that the preceding comments on the impotence of the states were written prior to the exercise by Congress of its partial preemptive powers, which reduced significantly the discretionary authority of the states and, by implication, their political subdivisions'. Yet no scholar has recently suggested that the states have become powerless.

The United States has undergone a constitutional paradox since Congress began to exercise its partial preemptive powers in 1965. The states have both less and more discretionary authority today than prior to 1965. In terms of the ability to exercise a wide range of formal powers without national constraints, the states are weaker today because of congressional and judicial preemption. Yet the states are exercising powers today that they generally did not exercise before 1965. In other words, the universe of exercised powers has been expanded tremendously by partial federal preemption and has resulted in the states exercising new powers at the same time that they were losing freedom to exercise certain powers because of total federal preemption.

In effect, partial federal preemption has pressured the states into undertaking new regulatory activities, resulting in an overall expansion of their exercised powers. In employing its powers of partial preemption, Congress relies upon the states to conduct regulatory programs meeting or exceeding minimum national standards, and the states generally possess relatively wide discretionary authority in administering such programs.

Changing Roles

The expansion of national power via conditional grants-in-aid and partial federal preemption has produced a number of significant changes in the roles of Congress, president, federal bureaucrats, U.S. judiciary, state governor, state legislature, state bureaucrats, local government chief executives and governing bodies, local bureaucrats, interest groups, and citizens. Congress often simultaneously employs conditional grants-in-aid and partial preemption to achieve national policy goals.

Congress no longer confines its attention exclusively to foreign affairs, national defense, and major public-works projects such as the Boulder Dam, and has become involved deeply in designing programs to solve traditional state and local government problems in urban and rural areas throughout the nation. In part, Congress has responded to the pressures of interest groups and has also generated interest-group pressures through congressional activism.

As chief executive, the president is responsible for budgeting and directing myriad federal domestic programs and is the object of intense pressuring by interest groups and citizens as federal partial preemption becomes more common.

The role of federal bureaucrats, although their numbers have remained nearly constant since the end of World War II, has been enhanced dramatically as Congress typically enacts "skeleton" partial-preemption laws outlining a new program or policy and authorizes administrative agencies to draft and promulgate implementing rules and regulations. The responsibilities of federal bureaucrats include reviewing and accepting or rejecting state and local government applications for federal grants-in-aid and analyzing state plans for conformance to federal standards under partial-preemption statutes prior to delegating primacy in regulation to the states.

The U.S. judiciary continues to play its customary referee role but more significantly has become deeply involved in broad policy-making in areas such as public schools and the environment, even to the point of establishing judicial receivership of a public school system, as described in Chapter 6.

Partial federal preemption of traditional state responsibilities has changed the balance of power between the governor and the state legislature as various federal partial-preemption statutes, and accompanying rules and regulations, delegate powers to governors that are not assigned to governors by their respective state constitutions and statutes. The new roles of governors are described in Chapter 5.

Partial federal preemption has forced state legislatures to amend statutes to bring them into conformity with federal standards or lose responsibility for the partially preempted function and possibly federal grants-in-aid.

Initiation of new programs by states in response to partial federal preemption has increased the importance of state bureaucrats administering such programs because they develop and promulgate implementing regulations. In developing such regulations, state bureaucrats must work closely with their federal counterparts, who are required by preemption laws to review state rules and regulations for their conformance with federal minimum requirements. Extensive negotiations between bureaucrats on the two planes of government are often essential for the development of acceptable state regulations.

Local government chief executives do not receive grants of power from federal partial-preemption statutes but are subject to the provisions of the statutes and their implementing rules and regulations. The federal standards are typically administered by the state government, and local chief executives may have to seek clarification or waivers of the standards or extension of time for their governments to meet the standards.

Local governing bodies are affected by federal preemption statutes to the extent that local public facilities do not meet minimum federal standards such as air and water quality, and the governing bodies must appropriate funds for necessary improvements to existing facilities and/or construction of new facilities. Chapter 7 examines the federal mandates to state and local governments, and addresses the question whether states and their political subdivisions should be reimbursed for the costs of complying with the mandates.

The expansion of national government activities and the increasing importance of interest groups, public and private, are correlated positively. As the national government became involved extensively in traditional state and local governmental responsibilities, it was natural that interest groups would transfer part of their attention to Washington, D.C. In particular, interest groups unable to achieve their goals on the local and state planes have focused their resources on Congress, the president, and the bureaucracy, with varying degrees of success.

Economic interest groups have typically worked against proposed federal regulation in the belief that they would be more successful in influencing state regulators and that state regulation might not be as stringent as federal regulation. A principal exception has been the automobile industry, which lobbied for total federal preemption of motor-vehicle safety standards and regulation of emissions from motor vehicles. The industry was concerned that absent total federal preemption of emissions, the various manufacturers would have to build different engines for sale in states with varying emission standards. Similarly, the trucking industry and the Teamsters Union lobbied Congress to preempt totally maximum truck sizes and weights, a subject examined in Chapter 4.

Preemption Criteria

Considerable controversy has swirled around the questions of when and under what conditions Congress should preempt the authority of the states and their political subdivisions. Concern that too much political power had shifted from the states to the national government led President Dwight D. Eisenhower in 1953 to appoint the Commission on Intergovernmental Relations to conduct a study of the federal system.

In its 1955 report, the commission identified the following conditions justifying federal preemption:

(a) When the National Government is the only agency that can summon the resources needed for an activity. For this reason the Constitution entrusts defense to the National Government. Similarly, primary responsibility for governmental action in maintaining economic stability is given to the National Government because it alone can command the main resources for the task.

(b) When the activity cannot be handled within the geographic and jurisdictional limits of smaller units, including those that could be created by compact. Regulation of radio and television is an extreme example.

(c) When the activity requires a nationwide uniformity of policy that cannot be achieved by interstate action. Sometimes there must be an undeviating standard and hence an exclusively national policy, as in immigration and naturalization, the currency, and foreign relations.

(d) When a State through action or inaction does injury to the people of other States. One of the main purposes of the commerce clause was to eliminate State practices that hindered the flow of goods across State lines. On this ground also, national action is justified to prevent unrestrained exploitation of an essential natural resource.

(e) When States fail to respect or protect basic political and civil rights that apply throughout the United States.[7]

To a large extent, the conditions identified by the commission are a restatement of the delegated or expressed powers of Congress, including the Fourteenth Amendment.

In 1984, the U.S. Advisory Commission on Intergovernmental Relations released a report containing five principles to guide Congress in exercising its powers of preemption:

1) to protect basic political and civil rights guaranteed to all American citizens under the Constitution;
2) to ensure national defense and the proper conduct of foreign relations;
3) to establish certain uniform and minimum standards in areas affecting the flow of interstate commerce;
4) to prevent state and local actions which substantially and adversely affect another State or its citizens; or
5) to assure essential fiscal and programmatic integrity in the use of federal grants and contracts into which state and local governments freely enter.[8]

It is instructive to compare the 1955 views of the Commission on Intergovernmental Relations and the 1984 views of the Advisory Commission on Intergovernmental Relations with the "Fundamental Federalism Principles" outlined by President Ronald Reagan in 1987.

(a) Federalism is rooted in the knowledge that our political liberties are best assured by limiting the size and scope of the national government.
(b) The people of the States created the national government when they delegated to it those enumerated governmental powers relating to matters beyond the competence of the individual States. All other sovereign powers, save those expressly prohibited the States by the Constitution, are reserved to the States or to the people.
(c) The constitutional relationship among sovereign governments, State and national, is formalized in and protected by the Tenth Amendment to the Constitution.
(d) The people of the States are free, subject only to the restrictions in the Constitution itself or in constitutionally authorized Acts of Congress, to define the moral, political, and legal character of their lives.
(e) In most areas of governmental concern, the States uniquely possess the constitutional authority, the resources, and the competence to discern the sentiments of the people and to govern accordingly. In Thomas Jefferson's words, the States are "the most competent administrations for our domestic concerns and the surest bulwarks against antirepublican tendencies."
(f) The nature of our constitutional system encourages a healthy diversity in the public policies by the people of the several States according to their own

conditions, needs, and desires. In the search for enlightened public policy, individual States and communities are free to experiment with a variety of approaches to public issues.

(g) Acts of the national government—whether legislative, executive, or judicial in nature—that exceed the enumerated powers of that government under the Constitution violate the principle of federalism established by the Framers.

(h) Policies of the national government should recognize the responsibility of—and should encourage opportunities for—individuals, families, neighborhoods, local governments and private associations to achieve their personal, social, and economic objectives through cooperative effort.

(i) In the absence of clear constitutional or statutory authority, the presumption to sovereignty should rest with the individual States. Uncertainties regarding the legitimate authority of the national government should be resolved against regulation at the national level.[9]

Structuring Nation-State Relations

Constitutional authorization for Congress to exercise powers of total and partial preemption without restrictions or guidelines has produced a wide variety of structural arrangements in nation-state relations. In addressing a major problem considered to be of national importance, Congress tends to develop a solution de novo. To date, there has been no major comprehensive study identifying and assessing (1) the effectiveness of the various structural approaches employed by Congress to preempt partially or totally the powers of the states and their political subdivisions or (2) the impact of federal preemption upon the viability of subnational governments.

The heart of a federal system is an *Imperium in Imperio,* an empire within an empire, with legislative bodies on at least two planes of government exercising relatively autonomous political powers. Two types of concurrent powers, a subject examined in Chapter 5, are authorized by the Constitution. The power to tax represents one type, and Congress lacks authority to preempt formally the taxing powers of the states unless the exercise of such powers places an undue burden on interstate commerce.

The other type of concurrent powers exercised by the states is subject to partial or total preemption by Congress. The power of Congress to preempt the states relative to these concurrent powers is highlighted by Article VI of the Constitution, stipulating that "this Constitution, and the laws of the United States which shall be made in pursuance thereof . . . shall be the supreme law of the land; . . . anything in the Constitution or laws of any State to the contrary notwithstanding." In effect, certain concurrent powers are coordinate powers, and other concurrent powers are subordinate, subject to total or partial preemption by Congress.

Congress has possessed the power to preempt totally certain concurrent powers since 1789 but did not exercise such a power until 1898 when state bankruptcy laws were nullified. The second exercise of the power of total preemption occurred with the enactment of the Atomic Energy Act of 1946. Whereas the national government possesses the ability to regulate bankruptcies without assistance from the states and their subdivisions, experience with the Atomic Energy Act of 1946 reveals a need for assistance by subnational units, as described in Chapter 4.

Congress has recognized that the states can play significant roles in the administration of total-preemption statutes and has amended several — Atomic Energy, Grain Standards, Railroad Safety — by authority the responsible federal administrator to make limited regulatory turnbacks to the states. In addition, Congress has authorized the governor of one state to petition the Secretary of Transportation for removal of preemption and also authorized the governor or state legislature to veto a federal administrative decision based upon a total-preemption statute, subject to a veto override by Congress.

One of the most interesting types of federal preemption is *contingent preemption,* as illustrated by the Federal Voting Rights Act of 1965, described in Chapter 4. Under provisions of this nationally suspensive law, a state or a local government becomes subject to the act only if two conditions prevail.

The major irritant in nation-state relations is federal mandating of state laws. Particularly galling to subnational governments is the decision of the Supreme Court in *Garcia,* upholding the extension of provisions of the Fair Labor Standards Act to employees of states and their subdivisions.[10]

Partial federal preemption of traditional state and local responsibilities has become common since 1965 and has worked a revolution, albeit a relatively silent one, in intergovernmental relations. Chapter 5 describes the variety of partial-preemption statutes enacted by Congress, including those creating an *Imperium in Imperio,* adopting a state standard, authorizing additional uses as determined by a state for a federally regulated product, combining partial preemption and *Imperium in Imperio,* and providing for state transfer of regulatory responsibility to the national government.

In effect, under partial preemption an *Imperium in Imperio* exists at the sufferance of Congress, which in its wisdom may decide to assume total responsibility for a regulatory function. The major difference between a true *Imperium in Imperio* and one established by minimum standards partial-preemption statutes is that the latter's establishment is dependent upon a state's voluntarily agreeing to submit a plan to the appropriate federal agency and to accept the primacy delegated to the state by the agency.

The Accountability-Responsibility Problem

Partial federal preemption creates a degree of confusion about the respective powers of the states, and Congress has produced such a complex intertwining of the powers of the two planes that it is difficult for government officials, as well as citizens, to determine which plane is responsible for solving major public problems.

If a genuine system of "dual" federalism existed with no shared powers, citizens would experience relatively little difficulty in identifying the plane responsible for a function or a functional component. The general lack of congressional interest in exercising powers of preemption on a regular basis until the latter part of the 1960s preserved in general a system of governance in which accountability and responsibility could be fixed with relative ease. Conditional grants-in-aid did allow subnational government officials to blame the federal government for certain unpopular actions by maintaining that they were "mandated" to take the actions. In fact, the "mandates" were conditions-of-aid that could have been avoided by failing to apply for or accept grants-in-aid from the national government.

Partial federal preemption does subject the States to national controls, but the extent and variety of these controls vary considerably from one preemptive statute to another, as outlined in Chapter 5. While one can argue that the system may function more effectively if preemptive statutes are tailored to address each problem in the most effective manner, one product of this approach is citizen confusion.

Federal preemption, total and partial, reduces citizen control of government as the decision-making forum is shifted from local governments and the states to Congress. This disadvantage of federal preemption may be offset in the eyes of many citizens by advantages that can flow from federal preemption. In Chapter 7, suggestions are advanced to clarify responsibilities under partial-preemption statutes.

Federal Preemption and Goal Achievement

The basic justification for the exercise of preemptive powers by Congress is the solution of major public problems in the most effective and efficient manner. To date, there have been relatively few studies of the effectiveness of the various types of partial and total preemption employed by Congress.

Studies of one total-preemption program — the Agreement States Program in the nuclear area — have reached a positive conclusion that the program is effective and popular with the states. Relative to partial-preemption statutes, the general public is aware that the air-quality and water-quality preemptive statutes have failed to achieved their goals because Congress has been forced to grant extensions of time for the achievement of mandated standards by the states and their subdivisions.

Chapter 7 examines the question whether Congress, in mandating the achievement of statutory goals by specific dates, was realistic in view of the fact that Congress did not take into account the technical feasibility of achieving certain standards or the financial and political ability of the states and local governments to comply with the standards by the specified dates.

Congressional Responsiveness

The Constitution originally had a built-in safeguard ensuring that Congress would not enact preemptive statutes that were unwanted by the states. Election of U.S. senators by state legislatures was an effective guarantee that states could indirectly veto actions of the popularly elected House of Representatives. The Constitution of the Federal Republic of Germany currently provides that members of the Bundesrat (upper house) of Parliament are elected by the Länder (states).

Jackson Pemberton, letting the authors of the Constitution speak for him, attributed the fundamental changes in federal-state relations to the adoption of the Seventeenth Amendment.

We noted with concern that the universal nature of legislatures is to legislate too much, and that unless some opposing force were supplied, the United States Congress would eventually infringe every State prerogative until the rights of the people vested in the States were consumed. We talked much of the need for Senators to preserve the sovereignty of their States because they were the best defenders of the rights the people had already lost to their States' governments. Hence, Senators were elected by the State legislature, were to answer to the State, and were to represent the interests of the State in the Congress. Amendment XVII destroyed that balance and the Senate became another House.[11]

While the Seventeenth Amendment removed a safeguard against preemptive actions by Congress, the amendment was ratified in 1913 and Congress did not commence to exercise its preemptive powers on a regular basis until 1965. The reasons for the sharp increase in the enactment of preemptive statutes are described in Chapters 4 and 5.

A focal point of this study is congressional responsiveness to the concerns of the states and their subdivisions. Chief Justice John Marshall of the U.S. Supreme Court wrote in 1824, relative to the interstate commerce power, that "the wisdom and the discretion of Congress, their identify with the people, and the influence which their constituents possess at elections, are . . . the sole restraints on which they have relied to secure them from its abuse.[12] In 1985, Justice Harry A. Blackmun of the Supreme Court modified the Marshall statement and wrote in *Garcia* that while the reach of the commerce power of Congress is great, "the political process ensures that laws that unduly burden the States will not be promulgated."[13] The Blackmun thesis can be extended to preemptive decisions of the Supreme Court, a subject examined in detail in Chapter 6. If the Court misinterprets the intent of Congress and holds a statute to be preemptive, Congress is free to amend the statute to remove the preemption.

The growing criticism of the categorical grant-in-aid system in the early 1960s induced President Lyndon B. Johnson to initiate a number of administrative actions. Similarly, President Richard M. Nixon proclaimed his "New Federalism" policy, which was designed to shift political power to the subnational governments. President James E. Carter, a former governor of Georgia, was particularly sensitive to federal regulations, and the deregulation movement commenced during his administration.

The most successful president in persuading Congress to shift authority to the states and reducing the volume of federal regulations affecting the states was Ronald Reagan. His "New Federalism" program, discussed in Chapter 3, emphasized replacement of categorical grants-in-aid with block grants, deregulation, and an accelerated delegation of primacy under partial-preemption statutes to the states. Although states generally have welcomed these changes, objections have been raised against the reduction in federal financial assistance provided to subnational governments in an era when these units are mandated by preemptive statutes to meet specified minimum standards.

Federalism Theory

The theory of American federalism is mentioned prominently in writings on the American political system, but the references are often little more than general phrases such as *dual* federalism and *cooperative* federalism. Dissatisfaction with the explanatory values of these descriptors led in the 1950s and 1970s to a myriad of new descriptors. In 1984, William H. Steward identified 497 such figurative descriptions.[14]

The theory of dual federalism is easy to describe in terms of the complete separation of state and national powers. Similarly, the theory of cooperative federalism can be defined readily as the cooperative activities of the three planes of government. Unfortunately, neither theory adequately explains American federalism two hundred years after its inauguration.

As described more completely in Chapter 2, Congress possesses certain exclusive powers that it is authorized to exercise and the states are forbidden to exercise. Furthermore, the states possess certain powers — such as the provision of services and control of local governments — that are not generally subject to direct national control, as Congress is not given these powers. These facts are in accord with the theory of "dual" federalism.

"Cooperative" federalism also continues to exist, the Internal Revenue Service and state tax and finance departments exchanging computer tapes of income tax returns, the Federal Bureau of Investigations operating a fingerprint service for state and local police, and Congress providing grants-in-aid to subnational units.

Neither theory, however, takes account of the increasing use of preemptive powers by Congress. In effect, the national legislature has produced a "silent" revolution in the American federal system by employing its powers of total and partial preemption to structure new relationships between the national government and the states.

    Daniel J. Elazar, who has made important contributions to fed-
eralism theory, pointed out in 1987: "[T]he center-periphery model of
statehood is being challenged by the champions of a new model,
which views the polity as a matrix of overlapping, interlocking units,
powers, and relationships. The efforts to come to grips intellectually
with all of these phenomena have been slower than the movement in
the real world. The accepted intellectual models have tended to lag
behind actual developments."[15]

    A full appreciation of the complexities and dynamics associated
with the ever-changing division and sharing of governmental powers
cannot be gained from existing federalism theory, which tends to focus upon the paradigms of centralization and noncentralization of
political power. Such a linear view of political power is useful in
positing the extremes but is not helpful in promoting an understanding of the nuances of a complex system with various elements of
centralization, noncentralization, and decentralization.

    Although federalism is an abstract organizational principle that
does not determine precisely the boundary line between national and
state powers, we can identify three broad spheres of power: a nation-
controlling sphere, a state-controlling sphere, and a shared national-
state sphere. In practice, the shared national-state sphere may also
involve general-purpose local governments. The goal of the drafters
of the Constitution to achieve "a more perfect Union" has been
achieved in the sense that the planes of government have become
more unified through interlinkages.

    A review of congressional total- and partial-preemption statutes
reveals a new synthesis of elements to be incorporated in a modified
theory of federalism that will have greater explanatory value than
existing theories. More than a separation of all political powers between two planes of government and interplane relations must be
embodied in a dynamic theory of federalism. The intertwining of
regulatory programs, produced by incentives and prescriptions, and
constantly changing relationships between the planes are the key characteristics of functioning federalism in the late twentieth century.

    I suggest that a comprehensive theory of dynamic federalism
must encompass elements of *Imperium in Imperio,* cooperative relationships, informal federal preemption, total federal preemption, and
partial federal preemption, which are examined in the following chapters. Chapter 7 reviews current federalism theory in more detail and
spells out suggested revisions.

Fiscal Implications of Federal Mandates

Local governments have long complained about state mandates requiring the governments to undertake certain activities or to provide services meeting minimum state standards and have sought reimbursement for the costs associated with mandate compliance.[16] Today, the states and local governments seek reimbursement of the costs incurred in complying with federal mandates.

With the termination of the federal general revenue-sharing program for general-purpose local governments at the end of 1986 and reductions in federal grants-in-aid to these units in the 1980s, many substate units are experiencing financial problems. Responding to the problems of these local governments and the complaints of the states, Senator David F. Durenberger of Minnesota and other senators introduced an Intergovernmental Regulatory Relief Act, requiring the national government to reimburse subnational governments for all additional directs costs imposed by federal mandates subsequent to enactment of the proposed law.[17] In Chapter 7, I develop a typology of federal mandates and offer suggestions regarding the mandates that merit reimbursement by Congress. The in-depth analysis of metamorphic federalism begins in Chapter 2, where I examine congressional use of incentives — conditional grants-in-aid and tax credits to persuade states and local governments to implement national policies.

II

From Confederation to Federation

he governmental system of the United States underwent a major metamorphosis during the period 1776–1781 as the Declaration of Independence led to the establishment of thirteen new and independent states that formed a loose coalition under the Continental Congress to prosecute the Revolutionary War against the United Kingdom. In 1781, this coalition was transformed by a written document — the Articles of Confederation and Perpetual Union — into a confederation with a weak central government and dominant state governments. The inadequacies of the Articles were demonstrated within a period of four years and led to the transformation of the governmental system in 1789 into the first federal system in the world. This system has been undergoing continuous change as the result of constitutional amendments, judicial decisions, and statutory elaboration.

Fear of a strong national government was responsible for both the initial adoption of a confederate form of government and the subsequent development and adoption of the innovative federate system. The struggle between advocates of a strong national government and their opponents — states' rights advocates — continues to this day. The dramatic expansion of the powers of the national government during the Great Depression struck fear in the hearts of the more conservative elements in the nation and led to many proposals in the immediate post–World War II period to return power to the states. Relatively few successful initiatives to strengthen the position of the states were implemented until President Nixon was able to convince Congress to enact several of his "New Federalism" proposals into law.

The resignation of President Nixon in 1974 ended effective efforts to alter the nature of the federal system fundamentally until the inauguration of President Ronald Reagan in 1981. President Reagan developed his own "New Federalism" proposals and experienced considerable success in implementing several of his recommendations in 1981, a subject examined in Chapter 3.

However, throughout the Nixon and Reagan presidencies, certain centralization trends continued. To a large extent, these trends are traceable to the Water Quality Act of 1965, the first partial-preemption statute, which established minimum national standards and provided for assumption of federal responsibility for water-pollution abatement if a state failed to adopt and implement a water-pollution-abatement plan meeting national standards.[1] Federal preemption has attracted relatively little scholarly attention but has had a major impact upon the nature of the federation. I examine this topic in detail in Chapter 5.

This chapter examines the development of the Articles of Confederation and Perpetual Union, the weaknesses of the Articles, the establishment of the federal system, the expansion of the powers of the national government, and the intent of the framers of the Constitution.

The Articles of Confederation

Under a confederacy, the states possess all powers not denied to them by their respective constitutions, and the national government possesses only powers expressly delegated to it by the states. Although one might assume that the newly independent states would have readily agreed to the formation of a confederation since they would retain ultimate control of the system, there was strong opposition by the states to giving up any of their powers to a national body, no matter how weak its powers might be. Leading figures, including Samuel and John Adams of Massachusetts and Thomas Jefferson and Patrick Henry of Virginia, strongly opposed any movement to restrain the freedom of state legislatures.[2]

Nevertheless, in 1777, the second Continental Congress, a unicameral body with equal state representation, submitted the Articles of Confederation and Perpetual Union to the thirteen states for ratification. Eight states ratified the document in 1778, and four states approved the Articles the following year. Maryland withheld its approval of the document until 1781 because of Virginia's claim to the "western lands." In 1781, Virginia acceded to Maryland's position by ceding these lands to the Union, Maryland accepted the Articles, and they became effective.

Major Provisions

The most important provision in the Articles stipulated that "each State retains its sovereignty, freedom and independence, and every power, jurisdiction and right, which is not by this confederation expressly delegated to the *u*nited States in Congress, assembled."[3] Notice that the title describes the new government as "united," the initial lowercase signifying that the new system on the national level was composed of states united for express purposes. The above stipulation is the heart of any confederation, and the nature of the confederation is determined by the powers expressly delegated to the new unicameral Congress. Article III of the Articles described the mutual relations of the states as "a firm league of friendship with each other."

Members of Congress were appointed by their respective state legislatures, and each state had one vote in the congress, regardless of the number of members representing the states. Each state was authorized to appoint from two to seven delegates, who were subject to being recalled at any time. No delegate could serve for more than three years during any six-year term of Congress.

Relatively few powers were delegated expressly by the states to Congress. It was empowered, however, to borrow and coin money, declare war, establish a postal system and standards of weights and measures, negotiate treaties with other nations, and regulate relations with Indians. Congress also could fix quotas for each state to furnish men and money for the army, but lacked authority to levy taxes or to regulate interstate commerce.

Major Defects

Experience quickly revealed that the confederation suffered from a number of defects in its fundamental document. Specifically, Congress was (1) dependent upon voluntary contribution of funds by states, which often were not sent; (2) powerless to regulate commerce among the states; (3) unable to enforces its laws, which individual states were free to ignore; (4) hampered in obtaining foreign credit; and (5) unable to suppress domestic disorders.

Lacking the power to tax, the paper money issued by congress became worthless, and several states began to issue their own paper currency. States began to erect trade barriers that began to strangle interstate commerce. Firewood from Connecticut and cabbage from New Jersey are examples of commodities taxed by New York in this period.[4] In addition, the moneyed and property interests were disturbed greatly by Shays's Rebellion in western Massachusetts in 1786, which resulted in Captain Shays and his supporters occupying most of Massachusetts west of Worcester until the rebellion was suppressed by the commonwealth of Massachusetts.[5] Shays demanded lower taxes, suspension of mortgage foreclosures, and cheap paper money. In that year, New Hampshire had to call out its militia to disperse a mob that was attempting to coerce members of the General Court to authorize the printing of paper money.[6]

The defects of the Articles became more apparent with the passage of each year, and by 1785, the boundary commissioners of Maryland and Virginia recommended that each state send delegates to a meeting in Annapolis the following year to discuss remedying the defects. Although the conference was attended by delegates from only five states, the conference urged Congress to call a convention to meet in Philadelphia in 1787 for the purpose of reforming the Articles of Confederation and Perpetual Union. With reluctance, Congress called the convention.

The Constitution of the United States

The Constitutional Convention met from May to September 1787 in Philadelphia, and delegates from all states except Rhode Island participated. Taking a middle course between perpetuating the confederation by reforming the Articles and establishing a unitary or centralized national governmental system, the delegates discarded the Articles and drafted a Constitution providing for a new governmental system — a federal system with powers divided between the thirteen states and Congress. (See Figure 2.1.)

The new fundamental document reflected the sharp divisions within the Union, with several compromises made between the large and small states, the northern and southern states, and the eastern and western states. The dispute over equal state representation (the "small state" or "New Jersey" plan) and representation according to population (the "large state" or "Virginia" plan) led to the famous Connecticut Compromise, converting Congress from a unicameral to a bicameral body, one house based upon equal representation for each

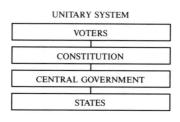

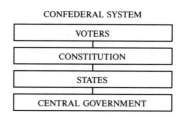

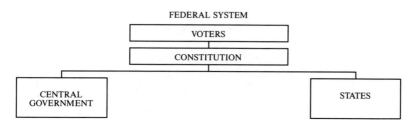

FIG. 2.1. *Systems geographically distributing political power*

state, the other house generally based on representation in accordance with the population of each state.

Power Distribution

Since a federal system involves the distribution of functional responsibilities between two planes of government, the drafters of a federal constitution have three options. First, they may assign specific functional responsibilities to each of the two planes. Second, specific functions can be made the responsibility of the national plane, all other powers, except prohibited ones, reserved to the states. Third, the states may be granted specific powers and all other powers, except prohibited ones, reserved to the national government.

The Constitutional Convention of 1787 decided to have the Constitution delegate only enumerated, or express, powers to Congress. Included among the enumerated powers are exclusive ones—foreign affairs, coinage of money, post offices, and declaration of war—which states are forbidden to exercise.[7] Although the Constitution did not explicitly stipulate it, the assumption of the drafters was that all other powers would be reserved to the states unless specifically prohibited. The Tenth Amendment makes this assumption explicit.

Congress and the states were denied other powers: bills of attainder, ex post facto laws, granting of titles of nobility.[8] In addition, Congress was forbidden to exercise certain other powers: laying duties on exports from any state, giving preference to the ports of one state, requiring vessels bound to or from a state to pay duties in another state, drawing money from the Treasury without an appropriation, or prohibiting the importation of slaves into any state prior to the year 1808.[9]

States were denied the power to "enter into any treaty, alliance, or confederation; grant letters of marque and reprisal; coin money; emit bills of credit; make any thing but gold and silver coin a tender in payment of debts; . . . or law impairing the obligation of contracts."[10]

The Constitution provides for two types of *concurrent* powers. The first includes the power to tax, which is not subject to formal preemption by Congress.[11] The second includes powers granted expressly to Congress and not prohibited to the states (the regulation of commerce among the states is an example). In the event of a direct conflict between a federal statute and a state statute, the supremacy clause of the Constitution provides for the prevalence of federal law by nullifying state law.[12] In other words, the exercise of this type of concurrent power by a state is subject to complete or partial preemption by Congress.

The Constitution also contains a list of powers that states may exercise only with the consent of Congress. Examples include the levying of import and tonnage duties, keeping troops in time of peace, and entering into compacts with other states.[13] The U.S. Supreme Court, however, has not interpreted these powers (Article I, Section 10) to mean that in all cases they may be exercised only with the consent of Congress. The Supreme Court held in *Virginia v. Ten-*

nessee (1893) that congressional consent is required only if states desire to enter into "political" compacts affecting the balance of power between the states and the Union, and in 1975 the Court ruled that the prohibition of levying "imposts or duties on imports" without the consent of Congress does not prohibit the levying of a property tax on imported products.[14] In 1986, the Court opined that the imposition of an ad valorem property tax by North Carolina on imported tobacco stored in customs-bonded storehouses for future domestic manufacture did not violate the import-export clause of the Constitution and was not preempted by a congressional statute.[15]

Ratification Campaign
There was strong opposition to the proposed Constitution in the thirteen states. Recognizing the near impossibility of securing the approval of all states for the new fundamental document, the drafters stipulated that the Constitution would become effective when ratified by the conventions of nine states.[16] The Articles of Confederation and Perpetual Union, of course, stipulated that the Articles could be amended only with the unanimous consent of the member states.

To help overcome the strong antifederal opposition in the state of New York, Alexander Hamilton, John Jay, and James Madison wrote a series of letters to the editors of New York state newspapers, explaining the provisions of the various articles of the proposed Constitution, the prohibitions incorporated to protect individual liberties, and the sections designed to ensure that the states would retain important powers. These letters have been published as *The Federalist Papers* and remain the best explanation of the original design of the Constitution.

According to James Madison, in *The Federalist Number 45,* "The powers delegated by the proposed Constitution to the federal government are few and defined. Those which are to remain in the State governments are numerous and indefinite."[17] Madison, of course, was referring in particular to the police power, a broad power allowing states to regulate persons and property in order to protect and promote public health, public safety, public morals, public welfare, and public convenience.

Hamilton, in *The Federalist Number 17,* assured readers that "it will always be far more easy for the State governments to encroach upon the national authorities than for the national government to encroach upon the State authorities. The proof of this proposition turns upon the greater degree of influence which the State governments, if they administer their affairs with uprightness and prudence, will generally possess over the people."[18] Madison added, in *The Federalist Number 46,* that "a local spirit will infallibly prevail much more in the member of Congress than a national spirit will prevail in the legislatures of the particular States."[19]

Minority members of the convention, convened in Pennsylvania to consider the proposed Constitution, issued a strong dissent and maintained that "the powers vested in Congress . . . must necessarily annihilate and absorb the legislative, executive, and judicial powers of the several States, and produce from their ruin one consolidated government, which from the nature of things will be *an iron handed despotism,* as nothing short of the supremacy of despotic sway could connect and govern these United States under one government."[20]

The minority report assailed in particular the "complete and unlimited" power of Congress "over the *purse* and the *sword,*" and predicted:

As there is no one article of taxation reserved to the state governments, the Congress may monopolize every source of revenue, and thus indirectly demolish the state governments, for without funds they could not exist; the taxes, duties, and excises imposed by Congress may be so high as to render it impracticable to levy further sums on the same articles, but whether this should be the case or not, if the state government should presume to impose taxes, duties, or excises on the same articles with Congress, the latter may abrogate and repeal the laws whereby they are imposed, upon the allegation that they interfere with the due collection of their taxes, duties, or excises, by virtue of the following clause, part of section 8th, article 1st, *viz.* "To make all laws which shall be necessary and proper for carrying into execution the foregoing powers, and all other powers vested by this Constitution in the government of the United States, or in any department or officer thereof."[21]

Although the above statement proved to be inaccurate in its totality, the fear expressed by the minority members was partially realized in 1942 when the Congress raised income tax surtaxes sharply, the highest rate set at 91 percent. These exceptionally high rates continued in effect until 1962 and effectively preempted the ability of states to levy income taxes at rates exceeding the nominal. In the period 1945 to 1962, a sharp increase occurred in federal conditional grants-in-aid, which enable Congress to exercise de facto control over many state and local governmental activities, a subject examined in Chapter 3.

Publius's assurances that the proposed Constitution limited the powers of the national government did not overcome the fears of a strong centralized government held by the Anti-Federalists. To gain the approval of the larger states, proponents agreed that the adoption of constitutional amendments containing a Bill of Rights would be the first item of business of the new Congress under the Constitution. Thomas Jefferson, in a letter to Madison, implied that the convention in Virginia should not ratify the proposed fundamental law unless a Bill of Rights was incorporated in the document.[22] The conventions in Massachusetts, New York, and Virginia ratified the proposal with the condition that a Bill of Rights be added as soon as the Constitution became effective. New Hampshire, in June 1787, also recommended the adoption of amendments and became the ninth state to ratify the proposed document. The new governmental system became effective early in 1789.

To make crystal clear that Congress possessed only enumerated powers, the Tenth Amendment provides that "the powers not delegated to the United States by the Constitution, nor prohibited by it to the States, are reserved to the States respectively, or to the people." This division-of-powers approach to government—an *Imperium in Imperio*—is often labeled *dual* or *layer-cake* federalism. In practice, as is well known, there is a sharing of many powers—a marble or "rainbow" cake—by the three principal levels of government—federal, state, and local—rather than the complete division of powers suggested by the term *dual federalism*.[23]

Expansion of National Powers

Thomas Jefferson was sensitive to the problem of nation-state conflicts based on one plane of government encroaching upon the powers of the other plane. In 1814, he wrote, "I have always thought where the line of demarcation between the powers of the General and the State governments was doubtfully or indistinctly drawn, it would be prudent and praiseworthy in both parties, never to approach it but under the most urgent necessity."[24]

However, since 1789, the federal sphere of power has been broadened appreciably by accretions of power resulting from constitutional amendments, statutory elaboration of delegated powers, and judicial interpretation, and has produced a continuing ideological debate over the proper roles of the national government and the states. (See Figure 2.2.)

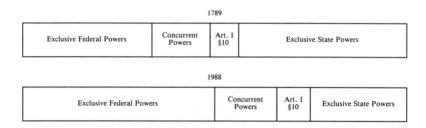

FIG. 2.2.   Distribution of powers, U.S. Constitution, 1789 and 1988 (based on a "zero sum" model where an increase in the powers of the federal government results in a corresponding decrease in the powers of the states [see also Chapter 7])

Constitutional Amendments

The Fourteenth Amendment — with its due process of law, privileges and immunities, and equal protection of the laws clauses — was the first constitutional amendment directly restricting the powers of the states. The amendment has served as the basis for numerous federal court decisions striking down as unconstitutional actions taken by states, including state laws enacted under the reserved police power. The federal courts have also interpreted the privileges and immunities clause to include the First Amendment's guarantees. Judicial preemption of state and local laws is examined in Chapter 6.

The Fifteenth Amendment, adopted in 1870, prohibits the abridgment of the right to vote "because of race, color, or previous condition of servitude." This amendment and the Fourteenth Amendment currently serve as the constitutional basis for the Voting Rights Act of 1965, as amended, an act discussed in greater detail in Chapter 4.

Whereas the Fourteenth Amendment provides the basis for federal judicial intervention in what previously had been the affairs of the states, the Sixteenth Amendment's authorization for Congress to levy a graduated income tax gave Congress power to raise sufficient funds to finance 492 categorical grant-in-aid programs for state and local governments.[25] Because of the conditions attached to the grants, Congress and the federal administration have considerable influence over reserved-power matters. Informal or de facto federal preemption by means of conditional grants-in-aid is explored in Chapter 3.

Statutory Elaboration

Congress failed to exercise a few of the delegated powers for many decades. To cite two examples, Congress did not use its power to regulate interstate commerce in a comprehensive manner until passage of the Interstate Commerce Act of 1887, and Congress did not use its supersessive power to nullify all state bankruptcy laws until 1898.

During the past three and a half decades, Congress has increasingly used its powers of partial and total preemption to supersede state laws. The Atomic Energy Act of 1946, for example, totally preempted responsibility for the regulation of ionizing radiation until a 1959 amendment authorized the Atomic Energy Commission (now the Nuclear Regulatory Commission) to enter into agreements with states to allow states to assume certain regulatory responsibilities.[26] Twenty-nine states have assumed such responsibility, a subject addressed in Chapter 4 in terms of its implications for intergovernmental cooperation and conflict. To cite one other example of complete supersession by Congress, the Uniform Time Act of 1966 totally preempted responsibility for determining the dates on which standard time is changed to daylight saving time (and vice versa).[27]

The most important preemptive actions by Congress have involved environmental protection. By the mid-1960s, Congress had decided that a number of environmental problems could not be eliminated by reliance upon state and local governmental action encouraged by the "carrots" of federal grants-in-aid. Two preemptive acts — the Water Quality Act of 1965 and the Air Quality Act of 1967 — marked a new phase in congressional use of its powers of supersession.[28]

The Water Quality Act required each state to adopt "water quality standards applicable to interstate waters or portions thereof within such State" as well as an implementation and enforcement plan. The administrator of the Environmental Protection Agency (EPA) is authorized to promulgate water-quality standards, which become effective at the end of six months if a state fails to establish and enforce adequate standards. The federal role was strengthened by other statutory enactments, particularly the Federal Water Pollution Control Act Amendments of 1972, which established July 1, 1977, as the deadline for the secondary treatment of sewage and July 1, 1983, as the date for achieving "water quality which provides for protection and propagation of fish, shellfish, and wildlife," and required the elimination of the "discharge of pollutants into navigable waters by 1985."[29] The Air Quality Act of 1967 established a similar procedure relative to state responsibility for air-pollution abatement with the exception of emissions from new motor vehicles.[30] The implications of these two acts are discussed in greater detail in Chapter 5.

Judicial Interpretation

As is well known, since the development of the doctrine of implied powers in *McCulloch v. Maryland* and the doctrine of the continuous journey in *Gibbbons v. Ogden,* the Supreme Court has tended to interpret national powers broadly.[31] In 1885, Woodrow Wilson wrote: "Congress must wantonly go very far outside of the plain and unquestionable meaning of the Constitution, must bump its head directly against all right and precedent, must kick against the very pricks of all well-established rulings and interpretation, before the Supreme Court will offer its distinct rebuke."[32]

Whereas the decisions of the Supreme Court limiting the police power of the states relative to economic matters have been well publicized, less public attention has been paid to the recent court decisions extending the First Amendment guarantees by partially preempting state corrupt-practices laws limiting political campaign contributions and expenditures.

State corrupt-practices acts since 1976 must conform to the guidelines laid down by the Supreme Court in *Buckley v. Valeo,* a case involving the Federal Election Campaign Act of 1971 and its amendments of 1974. In this case, the Court upheld individual-contribution limits, disclosure and reporting provisions, and public-financing provisions, but ruled "that the limitations on campaign expenditures, on independent expenditures by individuals and groups, and on expenditures by a candidate from his personal funds are constitutionally infirm."[33]

Regarding the limitations on personal expenditures by candidates, the Court ruled that the limitation "imposes a substantial restraint on the ability of persons to engage in protected First Amendment expression."[34] The Court added:

The candidate, no less than any other person, has a First Amendment right to engage in the discussion of public issues and vigorously and tirelessly to advocate his own election and the election of other candidates. Indeed, it is of particular importance that candidates have the unfettered opportunity to make their views known so that the electorate may intelligently evaluate the candidates' personal qualities and their positions on vital public issues before choosing among them on election day.[35]

Two years later, the Court struck down a Massachusetts law restricting a corporation's contributions to referendum campaigns involving issues "that materially affect its business, property, or assets" by holding that a corporation under the First Amendment could spend funds to publicize its views in opposition to a proposed constitutional amendment authorizing the state legislature to levy a graduated income tax.[36] These rulings have had a major impact on the nature of political campaigns by making it extremely difficult for candidates who are not exceptionally wealthy to win a seat in Congress or a governorship unless they are incumbents. In addition, these rulings have led to a proliferation of political action committees that provide a significant portion of the funds expended in political campaigns for office and in initiative and referendum campaigns.

The controversial nature of many Supreme Court decisions during the past three and a half decades and enactment of total- and partial-preemption statutes by Congress since 1965 have generated a major debate about whether the Court and Congress are adhering to the intent of the drafters of the Constitution.

The Intent of the Framers

The constitutional debate opened in 1985 by Attorney General Edwin Meese III regarding the intent of the framers of the Constitution has ensured that important issues of federalism are discussed in public forums. Addressing the American Bar Association in 1985, the attorney general argued:

A jurisprudence seriously aimed at the explication of original intention would produce defensible principles of government that would not be tainted by ideological predilection. A Jurisprudence of Original Intention also reflects a deeply rooted commitment to the idea of democracy. The Constitution represents the consent of the governed to the structure and powers of the government. To allow the court to govern simply by what it views at the time as fair and decent, is a scheme of government no longer popular; the idea of democracy has suffered. The permanence of the Constitution is weakened. A Constitution that is viewed as only what the judges say it is, is no longer a constitution in the true sense.[37]

Justice William J. Brennan, Jr., of the Supreme Court responded to the attorney general's speech and rejected his views in strong terms:

There are those who find legitimacy in fidelity to what they call "the intentions of the Framers." In its most doctrinaire incarnation, this view demands that Justices discern exactly what the Framers thought about the question under consideration and simply follow that intention in resolving the case before them. . . . It is arrogant to pretend that from our vantage we can gauge accurately the intent of the Framers on application of principle to specific, contemporary questions. . . . Typically, all that can be gleaned is that the Framers themselves did not agree about the applications or meaning of particular constitutional provisions, and hid their differences in cloaks of generality.[38]

Judge Robert H. Bork of the United States Court of Appeals for the District of Columbia Circuit entered the debate:

In short, all an intentionalist requires is that the text, structure, and history of the Constitution provide him not with a conclusion but with a premise. That premise states a core value that the framers intended to protect. The intentionalist judge must then supply the minor premise in order to protect the constitutional freedom in circumstances the framers could not foresee. . . . Thus, we are usually able to understand the liberties that were intended to be protected. We are able to apply the first amendment's free press clause to the electronic media and to the changing impact of libel litigation upon all the media; we are able to apply the fourth amendment's prohibition on unreasonable searches and seizures of electronic surveillance; we apply the commerce clause to state regulation of interstate trucking. . . . At the very least, judges will confine themselves to the principles the framers put into the Constitution. Entire ranges of problems will be placed off-limits to judges, thus preserving democracy in those areas where the framers intended democratic government. That is better than any non-intentionalist theory can do.[39]

Professor H. Jefferson Powell, of the University of Iowa Law School, published a major article in 1985 examining the cultural factors influencing legal interpretation when the Constitution was adopted and concluded: "[T]he claim or assumption intentionalism was the original presupposition of American constitutional discourse . . . is historically mistaken."[40]

Nevertheless, the constitutional debate opened by the attorney general is a healthy sign that the American governance system remains vigorous and that important issues of federalism are debated continually, even if each side labels the other with pejorative terms.

It is difficult to argue against the Meese contention that constitutional change should be made by the elected representatives of the people. One could extend the debate further by advocating formal constitutional change only with the direct consent of the electorate, the practice in all states except Delaware.

Judge-made law can not be avoided in its entirety because constitutional provisions are framed in general terms and it is impossible to divine the precise intention of the framers when the provisions were drafted. Furthermore, as critics of Meese correctly point out, many issues coming before the judiciary today have been generated by urbanization and industrialization, phenomena not in existence at the time of the convention that drafted the Constitution. I examine federal preemption by judicial interpretation of the Constitution in Chapter 6.

Summary

The major purposes of this chapter have been to examine the adoption of the Articles of Confederation and Perpetual Union, document briefly their defects, describe the distribution of powers between Congress and the states under the Constitution, analyze the reasons for the expansion of the powers of the federal government, and describe the argument over the intent of the framers of the Constitution.

This background material will promote the proper understanding of the nature of informal, total, and partial federal preemption, topics that are analyzed in the following three chapters. I have characterized the use of conditional grants-in-aid by Congress as *informal,* or de facto, federal preemption since the federal government thus gains influence and/or control over certain aspects of traditional state and local activities. Chapter 3 will also examine briefly the use of federal tax credits as a device to secure the compliance of the states with federal objectives.

III

Informal Federal Preemption

lthough formal-preemption powers have been possessed by Congress since 1789, reliance on the power to achieve national goals did not become common until 1965. Initially, Congress sought to achieve national goals by assisting states through land grants and in 1887 made the first financial grant-in-aid to the states. The early land and money grants did not limit the discretionary authority of the states. The attachment by Congress of conditions to grants-in-aid for states and local governments became relatively common in the 1930s and began to influence significantly state and local policy-making.

We refer to this type of federal preemption as informal preemption because it is not based upon the exercise of preemptive powers by Congress. Instead, states and local governments in effect initiate a type of preemption by voluntarily applying for and accepting conditional federal grants-in-aid, thereby becoming bound by national policy directives. In addition, states have enacted laws in response to federal laws providing tax credits for private individuals and business firms if states enact laws paralleling federal laws on the same subjects. Conditional grants-in-aid and tax credits reduce the ability of states and their subdivisions to administer covered programs in their own discretion.

A striking feature of the 1950s and the 1960s was the explosion in the number of grants-in-aid programs and the funds given to subnational units by the federal government. The proliferation of grant programs generated considerable criticism, and the Johnson and

Nixon administrations attempted to respond to the criticism. The Reagan administration launched a major attack on federal involvement in traditional state and local governmental activities and achieved a degree of success in modifying the national government's intergovernmental role.

Conditional grants-in-aid are not the only form of national financial assistance to state and local governments. The federal government also provides assistance in the form of in-lieu property-tax payments, loans, exemption of interest paid on municipal (state and local) bonds from federal income tax, services-in-aid (e.g., the FBI fingerprint service), commodities-in-aid (e.g., food stamps), and technical assistance.

This chapter traces the historical development of informal preemption in the form of conditional grants-in-aid, examines the criticisms of the grant-in-aid system and the federal response to the criticisms, explores informal federal preemption in the form of targeted tax credits, and briefly reviews the impact of the "Reagan Revolution" on the intergovernmental system. In addition, it considers the impact of declining federal financial assistance on subnational governments.

Historical Development of Federal Categorical Grants-in-Aid

Neither the Articles of Confederation nor the Constitution specifically authorizes Congress to make land and/or financial grants to states and local governments. Nevertheless, Congress enacted the Northwest Ordinance of 1785, which reserved one square mile in each township for educational purposes in the area covered by the ordinance.[1] The next major land grant, however, did not occur until the Morrill Act was enacted by the Congress in 1862 to encourage states to establish colleges of agricultural and mechanical arts.[2] On two occasions in the nineteenth century, the U.S. Treasury surplus was distributed to the states. These distributions were one-time disbursements of cash, and no provision was made for a continuing program of sharing national revenue with the states.

A major constitutional challenge to conditional grants to states was resolved in 1866 when the Supreme Court, in *McGee v. Mathias,* ruled that "it is not doubted that the grant by the United States to the State upon conditions, and the acceptance of the grant by the State, constitutes a contract. . . . The contract was binding upon the State, and could not be violated by its legislation without infringement of the Constitution."[3]

Whether Congress could use the grant device in effect to require States to exercise their reserved powers to implement provisions of the Maternity Act was the subject of a 1922 Supreme Court decision in *Massachusetts v. Mellon;* the Court held that the act was constitutional.[4]

Conditional Grants-in-Aid

Conditional grants-in-aid generally require the recipient state or local government to provide matching funds, often on a two-thirds-federal, one-third-state-or-local basis. Continuing grants-in-aid to subnational units are traceable in origin to the Hatch Act of 1887, which provided grants to states to promote the establishment of agricultural experiment stations at state colleges of agriculture.[5]

The first condition attached to a grant program, a type of de facto partial preemption, dates to the Carey Act of 1894, which required the preparation of a comprehensive plan for the irrigation of arid land as a condition for the receipt of federal funds.[6]

Federal inspection of state programs administered in part with federal moneys and state matching requirements originated with the Weeks Act of 1911, providing national grants to states for state forestry programs.[7] The next major innovation in the use of the grant-in-aid device was contained in the Federal Road Aid Act of 1916, which contained the first "single state agency" requirement by mandating that the highway program aided with federal moneys be administered by a state highway department.[8] The 1921 amendments to this act went one step further in extending federal influence by stipulating that state highway departments receiving federal funds were subject to an evaluation of their competence by the secretary of agriculture.[9] Although this federal condition did not prove controversial, employment of the "single state agency" provision in the Social Security Act of 1935 has caused rifts in federal-state relations.[10]

Congress's concern with the competence and political neutrality of state and local governmental employees administering programs funded in part with national moneys led to the incorporation of a provision in the Social Security Act of 1935 requiring that subnational employees administering programs under the act must be selected and promoted in accordance with the merit principle.[11] The Hatch Acts of 1939 and 1940 forbid any state or local employee receiving part or all of his salary from federal funds from engaging in partisan political action.[12]

Viewing local governments as creatures of the states, Congress initially channeled funds only to the states. The first federal grant-in-aid provided directly to local governments, thereby completely by-passing the states, was authorized by the United States Housing Act of 1937.[13]

Growth of Federal Grants-in-Aid

Federal financial assistance for state and local governments in the late 1980s has become essential to their continued fiscal health. This situation represents a dramatic change from the period prior to 1915 when all federal aid to states totaled less than $5 million annually.[14] The Federal Road Aid Act of 1916 produced a sharp rise in federal aid to states, to approximately $100 million per year in the period 1918 to 1930, with highway aid accounting for approximately 80 percent of the total. Responding to the multiple problems associated with the Great Depression of the 1930s, federal grants-in-aid to states increased sharply yet amounted to less than 10 percent of federal appropriations each year.

Although twenty-nine programmatic categories of federal aid were authorized by Congress in the period 1946 to 1960,[15] an explosion in federal aid occurred, beginning in fiscal 1960 when such grants to state and local governments increased by approximately 15 percent annually from $7 billion to over $91 billion in fiscal 1980.[16] Thirty-nine of the ninety-five program categories were authorized in the period 1961 to 1966.[17]

Tables 3.1 and 3.2 reveal the trends in sources of state and local governmental revenues and expenditures by function in the period fiscal year 1972 to fiscal year 1986. Federal financial assistance to subnational units during this time period increased by an average of 9.6 percent annually, although such assistance declined as a percentage of total state and local revenue, from 16.5 percent to 14.4 percent. Total state and local governmental spending increased yearly by an average of 10 percent in the same period, a rate of increase slightly greater than the rate of increase in federal financial assistance.

The proportion of federal fiscal assistance has varied by function over the decades. The early grants were related generally to agriculture, including the Federal Road Aid Act of 1916, which was designed to facilitate the transport of farm crops to markets. Enactment of the Social Security Act in 1935 changed the proportion of aid devoted to

Table 3.1. State and local government revenue, by source, fiscal years 1972 to 1986

Source	Distribution (%)				Average Annual Increase (%)	
	1985–86	1981–82	1976–77	1971–72	1984–85 to 1985–86	1971–72 to 1985–86
Revenue, total	100.0	100.0	100.0	100.0	8.8	10.7
General revenue, total	83.9	83.6	84.6	87.7	7.2	10.1
Intergovernmental revenue from the federal government	14.4	15.9	18.5	16.5	6.5	9.6
Taxes	47.6	48.8	52.1	57.3	6.5	9.2
Property	14.3	15.0	18.5	22.2	7.7	7.2
Sales and gross receipts	17.2	17.2	17.9	19.8	6.8	9.6
General	11.6	11.1	10.8	10.7	7.6	11.3
Motor fuel	1.8	1.9	2.7	3.8	5.6	5.0
Other	3.8	4.1	4.5	5.2	5.3	8.2
Income	12.0	12.1	11.4	10.4	5.4	11.9
All other taxes	4.1	4.6	4.2	5.0	4.2	9.0
Charges and misc. general revenue	19.8	18.9	14.0	13.9	9.6	13.5
Utility and liquor stores	6.0	6.2	5.0	5.3	5.3	11.7
Insurance trust	12.1	10.3	10.4	7.1	23.0	15.0

Source: U.S. Bureau of the Census, *Governmental Finances in 1985–86* (Washington, D.C.: Government Printing Office, 1987), p. xi.

Table 3.2.   State and local government expenditure, by function, fiscal years 1972 to 1986

Item	Distribution (%)				Average Annual Increase (%)	
	1985–86	1981–82	1976–77	1971–72	1984–85 to 1985–86	1971–72 to 1985–86
Expenditure, total	100.0	100.0	100.0	100.0	9.2	10.0
Education	29.3	29.6	31.8	34.4	9.4	8.8
Public welfare	10.7	11.1	11.1	11.2	7.3	9.7
Utility and liquor stores	9.1	9.2	6.9	6.0	9.2	13.3
Health and hospitals	7.5	7.7	7.0	6.8	7.9	10.7
Highways	6.9	6.6	7.2	10.1	9.7	7.0
Insurance trust	6.5	7.5	8.1	5.6	5.1	11.2
Interest on general debt	5.2	3.8	3.5	3.2	14.3	13.9
Governmental administration	4.4	4.3	4.1	3.9	10.1	10.9
Police protection	3.2	3.1	3.2	3.2	8.3	10.0
Sanitation	2.7	2.9	2.7	2.5	10.0	10.5
Correction	2.1	1.6	1.3	1.1	16.5	15.0
Housing and community development	1.6	1.5	1.1	1.5	8.7	10.5
All other	11.0	11.0	11.9	10.6	9.4	10.3
Exhibit: Salaries & wages	35.7	36.4	38.9	41.7	8.4	8.8

Source: U.S. Bureau of the Census, *Governmental Finances in 1985–86* (Washington, D.C.: Government Printing Office, 1987), p. xi.

Table 3.3.   Number of categorical grants, by type, selected fiscal years

	1975		1978		1981		1987	
	Number	Percent	Number	Percent	Number	Percent	Number	Percent
Formula-based								
Allotted formula	96	21.7	106	21.5	111	20.8	94	22.3
Project grants subject to formula allocation	35	7.9	47	9.6	42	7.9	23	5.5
Open-end reimbursement	15	3.4	17	3.5	20	3.8	17	4.0
Total formula-based	(146)	(33.0)	(170)	(34.6)	(173)	(32.4)	(134)	(31.8)
Project	296	67.0	322	65.4	361	67.6	288	68.2
Total	442	100.0	492	100.0	534	100.0	422	100.0

Source: *A Catalog of Federal Grant-in-Aid Programs to State and Local Governments: Grants Funded FY 1987* (Washington, D.C.: U.S. Advisory Commission on Intergovernmental Relations, 1987), p. 3.

Table 3.4. Number of categorical grant programs, by type and administering agency, FY 1984 and FY 1987

	1984 Total		Total		1987 Formula		Project		Change in Total Number 1984–1987
	Number	Percent	Number	Percent	Number	Percent	Number	Percent	
Agriculture	36	9.2	36	8.5	20	14.9	16	5.6	∶∶
Appalachian Regional Commission	13	3.3	13	3.1	∶∶	∶∶	13	4.5	∶∶
Commerce	21	5.4	20	4.7	3	2.2	17	5.9	−1
Education	87	22.2	92	21.8	29	21.6	63	21.9	+5
Energy	11	2.8	12	2.8	6	4.5	6	2.1	+1
Environmental Protection Agency	28	7.1	31	7.3	7	5.2	24	8.3	+3
Federal Emergency Management Agency	19	4.8	18	4.3	1	0.8	17	5.9	−1
Health and Human Services[a]	(73)	(18.6)	(86)	(20.4)	(23)	(17.2)	63	(21.9)	+13
Family Support Administration	7	1.8	7	1.7	3	2.4	4	1.4	∶∶
Health Care Financing Administration	5	1.3	4	0.9	2	1.5	2	0.7	−1
Human Development Services	31	7.9	33	7.8	17	12.7	16	5.6	+2
Public Health Services	30	7.7	42	10.0	1	0.8	41	14.2	+12
Housing and Urban Development	10	2.6	12	2.8	3	2.4	9	3.1	+2
Interior	15	3.8	14	3.3	6	4.5	8	2.8	−1
Justice	7	1.8	15	3.6	3	2.4	12	4.2	+8
Labor	15	3.8	15	3.6	8	6.0	7	2.4	∶∶
Transportation	34	8.7	35	8.3	20	14.9	15	5.2	+1
Other[b]	23	5.9	23	5.5	5	3.7	18	6.3	∶∶
Total categoricals	392	100	422	100	134	100	288	100	+30

Source: *A Catalog of Federal Grant-in-Aid Programs to State and Local Governments: Grants Funded FY 1987* (Washington, D.C.: U.S. Advisory Commission on Intergovernmental Relations, 1987), p. 7.

[a]Numbers in parentheses indicate the total number and percent of grants in the area of health and human services.

[b]FY 1987 includes ACTION, Department of Defense, Federal Mediation and Conciliation Service, National Foundation for Arts and Humanities, National Archives and Records Administration, Nuclear Regulatory Commission, and Veterans Administration.

agriculture and highways by establishing a new social-services program. Approximately 60 to 65 percent of federal grants were dedicated to health, labor, and welfare in the period 1950 to 1955, with welfare payments accounting for about 50 percent of the funds.[18] The National Defense and Interstate Highway Act (1956) changed the mix of aid and resulted in the bulk of the funds being devoted to highways.[19] "Great Society" programs enacted by Congress during the Johnson administration emphasized once again health, labor, and social-service programs.

Categorical grants-in-aid assume one of two forms—formula or project. The former provides for the distribution of federal funds to subnational units on the basis of a formula composed of several factors, such as population and per capita income. The latter refers to capital projects such as sewerage plants and light rail systems. Table 3.3 depicts the changes in the number of categorical grants by type in the period 1975 through 1987.

Table 3.4 contains a breakdown of the number of categorical grants by federal agencies in fiscal years 1981 and 1984. The sharp reduction in the number of education, health and human services, and labor categorical grants are the product of the adoption of block grants, a topic discussed in a subsequent section. Dr. Carl W. Stenberg, executive director of the Council of State Governments, attributed "the presence of so many separate or functionally related programs administered by various agencies" to "differences in individual missions and clienteles."[20]

Criticisms of Categorical Grants-in-Aid

The initial grant-in-aid programs generated relatively little controversy. By 1920, however, strong Democratic and Republican opposition to such aid developed, and charges frequently were made that "sovereign" states were being dictated to by unelected federal bureaucrats. The early opposition also stressed that the power to tax and the power to spend should not be separated, that grants are in effect bribes to state and local governments to carry out national programs, and that the wealthier states should not be taxed by Congress to fund the provision of services in the poorer states.[21]

Continuing concern with federal grants-in-aid led the Commission on Intergovernmental Relations, in 1955, to caution that "the

National Government must refrain from taking over activities that the States and their subdivisions are performing with reasonable competence, lest the vitality of state and local institutions be undermined."[22]

Proponents of fiscal assistance to subnational units stressed that such aid fosters cooperative services by governments on three planes, helps to overcome inflexible constitutional provisions, assists subnational units to finance services they otherwise could not afford to provide, promotes tax equity by redistributing tax resources nationally, enables these units to preserve their viability, and improves the quality of state and local governmental administration.[23]

A southern governor wrote to me in 1987 that "grants-in-aid generally give the State the option to conform in its own way to federal mandates rather than being instructed by federal legislation on exactly how compliance will be dealt with. This flexibility is certainly much better than a comprehensive federal statute outlining what will be done."

While the early pro and con arguments tended to be ideological in nature, commencing in the 1960s the arguments focused more heavily on the administrative discretion of subnational units, economy and efficiency in service provision, programmatic accountability, citizen understanding, and effectiveness in achieving programmatic goals.

Post-1960 Criticisms

The sharp growth in the number of narrow categorical grant-in-aid programs and funding for such programs in the late 1950s and 1960s generated considerable controversy over the impact of such programs on state and local governments.[24] In particular, critics were disturbed by the fact that Congress was attempting to influence traditional state and local governmental activities that previously had not been eligible for federal conditional grants-in-aid.

In 1978, the U.S. Advisory Commission on Intergovernmental Relations issued a report noting that "at least through the 1950s, federal assistance activities were confined by an effort to restrict aid to fields clearly involving the national interest or an important national purpose."[25] However, "the concept of the national interest lost most of its substantive content" subsequent to 1965 with "any action passed by both legislative chambers and signed by the President being accepted as appropriate."[26]

State and local governmental officials, while welcoming the federal funds, were disturbed by the impact that narrow categorical grants-in-aid were having on subnational units and cited twenty undesirable effects.[27]

1. *Reduction in the discretionary authority of state and local governments.* Not surprisingly, subnational governmental officials objected to conditions that in their judgment unduly limited their discretion and resulted in poorer-quality services and/or higher administrative costs.

Charles L. Schultze questioned in 1976 whether major national purposes are served by conditional grants-in-aid and maintained that the grants "simply reflect the substitution of the judgment of federal legislators and agency officials for that of state and local officials."[28]

2. *Federal bureaucratic dominance.* Congressional conditional grant-in-aid programs greatly increase the authority of federal bureaucrats over subnational governments by granting the bureaucrats a veto power over state and local governmental plans, policies, and implementation of federally assisted programs. Evoking fears of administrative imperialism, Senator James L. Buckley stressed in 1978: "The federal bureaucracy has grown into what is essentially a fourth branch of government that has become virtually immune to political direction or control. It is peopled by men and women who are now possessed of broad discretionary power over many areas of American life — so many, in fact, that one begins to wonder to what extent ours can still be described as a government of laws rather than of men."[29] Buckley is convinced that only by reducing federal involvement in the governance process, shifting responsibilities to the states and their subdivisions, will it be possible to "expand the amount of time that the President and members of Congress can devote to each of the matters for which they remain responsible."[30]

3. *Gubernatorial-legislative relations.* Conditional grants-in-aid have strengthened the position of the governor vis-à-vis the legislature in the typical state since most federal grants are applied for and received by executive agencies under the control of the governor.

A survey of state budget officers by the U.S. Advisory Commission on Intergovernmental Relations revealed that federal grants requiring no state matching or only in-kind matching "strengthens the discretionary power of the Governor and administrators and weakens the Legislature's control over the budget and administration."[31] In consequence, several state legislatures enacted statutes stipulating that federal funds could not be expended in the absence of an appropriation by the legislature. Courts in Colorado and New Mexico, however, ruled that such funds are not subject to legislative reappropriation since they are "custodial funds" controlled exclusively by the executive branch.[32] On the other hand, the New York Court of Appeals held that federal funds are subject to appropriation by the legislature.[33]

In 1973, the Supreme Court ruled that a state's constitutional spending prohibitions were not preempted and that whether a federal grant-in-aid falls within the state prohibition is a matter of state law, not federal law.[34] Six years later, the Court refused to overturn a decision of the Pennsylvania Supreme Court that a state law mandating that all federal funds be deposited in the general fund of the commonwealth was a valid exercise of legislative power.[35]

4. *Greater subnational bureaucratic independence.* Closely related to the above criticism was the concern expressed by many elected state and local officials and observers that administrative agencies on the state and local level apply for and receive federal funds that enable them to be more independent of elected officials and thereby evade in part regular budgetary and personnel controls. The criticism was advanced as early as 1940 by G. Homer Durham, who wrote that "some of the largest and politically most powerful state agencies, such as highway Administration with an almost total absence of merit personnel, are no longer dependent on their operating jurisdictions for funds."[36]

5. *Budget distortions.* The adverse impact of federal fiscal assistance upon the ability of subnational units to determine their own priorities and the resulting distortion of the spending patterns of these units disturbed many observers. Since most grants require a nonfederal match—typically on a two-thirds-federal, one-third-nonfederal basis—there was a natural tendency for state and local governmental officials to seek the type of federal grants that would maximize their matching funds.

A 1980 U.S. General Accounting Office report concluded that local governments experiencing a fiscal crisis or taxpayer revolt are unable to reduce spending for federally supported activities without losing the federal aid and may have to eliminate programs not supported by federal grants or not institute needed reductions in any program.[37]

6. *Promotion of increased state-local spending.* Since most federal grant-in-aid programs require a nonfederal match, total government spending is increased above the level of spending that would otherwise occur. In other words, federal matching requirements stim-

ulate greater subnational spending, which is one of the objectives of matching federal grant-in-aid programs.

7. *Agency-client group relationships.* The proliferation of federal grant programs is attributable in large measure to interest groups that subsequently establish what amount to agency-client relationships. These groups have individualistic goals and by promoting categorical grant programs to achieve these goals, make it more difficult for state and local governments to integrate administratively related programs in the most effective manner.

8. *Ineffective review of proposed federal spending.* The great political power of many interest groups in the national capital results in congressional approval of many proposed grant-in-aid programs promoted by the groups. Writing in 1940, Professor V. O. Key, Jr., emphasized that "the strength of these pressure groups, rather than any rational consideration of governmental finance, has been the controlling factor behind federal and state aid."[38]

9. *Conflicting grant objectives.* Responding to pressures from divergent interest groups, Congress enacted many grant-in-aid programs with goals that conflicted in part with the goals of other grant-in-aid programs. The outstanding example is in the area of transportation. Highway improvements, especially the interstate system, encourage citizens to use their private motor vehicles rather than public transportation in urbanized areas and to use their motor vehicles in lieu of passenger trains for longer journeys. As traffic was diverted from public-transportation facilities, the operators were forced to reduce services and increase fares, which in turn promoted an additional decline in their traffic and revenues.

10. *Overlapping and duplicative grants.* The U.S. Advisory Commission on Intergovernmental Relations cited as the "classic case" illustrating this criticism "federal grants for water and sewer projects. No less than four such programs are available, administered by four different agencies."[39]

11. *Voluminous federal rules and regulations.* The expansion in the number of grant programs was accompanied by the issuance of voluminous and complex federal rules and regulations adopted by federal administrative agencies to implement the grant programs. Critics generally concluded that the delivery of services by subnational units was hindered and made more expensive by the vast array of rules and regulations.[40]

12. *Inadequate subnational advice on the framing of regula-*

tions. State and local government officials often complained that they received no advance notification of new federal rules and regulations for grant-in-aid programs until they read the proposals in the *Federal Register.* As a consequence, they were not accorded sufficient time to review the proposals and to offer constructive suggestions for their revision in many instances.

13. *Complex application procedures.* Subnational officials objected to unnecessarily complex procedures in the grant application process, including the requirement for multiple copies of applications, which significantly raised administrative costs.

14. *Insufficient federal field delegation.* Relatively tight administrative control of grant-in-aid programs by the Washington offices resulted in insufficient delegation of authority to federal field offices, which produced what observers considered too many levels of review of grant applications, requests for changes in approved plans, and required reports.

15. *Inflexible programmatic requirements.* The time that elapsed between the preparation of an application for a grant-in-aid and approval of the application could be as long as eighteen months, with the result that conditions might have changed significantly, necessitating programmatic revision for the most effective attainment of grant objectives, but approval for such revisions was difficult to obtain.

16. *The single-agency requirement.* Most federal grant-in-aid programs require that a single state agency be responsible for administration of each program, to fix responsibility and avoid programmatic duplication. This requirement proved to be highly controversial as many governors felt that their states lost the ability to reorganize their executive branches to achieve goals more effectively and economically. The Supreme Court in 1979 upheld the constitutionality of the requirement by denying a petition for a writ of certiorari.[41]

17. *Cross-cutting requirements.* With the passage of time, Congress began to add "cross-cutting" requirements to grant programs. Such requirements are not related to the goals of the particular programs but are designed to achieve other policy goals such as nondiscrimination and citizen participation. A western governor wrote to me in 1987 that the federal threat of loss of highway grants-in-aid if a state does not raise its minimum legal drinking age to twenty-one "amounts to little more than federal blackmail." The Supreme Court in 1987 upheld the requirement, writing that "even if Congress might

lack the power to impose a national minimum drinking age directly, we conclude that encouragement to state action found in § 158 is a valid use of the spending power."[42]

18. *The accountability problem.* Carl W. Stenberg highlighted the accountability problem associated with categorical grants-in-aid:

[T]he highly fragmented intergovernmental assistance program provides many buck-passing opportunities. Local officials can always blame the "feds" for unpopular actions or policy decisions such as fair share housing programs or community based corrections projects. Both can criticize the insensitivity, unwillingness, or inability of some States to provide needed assistance or authority to their local governments.[43]

19. *Impediments to state-local coordination.* The United States Housing Act of 1937 represented a new departure in intergovernmental relations; it provided for direct federal grants-in-aid to local governments, completely bypassing state governments.[44] The trend toward establishing direct federal-local fiscal relations became more pronounced in the 1960s when twenty-three of thirty-eight federal grant programs bypassed the states.

The establishment of direct federal-local financial relationships has been attributed by some observers to the failure of state governments to assume their urban responsibilities and play a major partnership role in the federal system. However, it must be pointed out that this charge obviously did not apply to all states, and progressive states such as California and New York launched urban programs that were later adopted by Congress.

States were highly critical of "bypassing" and maintained that they were in the best position to integrate state programs with federally aided local programs to achieve maximum results at the lowest costs.

20. *Impediments to local coordination.* Beginning with the Economic Opportunity Act of 1964, Congress made grants to private organizations, thereby bypassing local governments as well as state governments. In addition, the numerous grants made to various local governmental agencies made it extremely difficult for a local government to launch a coordinated attack upon local problems because of the restrictive conditions attached to the grants.

Federal Responses to the Criticisms

Responding to the mounting criticism resulting from the impact of greatly enlarged grant-in-aid programs and bypassing state and local governments, the federal government in the mid-1960s inaugurated new organizations and procedures. To achieve better program coordination, among other objectives, the Department of Housing and Urban Development and the Department of Transportation were created.

Excessive categorization of federal grant programs had confused too many state and local officials, augmented rather than alleviated by the catalogs issued by various federal grant agencies. Consequently, in 1967, the Office of Economic Opportunity was assigned responsibility for publishing a consolidated catalog of federal grant-in-aid programs, a responsibility later assumed by the Office of Management and Budget. A companion publication, the *Vice President's Handbook for Local Officials,* was prepared and distributed.

The Budget Bureau was directed by President Lyndon B. Johnson in March 1967 to study the consolidation of grants, simplification of grant-application procedures and financial accounting, and field-office structure and location.

To improve high-level communications, in 1965 President Johnson designated the Office of the Vice President as the contact point for local officials and the Office of Emergency Preparedness in the Executive Office as the contact point for governors. In 1969, President Richard M. Nixon, by executive order, transferred responsibility for federal-state relations to a newly created Office of Intergovernmental Relations under the vice president's supervision, to serve as a federal "ombudsman" to state and local governments.

In 1966, a procedure was established whereby governors and local chief executives were consulted by federal agencies prior to the issuance of new or revised grant regulations. The U.S. Advisory Commission on Intergovernmental Relations acted as an intermediary, channeling proposed changes to national associations of state and local officials and transmitting their comments and questions to the appropriate federal agencies.

A Budget Bureau (now Office of Management and Budget) directive required federal agencies to consult governors before designating planning and development districts. If a state had already established districts, new districts created by federal agencies were required to have the same boundaries unless there was strong justification for establishing different boundaries.

To improve interagency coordination between federal agencies, interagency agreements were developed, especially between the Office of Economic Opportunity and the Departments of Agriculture; Health, Education and Welfare; and Housing and Urban Development.

By executive order, President Johnson authorized the secretary of housing and urban development to issue orders convening all federal agencies operating in a city whenever it was apparent that greater coordination of federal programs was needed. A similar convener power was given to the secretary of agriculture with respect to federal programs having an impact on agricultural and rural development. These convener powers, however, were not utilized.

The passage of the Intergovernmental Cooperation Act of 1968 was a milestone in effectuating greater federal-state-local coordination by providing for dissemination of more information to state and local governments, authorization of federal agencies to waive the single-agency requirement and provide technical services to subnational units on a reimbursable basis, and periodic congressional review of grant programs.[45] The act authorized the head of any federal department or agency, upon request of the governor or other appropriate state official, to waive the single-agency requirement and approve a different administrative structure.

While the above actions helped to improve the administration of federal grant-in-aid programs, congressional authorization of block grants and general-revenues sharing—subjects examined in a subsequent section—has had a more significant impact upon the federal system.

Tax Credits

Congress can achieve national goals by persuading states to adopt uniform laws through the tax-credit device, a second type of informal federal preemption. In common with conditional grants-in-aid, tax credits offer incentives to states to accept national policies. A tax credit allows a taxpayer to deduct all or part of a credit from her federal income tax liability. Since a tax *deduction* allows a taxpayer only to deduct an amount from the taxpayer's gross income to determine taxable income, a tax credit is more valuable to a taxpayer than a tax deduction.

The first federal tax credit was authorized by the Federal Revenue Act of 1926, which allowed eligible taxpayers to take an 80 percent credit against the federal estate tax for estate or inheritance taxes paid to a state.[46] The congressional purpose was to persuade states without an inheritance or estate tax to adopt a uniform one and to persuade the other states to adopt a tax identical to the federal tax to achieve national uniformity. Failure of a state to adopt such a tax would result in all the tax revenue flowing to Washington. If a state adopted an inheritance or estate tax that did not conform with the federal law, the eligible taxpayers in the state would be denied a tax credit, and they would pressure the state legislature to bring the state tax into conformity with the federal law. This federal tax-credit program has been completely successful in achieving its purposes.

The second tax-credit program, authorized by the Social Security Act of 1935, was designed to establish a national system of unemployment insurance operated by the states.[47] Employers who pay unemployment taxes to a state are allowed a credit against their federal unemployment insurance tax of 90 percent of the taxes paid to a state, provided the state law conforms to the federal tax provisions. This tax-credit program was also successful in achieving its goal of establishing a national unemployment compensation system administered by the individual states.

The most recent example is the Economy Recovery Tax Act of 1981, which employed the tax-credit mechanism to promote the rehabilitation of homes in historical districts of cities and to assist public-transportation authorities.[48] To cite a specific example, a private corporation could purchase buses from a public-transportation authority for $10 million by using $2 million of its own funds and $8 million of the authority's funds. The private corporation held title to the buses, depreciated the total cost of the buses, and leased them for a modest fee to the authority, which was responsible for all maintenance and operating costs. The net results of the transaction were that the authority gained $2 million and that the private corporation took advantage of tax-deductible interest payments and accelerated depreciation over a five-year period. The tax-credit programs authorized by this act were not extended by Congress at the end of 1985 because of the growing size of the federal deficit and the loss of federal tax revenue.

A federal tax-credit program can be developed to replace one or all categorical grant-in-aid programs since the former is a type of informal federal preemption as effective as the latter in achieving national objectives. The major advantages of tax-credit programs are administrative in nature; that is, the programs can be administered by the Internal Revenue Service at a considerably lower cost than conditional grant-in-aid programs administered by specialized agencies of the federal government.

Block Grants and General-Revenue Sharing

Stringent criticisms of narrow categorical grants-in-aid and contentions by state and local government officials that federally aided programs could be administered more economically and effectively if the officials were granted additional discretionary authority led to the development of block grants and general-revenue sharing. The former, which grant subnational units less discretion than the latter, date to 1966. The general-revenue-sharing program was in effect from 1972 until the end of federal fiscal year 1986.

Block Grants

In 1949, the first Hoover Commission urged that "a system of grants be established based upon broad categories . . . as contrasted with the present system of extreme fragmentation," but the first block-grant program was not authorized by Congress until the Partnership for Health Act of 1966 was enacted.[49] In tracing the origins of this act, the U.S. Advisory Commission on Intergovernmental Relations reported that one formula Public Health Service "program in 1936 had become nine programs in 1966" and that there was a congressional preference for categorical health grants for the following reasons:

Proponents argued that categorical disease control programs resulted in the most highly targeted impact of limited federal financial aid. It was feared that adding funds to the general health grant would not achieve a greater impact in a particular program area, given the many competing demands on state and local health departments. Programs directed at specific health problems also demonstrated the responsiveness of the federal government to these problems, and to the constituencies which favored categorical grants, because success with Congress made it unnecessary to cope with the ambiguities of state legislative processes. Lastly, an increasing and permanent federal participation in the financing of health services naturally led to a desire on the part of Congress and administering officials to more actively shape state and local decisions regarding aided activities.[50]

Critics of categorical health grant-in-aid programs objected to the administrative burden placed upon the states by such programs and the obstacles posed to the development of balanced public-health programs. The congressional response to the criticism took the form of the collapse of nine formula-grant programs into a block-grant program designed to grant additional discretionary authority to the states while ensuring the achievement of national goals. State departments of public health quickly became strong supporters of the block-grant approach.

In 1968, Congress enacted the Omnibus Crime Control and Safe Streets Act, which Michael D. Reagan and John G. Sanzone referred to as being "so much subjected to 'creeping categorization' that it can best be described as a closely related set of categorical grants masquerading under a block grant guise by being run through a single federal agency . . . and by utilizing state planning agency structures as a device for federal-state interaction."[51]

In 1972, President Nixon proposed four "special revenue sharing" programs, and the 1974 Congress enacted one of the four proposed programs—community development.[52] The program is usually referred to as the community development block-grant program (CDBG), but differs from a conventional block-grant program in four respects: the eligible local government is required to submit only a simple application; the U.S. Department of Housing and Community Development may not reject the application; the recipient subnational unit is not subject to administrative audits by the department; and maintenance of effort and matching requirements do not pertain to the program.

Between 1966 and 1974, Congress consolidated thirty-two categorical grant-in-aid programs into block grants or a special revenue-sharing program. Congress in 1977 and 1978 formed new block-grant programs—insular areas, elderly, and forestry—by merging categorical-grant programs. The law-enforcement block-grant program was ended in 1980, but the Reagan administration in 1981 persuaded Congress to establish block-grant programs by amalgamating fifty-seven categorical grant-in-aid programs.[53]

Richard S. Williamson, assistant to President Reagan for intergovernmental affairs, in 1981 advanced five major reasons why the administration favored the block-grant approach:

First, our governmental system, at present, is not working. The federal government is overloaded, having assumed more responsibilities than it can efficiently or effectively manage. . . . It has crowded out state and local governments, treating them as if they were mere administrative provinces of the federal government. . . .

Second, the block grants will permit government decisions once again to be made by state and local officials who can be held *accountable* for those decisions. There has been a breakdown in accountability between decision-maker and voter. . . .

Third, significant administrative savings will result. The programs proposed for consolidation in just the health and social services areas alone encompass 437 pages of law and 1,200 pages of regulations. Once the awards for 6,800 separate grants are made, over 7 million man-hours of state and local government and community effort are required each year to fill out federally required reports. . . .

Fourth, block grants will result in greater innovation and permit the States to serve as true "laboratories of democracy." . . .

Finally, enactment of the block grants will reduce the impact of the budget cuts by permitting state and local officials to target diminishing resources to areas and individuals whose needs are the greatest.[54]

In 1984, the General Accounting Office released reports assessing the material-and-child-health block grant, preventive-health and health-services block grants, and education block grant. The office concluded that the block grants had achieved their objectives of according states greater flexibility in program administration and specifically noted that the education block grant "facilitates improvements in administrative procedures and planning and budgeting."[55] A 1986 report by SRI International reached a similar conclusion relative to the education block-grant program, noting that the program "reduced the local administrative burdens associated with the programs it replaced" and "enhanced local discretion over these federal funds."[56]

General-Revenue Sharing

Of all the programs enacted by Congress to assist state and local governments financially, the general-revenue-sharing program permitted the recipient units the greatest degree of discretionary authority. The State and Local Fiscal Assistance Act of 1972 appropriated $30.2 billion over a five-year period for the sharing of general federal revenue with the states and general-purpose local governments.[57]

General-revenue sharing was an entitlement program, and eligible units were not required to submit an application to the U.S. Treasury, provide matching funds, meet a maintenance-of-effort requirement, or submit to administrative audits by a federal agency.

The program was renewed in 1976 for five years, but states were dropped as eligible units when the program was renewed in 1980. The growing federal deficits induced Congress to allow the program to expire at the end of fiscal year 1986.

General-revenue sharing was very popular with elected state and local officials because of the relatively few restrictions on the spending of the federally shared revenue and the strengthening of the ability of elected officials to control bureaucrats since general-revenue sharing funds could not be spent by bureaucrats without an appropriation by the local governing body.

The "Reagan Revolution"

President Reagan's program to remake the intergovernmental system was labeled New Federalism, a term President Nixon had employed earlier. The latter sought to decentralize the governmental system of the United States by encouraging the return of functional responsibilities from the federal government to the states and their subdivisions and by increasing the financial capacity of subnational units. As explained earlier, general-revenue sharing and four special-revenue-sharing programs were the key mechanisms in his program for transferring federal revenue to the states and local governments.

While his New Federalism received widespread publicity, President Nixon's centralization initiatives did not receive much publicity. In particular, responsibility for income maintenance and for functions that have spillover costs from one unit to another were centralized during his administration, including regulation of air and water pollution and energy policy.[58]

President Reagan's New Federalism involved three key policies: continuation and expansion of economic deregulation begun under the Carter administration, a "swap" of certain functions between the national government and the states, and additional block-grant programs. In his 1980 acceptance speech at the Republican National Convention, Mr. Reagan stated: "Everything that can be run more effectively by state and local government we shall turn over to state and local government, along with the funding sources to pay for it. We are going to put an end to the money merry-go-round where our money becomes Washington's money to be spent by States and cities exactly the way the federal bureaucrats tell us it has to be spent."[59]

The president proposed that the national government assume responsibility for Medicaid and that the states assume responsibility for aid to families with dependent children and the food-stamp program. He also proposed turning back to the states thirty to forty programs in addition to the programs covered by his proposed block grants. To assist states to finance the "turnback" programs, the president suggested "tax turnbacks"; revenues from specified excise taxes—alcohol, cigarettes, and gasoline—would be made available to the states. Although the president maintained that his proposal was revenue-neutral, states began to fear that they would lose revenue under the proposal. As a consequence, considerable controversy developed over the proposal, and Congress failed to approve this Reagan initiative.

The Reagan administration continued the economic-deregulation program and expanded the scope of deregulation to include subnational units. As indicated earlier, Congress in 1981 consolidated fifty-seven categorical grant-in-aid programs into nine new or revised block-grant programs, thereby necessitating the revision of the existing rules and regulations to conform to the new block-grant format. The revised regulations total only 31 pages, compared to the previous 905 pages, in the *Code of Federal Regulations*. The Reagan administration also reviewed all other rules and regulations, and revised them to reduce the burden placed upon the states and local governments.[60]

Reviewing the results of deregulation, U.S. Comptroller General Charles A. Bowsher reported in 1986:

> Reduced federal regulatory control has enabled States to make gains in containing health care costs. For instance, under Medicaid, States are moving toward prepaid plans and States are using prospective payments for nursing home care.
>
> States have also moved decisively in areas where the federal government has stepped back. One example is the States' role in delivering emergency medical services under the preventive health and health services block grant. States strengthened their regulatory roles, and a number have created trust funds from traffic fines to finance local emergency medical services. Local officials are looking more to the States, not the federal government, to set the standards and provide assistance.[61]

Recognizing that the reduction in federal regulation of state and local governmental activities financed in part with federal funds might result in programmatic inefficiencies, the 1984 Congress enacted the Single Audit Act, designed to determine and report whether "the government, department, agency, or establishment has internal control systems to provide reasonable assurance that it is managing federal financial assistance programs in compliance with applicable laws and regulations."[62] The states are primarily responsible for arranging for each audit, and all subsequent audits by federal agencies must build upon the single state audit.

After reviewing the record of the Reagan administration, in 1984 the Urban Institute concluded:

[T]he Administration has reversed the trend of growing financial dependence of lower levels of government on the national government, put in place a grant structure that is less restrictive and provides less encouragement to local spending, challenged the assumption that there should be uniform national standards for public services, and more fully engaged the States as partners in the effort to contain domestic program costs.[63]

In 1986, President Reagan reviewed the accomplishments of his administration in economic growth, tax reform, deregulation, the environment, and other matters. With respect to the federal system, the president was critical of the tendency of the federal government to bypass the states and their subdivisions during the 1970s and added:

Today, we have reversed the trend toward centralization. State and local governments are again assuming their rightful role. . . .

Through block grants, we have been able to cut through Federal red tape and allow state and local officials to design and administer programs that make sense to them and their taxpayers. Accordingly, the budget I submitted contains proposals for new block grants, and maintains healthy funding levels for the ones already in place.

We are working with State and local government officials and organizations to compile a roster of major federal regulations for revision or elimination. We will also seek to standardize agency grant management practices that will reduce administrative costs and confusion.[64]

Not everyone has been pleased with the Reagan administration's initiatives. Democratic members of the United States Conference of Mayors, for example, released the results of a survey revealing that 80 percent of the surveyed cities indicated that the number of poor people has increased since 1982.[65] Mayor Ernest N. Dutch Morial of New Orleans stated that cities "are being left with the federal neglect of the poor, the hungry, the homeless, and the sick, with dwindling federal and state support and with little financial material of our own to work with."[66]

While not referring directly to President Reagan's New Federalism program, in late December 1986, Governor Victor Atiyeh of Oregon was highly critical of federal mandates and inflexible programmatic requirements:

In Oregon, we have found that we can care for thousands of elderly people in their own homes, instead of sending them to nursing homes. Not only do our older citizens retain their independence, but we have found that home care costs as little as one-third of the cost of institutional care. . . . But the federal Health and Human Services Department's Health Care Financing Administration (HCFA) apparently would rather see people in institutions than in their own homes.

At least, that is the conclusion one might draw from the inflexible requirements HCFA keeps handing us when we seek medicare and medicaid payments for elderly people who are receiving treatment at home. We have had to fight like the devil to convince HCFA to waive some of those requirements so we can get on with our program. You can look at any number of other federal-state programs and see the same thing: excessive red tape, too-many-strings-attached regulations and inflexible requirements that fail to take into account the innovation and individuality of state programs.[67]

The Federal-Mandate Problem

The Balanced Budget and Emergency Deficit Control Act of 1985 (Gramm-Rudman-Hollings Act), the expiration of the general-revenue-sharing program at the end of the 1986 federal fiscal year, and the growing numbers of federal mandates have aggravated the fiscal problems of many subnational units.[68] A 1986 survey of federal departments and agencies by the National Conference of State Legislatures revealed that twelve of the respondents listed a total of 145 federal laws mandating action by the states and that most of the mandates are post-1972.[69]

A 1986 joint survey by the National Governors' Association and the National Association of State Budget Officers discovered that "the majority of States passed along the Gramm-Rudman-Hollings cut of 4.3 percent onto their agencies without supplementing state dollars for lost federal dollars. Those few States that did supplement the cuts did so for human resource programs."[70]

Table 3.5 contains the results of a survey of state municipal leagues regarding the impact of the termination of federal revenue sharing and reduced federal grants-in-aid on municipalities. The table reveals that 60 percent of the respondents felt that the termination of revenue sharing in 1986 had a great impact upon their municipalities and that twelve municipal leagues reported that the impact was greatest on the smaller municipalities. In general, the reduction in federal grants-in-aid has not had as major an effect upon municipalities as the loss of federal revenue-sharing funds.

Table 3.5. Fiscal survey, state municipal league responses, 1987

Question	Region				Total
	Northeast	Midwest	South	West	
Impact of termination of revenue sharing					
Great	0	7	7	1	15
Some	6	2	1	1	10
Greater impact on smaller units	2	4	5	1	12
Impact of reductions in federal grants					
Great	2	1	6	2	10
Some	3	7	3	1	14
Should federal mandate reimbursement be required?					
Yes	6	9	9	2	26
No	0	1	0	0	1
How beneficial are federal block grants?					
Great	2	3	4	1	10
Some	2	6	4	1	13
Has the state replaced federal revenue-sharing funds?					
Yes	0	0	0	0	0
No	5	10	8	2	25
Has the state replaced the loss of federal grant funds?					
Yes	1	0	0	0	1
No	5	10	9	2	26

Not surprisingly, the responding municipal leagues, with one exception, want the federal government to reimburse municipalities for the costs associated with federal mandates. States to date have not come to the assistance of municipalities by replacing federal revenue sharing or the decline in federal grant-in-aid moneys.

A 1987 survey of state associations of counties produced very similar results. Interestingly, one county association in the South was opposed to federal reimbursement of the costs associated with clean-water mandates and pointed out that water-pollution abatement "is a local responsibility."

The ability of local governments to raise revenue through taxation and borrowing is limited in most states by various constitutional and statutory restrictions.[71] All states provide for full or partial property-tax exemptions, thirty-nine states limit local tax rates, twenty-two states limit tax levies, and three states have established local expenditure limits. In addition, constitutions and statutes in forty-six states establish debt limits for all or some general-purpose local governments. In forty-six states, long-term borrowing by local governments is subject to voter approval in a referendum, and in a number of states an extra-majority affirmative vote is required for the issuance of bonds.

Even if states and their subdivisions were free of constitutional borrowing and taxation restrictions, these units would be hesitant to raise taxes sharply or to borrow large sums of funds because of the "tax revolt" that erupted in the 1970s in many states.[72] Employing the initiative, voters in California in 1978 approved Proposition 13, limiting the general property tax. Idaho and Nevada voters in 1978 and Massachusetts voters in 1980 approved similar initiative propositions.

Intergovernmental Regulatory-Relief Bill

These developments at the subnational level have not gone unnoticed at the national level. Senator David F. Durenberger of Minnesota has introduced in each Congress in recent years an intergovernmental regulatory-relief bill.[73] In introducing his 1987 bill, the senator referred to the decrease in federal financial assistance to states and their subdivisions in the period 1980 to 1985: "Federal aid for clean water decreased 29 percent, clean air decreased 37 percent, bilingual education decreased 36 percent — the list goes on."[74] He added, "The clear message from Washington to State and Local governments has been 'we're counting on you,' but when it comes time to finance these new responsibilities the message from Washington is 'don't count on us.' No action represents this sentiment more clearly than the termination of the general revenue sharing program last year."[75]

In supporting the bill, cosponsor Senator Pete Wilson of California pointed out that there had been a 24 percent decline, in constant dollars, of federal financial assistance to subnational units in the period 1980 to 1987 and that there was a 60 percent reduction in federal funds for urban programs while the costs imposed upon these governments by federal mandates continued to increase.[76] Senator Wilson justified federal reimbursement of mandated costs:

If, in our judgment, a particular responsibility to be discharged at the state and local level is important enough to merit the enactment of federal legislation in order to require it, then, it seems only fair and right that such mandates should be accompanied by appropriate federal funding.

In recent years, Congress has often responded to problems without providing the adequate funding to carry them out—present mandates are estimated to cost state and local governments billions of dollars each year. If we now require federal reimbursement for all future federal mandates, we shall reform our low lack of realism and work to slow down the proliferation of regulatory requirements while bringing relief, much deserved relief, to those who labor at the state and local level.[77]

Summary and Conclusions

This chapter has examined the development of informal federal preemption through tax-credit programs and conditional grant-in-aid programs, criticisms of informal federal preemption, and administrative and political responses to the criticisms.

The combination of the reduction in federal financial assistance to subnational governments and the increase in federal mandating because of continued federal preemption of state and local governmental responsibilities raises important questions about the future of the federal system in the United States. While the regulatory relief provided by Congress and the president in the form of block grants has been welcomed by state and local government officials, the increased use of preemptive powers has created serious tensions in intergovernmental relations, often without solving the problems addressed by preemption, and have contributed to the financial problems of many political subdivisions.

Chapter 4 examines total preemption by Congress and decisions by the Supreme Court holding that states and their local governments lack authority to initiate actions in certain areas. With respect to congressional preemption, a typology and two case studies of total preemption are presented. Chapter 5 addresses the various types of partial federal preemption.

IV

Total Federal Preemption

ecognizing their inability to foresee all future developments, the writers of the Constitution decided to ensure that there would not be a static distribution of political power between Congress and the states by providing procedures for formally amending the Constitution, authorizing congressional preemption relative to several concurrent powers, and including the "supremacy of the laws" clause. The latter provides not only for the prevalence of a federal law if there is a conflict in the exercise of a concurrent power by the lawmaking body on each plane but also for nullification of a state law based upon a nonconcurrent reserved power if the law conflicts with a federal law based on a delegated power.

The exercise of formal preemptive powers by the Congress had a minimal impact on intergovernmental relations until 1965.[1] Federal regulation of interstate commerce did not prevent the states from exercising the police power, provided such exercise did not unduly burden commerce among the states. Support for this conclusion is based in part upon the January 1940 issue of *The Annals,* which was devoted to "Intergovernmental Relations in the United States" and contained no reference to formal federal preemption.[2] A similar volume of *The Annals,* published in 1974, contained several references to formal federal preemption.[3]

Although total federal preemption removes states' discretionary authority in a given regulatory area, the states on occasion will support and even urge Congress to assume total responsibility for a function. For example, the National Governors' Association adopted the following policy position for 1980–1981:

The Association is concerned with increasing costs to truckers as well as consumers resulting from the lack of uniformity in allowable vehicle weights and dimensions which still exists among many States. . . .

The Association urges that Congress immediately enact legislation establishing national standards for weight (80,000 gross; 20,000 per single axle; 34,000 for tandem) and length (60 ft.).[4]

In other instances, associations of state officials will call upon Congress to clarify the authority of a federal department or agency responsible for a totally preempted function. The National Conference of State Legislatures has expressed its concern about the danger to the public posed by the transportation of high-level nuclear wastes across their borders to a disposal site, maintained that the national government should be responsible "for the protection of the public against damages and personal injury incurred as the consequence of any accident in the transportation or disposal of high-level nuclear waste," and added:

The Nuclear Waste Policy Act authorizes the U.S. Department of Energy (DOE) to enter into written cooperation and consultation agreements with the States to address liability concerns of the States. However, the federal government (through its agent the U.S. Department of Energy) asserts that its liability for accidents incurred during the transportation or disposal of high-level nuclear waste is limited by existing federal law which, it claims, circumscribes its authority to protect the States.[5]

This chapter probes the nature of total federal preemption by developing a typology of formal preemption types and presenting two case studies involving complete assumption of regulatory authority by the federal government.

The Nature of Congressional Preemption

The major reasons for the sharp increase in federal preemptive action since 1965 are the growing recognition of the interstate nature of many public problems, the general failure of the states to launch effective corrective programs to solve the problems, the establishment of environmental and public-interest groups that have lobbied effectively in Washington, and concomitant public support for governmental action to solve environmental problems in particular.

Many federal laws contain an express provision for total federal preemption. The Flammable Fabrics Act stipulates that "this Act is intended to supersede any law of any State or political subdivision thereof inconsistent with its provisions."[6] Similarly, the United States Grain Standards Act forbids states or political subdivisions to "require the inspection or description in accordance with any standards of kind, class, quality, condition, or other characteristics of grain as a condition of shipment, or sale, of such grain in interstate or foreign commerce, or require any license for, or impose any other restrictions upon, the performance of any officials inspection function under this Act by official inspection personnel."[7] And the Radiation Control for Health and Safety Act of 1968 forbids state and local governments "to establish . . . any standard which is applicable to the same aspect of the performance of such product and which is not identical to the federal standard."[8]

A limited type of total preemption is illustrated by the Gun Control Act of 1968: "No provision of this chapter shall be construed as indicating an intent on the part of the Congress to occupy the field in which such provision operates to the exclusion of the law of any State on the same subject matter, unless there is a direct and positive conflict between such provision and the law of the State so that the two can not be reconciled or consistently stand together."[9] A similar provision is contained in the Drug Abuse Control Amendments of 1965.[10]

Many acts of Congress do not contain an explicit partial- or total-preemption section yet have been held by courts to be preemptive. In Chapter 6, we examine the criteria employed by the Supreme Court to determine whether an act of Congress is preemptive of state and/or local laws.

Is it possible for the states and their political subdivisions to receive relief from congressional preemptive acts and judicial decisions preempting the authority of subnational units? The answer is yes, according to Mr. Justice Harry A. Blackmun of the Supreme Court, who stressed in *Garcia v. San Antonio Metropolitan Transit Authority:*

[T]he principal and basic limit on the federal commerce power is inherent in all congressional action—the built-in restraints that our system provides through state participation in federal government action. The political process ensures that laws that unduly burden the States will not be promulgated. In the factual setting of these cases the internal safeguards of the political process have performed as intended.[11]

Not all observers of the American federal system agree with Justice Blackmun's position, and one of our purposes is to examine the question of how responsive Congress is to the states and their political subdivisions in providing relief from preemptive statutes that unduly restrict the discretionary authority of subnational units and impose added costs upon them. In the next two sections, I present a typology of fourteen varieties of total federal preemption and two case studies illustrating the degree of federal responsiveness to the concerns of state and local governmental officials relative to two completely preempted regulatory functions.

A Typology of Total Federal Preemption

An examination of the various total-federal-preemption statutes enacted by Congress reveals that there are fourteen distinctive types of complete assumption of regulatory authority by the federal government. In this section, I briefly identify each type; I shall use this typology for comparative purposes when I examine the various partial-federal-preemption statutes in Chapter 5. The purpose of the comparative typology is to assist analysts in drawing conclusions as to which type(s) of federal preemption is most effective in mobilizing the needed resources at least cost to achieve the objectives mandated by the preemption statutes.

No Need for State and/or Local Assistance
In addressing the bankruptcy problem, the Congress in 1898 decided to nullify completely the bankruptcy laws of the states and make the U.S. district court and the Supreme Court of the District of Columbia responsible for handling bankruptcy cases.[12] In 1933, Congress established the U.S. Bankruptcy Court to handle all bankruptcy filings in the United States.[13] By assigning total responsibility for this function to a U.S. court, Congress avoided the need to rely upon states or their political subdivisions for assistance in carrying out the function.

Responding to pressure from the domestic motor-vehicle manufacturers, who feared that they might have to develop different specialized emission control systems for each of the fifty states, Congress in 1967 completely preempted the right to establish emission standards for 1968 and subsequent model vehicles.[14] The Clean Air Amendments of 1970 represented a sharp break with the earlier approach to air-pollution abatement, which took into consideration the economic and technical feasibility of abatement controls. The amendments, for example, stipulated that 1975-model automobiles must achieve a 90 percent reduction of the 1970 standards for emission of carbon monoxide, hydrocarbons, and nitrogen oxides.[15] These standards were mandated without an analysis of the economic and technical feasibility of achieving the standards.

Although the federal government does not need the assistance of subnational units in ensuring that new motor vehicles meet the national emission standards, state emission programs are an essential part of state implementation plans (SIPs) for the attainment of air-quality goals, a subject addressed in the next chapter.

No State Economic Regulation Allowed

In deciding to enact laws implementing the total economic deregulation of the airline, trucking, and bus industries, Congress took action to ensure that there would be no state economic regulation of airlines and bus companies. The Airline Deregulation Act of 1978 added the following section to the Federal Aviation Act of 1958:

> Sec. 105. (1) (1) Except as provided in paragraph (2) of this subsection, no State or political subdivision thereof and no interstate agency or other political agency of two or more States shall enact or enforce any law, rule, regulation, standard, or other provision having the force and effect of law relating to rates, routes, or services of any air carrier having authority under title IV of this Act to provide interstate air transportation. (2) Except with the respect to air transportation (other than charter air transportation) provided pursuant to a certificate issued by the Board under section 401 of this Act, the provisions of paragraph (1) of this subsection shall not apply to any transportation by air of persons, property, or mail conducted wholly within the State of Alaska.[16]

The Motor Carrier Act of 1980 deregulated the trucking industry, and the Bus Regulatory Reform Act of 1982 deregulated the bus industry and also stipulated that there could be no state economic regulation of bus companies.[17]

During the Great Depression, a number of the states enacted price-maintenance laws as "fair trade" laws. According to the typical provisions of such laws, if a manufacturer signed an agreement with one retailer to maintain a fixed price for an article, the agreement became binding upon all retailers in the state. When questions were raised whether state legislatures possessed the authority under the Constitution to enact such laws in view of the commerce clause, Congress enacted the Robinson-Patman Act in 1936, validating such laws.[18] As part of the economic deregulation movement of the 1970s,

Congress repealed the authorization under the commerce clause for state legislatures to enact "fair trade" laws.

No Mandatory Retirement Age

Commencing with the Age Discrimination in Employment Act of 1967, Congress took action to protect older citizens against employment discrimination.[19] This act was amended in 1982 by Congress to prohibit employers' requiring employees to retire because of age.[20] As the amendment applied to states and their political subdivisions in their capacities as employers, protests were made by these governmental units with respect to the application of the amendment to fire fighters and police.

In 1986, Congress responded to the complaints by enacting the Age Discrimination in Employment Amendments, stipulating that it is not unlawful for a state or a political subdivision

to fail or refuse to hire or to discharge any individual because of such individual's age if such action is taken —

(1) with respect to the employment of an individual as a firefighter or as a law enforcement officer and the individual has attained the age for hiring or retirement in effect under applicable State or local law on March 3, 1983, and

(2) pursuant to a bonafide hiring or retirement plan that is not a subterfuge to evade the purposes of this Act.[21]

The provision sunsets automatically on December 31, 1993.

State and Local Assistance Needed

While the Atomic Energy Act of 1946, as amended, assigns complete responsibility for the regulation of nuclear power plants to the U.S. Nuclear Regulatory Commission, the lack of adequate resources makes the commission dependent upon subnational governments for emergency personnel and equipment to protect public health and safety in the event of a radioactive discharge at a nuclear generating station. A major controversy swirled around attempts to repeal a commission regulation requiring emergency planning around new civilian nuclear power plants, including establishment of ten-mile evacuation zones, before the plants are allowed to operate at full power.[22] We address this controversy in the context of intergovernmental relations as a case study in a later section of this chapter.

A second example of the dependence of the national government upon subnational units involves the ban imposed by Congress in the Safe Drinking Water Act Amendments of 1986 on the use of lead pipes, solder, and flux in any public water system.[23] The amendments direct states to enforce the prohibition "through State or local plumbing codes, or such other means of enforcement as the State may determine to be appropriate."[24] Failure of a state to enforce the lead ban may result in the loss of 5 percent of federal grants under the Safe Drinking Water Act. As of 1990, thirty-five states and the District of Columbia were enforcing the lead ban.

State-Activities Exception

In enacting the National Traffic and Motor Vehicle Safety Act of 1966, Congress totally preempted responsibility for establishing motor-vehicle safety standards. However, the act makes an exception for motor vehicles operated by a state or a local government by authorizing these units to establish "a safety requirement applicable to motor vehicles or motor vehicle equipment procured for its own use if such requirement imposes a higher standard of performance than that required to comply with the otherwise applicable federal standard."[25]

Limited Regulatory Turnbacks

Several total-federal-preemption statutes contain authorization for a federal official or agency to turn back limited regulatory responsibility to states. The U.S. Grain Standards Act is totally preemptive, as noted in an earlier section.[26] The act, however, authorizes the administrator of the Federal Grain Inspection Service to delegate to state agencies authority to perform official inspection and weighing.[27] Currently, eight states inspect and weigh grain at export-port locations, and an additional thirteen states perform these functions at interior locations. Since the states operate on a fee-for-service basis, they incur no costs that the Federal Grain Inspection Service must reimburse them for.

Similarly, the Hazardous and Solid Waste Amendments of 1984 allow the states to assume responsibility for the U.S. Environmental Protection Agency's hazardous-waste program.[28] Since 1976, the states have been partially preempted by Congress relative to hazardous-waste programs.[29] Nineteen states currently have assumed responsibility for such programs. As of 1990 forty-four states received authorization from the Environmental Protection Agency under the Resource Conservation and Recovery Act, but only Georgia had received authority from the agency under the Hazardous and Solid Waste Amendments.[30]

The Federal Railroad Safety Act of 1970 provides for state assumption of railroad inspections.[31] As of 1990, thirty-one states were participating in the State Safety Program, funded in part by the Federal Railroad Administration.[32]

The most successful major program involving states' voluntarily administering federal laws and regulations is the Agreement States Program of the Nuclear Regulatory Commission. The Atomic Energy Act of 1946, a total-federal-preemption statute relative to ionizing radiation, was amended in 1959 to authorize the former Atomic Energy Commission (now Nuclear Regulatory Commission) to enter into agreements with states under which a state would be allowed to assume certain regulatory responsibilities.[33] As of 1990, twenty-nine states had signed agreements with the Nuclear Regulatory Commission (NRC).

In contrast to partial-preemption statutes that assign regulatory responsibility to the states, provided they adopt standards at least as high as federal standards and enforce the state standards, the Agreement State Program simply requires that a state radiation-control program be compatible with, and not necessarily identical to, the commission's regulatory program.

In 1983, the National Governors' Association's Committee on Energy and Environment released the first comprehensive report on the Agreement State Program, containing the conclusion that the "program is one of the most successful state/federal partnerships yet established in terms of 1) the flexibility provided States in assuming regulatory responsibility, 2) successful state performance of regulatory duties, and 3) consultation with States in the preparation of new regulations."[34]

My survey of agreement states in 1987 produced a similar conclusion: All respondents reported excellent experience with the program, and no state had considered abandonment of the program. The only reservation mentioned by a few respondents referred to the lack of federal funding of the program. According to respondents, state regulation is preferable to NRC regulation because state personnel are more readily available to licensees with questions, licensing action is completed more rapidly, licenses are inspected more frequently and minor problems are corrected before they become major problems, state personnel spend less time in travel and thereby reduce the cost of inspections, and emergency personnel can respond more rapidly than NRC personnel.

New Mexico, however, returned responsibility to the Commission for the uranium-mill licensing program in 1986, primarily because of the cost of the program, which was diverting Radiation Protection Bureau personnel from other licensing responsibilities.[35]

Federal Mandating of State-Law Enactment

The Equal Employment Opportunity Act of 1972 and similar laws mandate that the states comply with the federal laws in the enactment of state laws, under the threat of civil or criminal penalties.[36] Since the *Garcia* decision in 1985, discussed in an earlier section, subnational governments must comply with the provisions of the Fair Labor Standards Act of 1938, as amended, or be subject to both civil and criminal penalties.[37] A similar mandate is contained in the Federal Mine Safety and Health Act of 1977.[38]

The Tax Equity and Fiscal Responsibility Act of 1982 mandates that state and local governments making income tax refunds to taxpayers must report information on the refunds to the Internal Revenue Service.[39]

Federal Promotion of Interstate Compact Formation

The Low Level Radioactive Policy Act of 1980 declares that "each State is responsible for providing for the availability of capacity either within or outside the State for the disposal of low-level radioactive waste generated within its borders," with the exceptions of such wastes generated by national defense or federal research activities.[40] The act promotes disposal of such wastes by encouraging the formation of interstate compacts for this purpose. However, such a compact "shall not take effect until the Congress has by law consented to the compact. Each such compact shall provide that every five years after the compact has taken effect the Congress may by law withdraw its consent."[41] Effective January 1, 1986, a compact may provide that only wastes generated within the region may be disposed of within the region.

A series of complex legal questions were raised by draft compacts, and in 1984, Assistant Attorney General Robert A. McConnell advised Chairman Strom Thurmond of the U.S. Senate Committee on the Judiciary that

given the authority of the commissions to assess civil penalties and to impose other sanctions, and their authority to enforce those penalties and sanctions through the federal courts, the compacts could possibly be challenged on the basis that such authority may be exercised only by "officers of the United States." It may be that the States intend only that the commissions exercise such authority by virtue of appropriate delegations of state law, and only through the state courts. Such content, however, is not clear on the face of the compacts. Moreover, . . . it is not entirely clear whether or to what extent, the States can by agreement make the compact enforceable only in the state or federal system.[42]

Responding to these problems, Congress enacted the Low-Level Radioactive Waste Policy Amendments Act of 1985, making changes in the 1980 act and granting the consent of Congress to seven interstate compacts.[43] Two additional compacts have been approved by Congress. In addition, several states initiated action to locate a site within their respective borders since the three states with disposal sites—Nevada, South Carolina, and Washington—may refuse to accept low-level wastes from the other states effective January 1, 1993.

Gubernatorial Petition for Preemption Removal

The Department of Transportation and Related Agencies Appropriation Act of 1986 stipulates that tolls for motor vehicles on any bridge connecting Brooklyn and Staten Island, New York, shall be collected only as vehicles exit the bridge in Staten Island.[44] However, the secretary of transportation is authorized to remove the limitation upon the petition of the governor of New York State.

State Veto of a Federal Administrative Decision

The Nuclear Waste Policy Act of 1982 authorizes the secretary of energy to select a site for the construction of a high-level radioactive waste facility, but the site may be vetoed either by the state governor or the state legislature.[45] Congress, however, may override the state veto.

In December 1987, Congress ignored the procedure for selecting a site outlined in the 1982 act and included in the Omnibus Budget Reconciliation Act for fiscal year 1988 an amendment to the 1982 act eliminating sites in Washington and Texas under consideration by the Department of Energy and in effect selecting a site in Nevada, subject to tests for suitability.[46]

Contingent Total Preemption

The Federal Voting Rights Act of 1965, as amended, contains national provisions that are not applied to a state or a local government unless two conditions exist. The act automatically applies to a state or local government if the U.S. attorney general has determined that as of November 1, 1964, a test or device has been employed to abridge the rights of citizens to vote because of race or color *and* the director of the United States Bureau of the Census has determined that less than 50 percent of the persons of voting age were registered to vote on November 1, 1964, or that less than 50 percent of the persons of voting age exercised the franchise in the 1964 presidential election.[47]

If a determination is made that the act applies to a state or political subdivision, the covered unit becomes subject to the preclearance requirement, forbidding the unit to enact or administer any change, no matter how minor, in its election system unless the attorney general of the United States, within sixty days of submission of a proposed change to him, fails to register an objection. Alternatively, a covered unit can seek the issuance, by the District Court for the District of Columbia, of a declaratory judgment that the change would not abridge the right to vote of citizens protected by the act.

Federal Title Assertion
Paradoxically, a total-preemption statute can grant authority to a state. The Abandoned Shipwreck Act of 1987 asserts a national-government title to each abandoned historic shipwreck and subsequently transfers the title to the state within which the shipwreck is located.[48]

Contingent Moratorium
Amendments to the Atlantic Striped Bass Conservation Act, enacted in 1986, require individual states to comply with the management plan developed by the Atlantic States Marine Fisheries Commission, which lacks enforcement powers, or be subject to a striped-bass fishing moratorium imposed by the U.S. Fish and Wildlife Service and the Marine Fisheries Service in the coastal waters of a noncomplying state.[49]

Cooperative Enforcement
As noted in an earlier section, Congress recognized that states could play a helpful role in the enforcement of several total-preemption statutes and amended these statutes to authorize the concerned federal agency administrator to turn back a limited amount of regulatory authority to states signing an agreement with the administrator.

A related type of total-preemption statute is the Age Discrimination in Employment Amendments of 1986, which authorize the Equal Employment Opportunity Commission to sign cooperative enforcement agreements with state or local fair-employment agencies.[50] Such agreements, however, do not provide for a limited turnback of regulatory authority.

Nuclear Evacuation Plans and Truck Size and Weight

While one could assume that the exercise by Congress of total preemptive powers would result in Congress and appropriate federal agencies being completely responsible for the preempted function, an intergovernmental problem may be caused by the total-preemption action because Congress is a government of enumerated powers and may lack essential complementary powers and resources to ensure that it is capable of executing successfully a preempted responsibility.

Nuclear Evacuation Plans

The dependence of the national government upon a state and a number of its political subdivisions for auxiliary support relative to a totally preempted function is illustrated by the problems surrounding nuclear power plants. In 1983, Governor Mario M. Cuomo of New York highlighted such a problem in his state in a letter he sent to Senator Daniel P. Moynihan of New York.

I am writing to request that you initiate a hearing process to: (1) achieve a clarification and a precise specification of the respective responsibilities of local, state, and federal governments for off-site emergency plans at our nation's nuclear plants, and (2) devise a federal system for the administration and funding of the extensive activities undertaken by all three levels of government in the implementation, and (3) examine the consequences of decisions required by this off-site emergency planning process.[51]

Continuing controversy relative to evacuation plans for the area around the Shoreham nuclear power plant under construction on Long Island led the governor in 1985 to write to Secretary of Energy John S. Herrington, objecting to the department's support of the Long Island Lighting Company's (LILCO) evacuation plans.

The emergency preparedness situation concerning the Shoreham plant is the result of scrupulous and deliberate decisions of the County of Suffolk and New York State not to adopt or implement an off-site emergency plan for Shoreham. These governmental decisions were reached through the exercise of police powers which are vested inherently in the state government and the local government to which the State has delegated those powers. The efforts of your Department to promote LILCO's emergency plan over the constitutionally sound objections of the State and local governments is an affront to the sovereignty of New York State and an injury to the people of New York.[52]

In his letter, the governor specifically quoted a statement by President Ronald Reagan that "this Administration does not favor the imposition of Federal Government authority over the objections of State and local governments in matters regarding the adequacy of an emergency evacuation plan for a nuclear power plant such as Shoreham."[53]

Although New York State and Suffolk County did not participate in federally supervised test evacuation plans for the Shoreham nuclear power plant, the initial federal evaluation of the test was positive, according to Roger B. Kowieski, chairman of the Regional Assistance Committee representing eight federal agencies, who stated that "[t]his was better than first drills at other nuclear plants."[54] Regional Director Frank P. Petrone, of the Federal Emergency Management Agency, however, stated that his agency was unable to give "reasonable assurance" that the public would be adequately protected in an emergency without the participation of New York State and area local governments.[55]

The adequacy of the evacuation plans made newspaper headlines on April 15, 1986, when Regional Director Petrone resigned and charged that Julius W. Becton, head of the agency in Washington, had applied pressure to have Petrone drop his conclusion from a soon-to-be-released report that he could not "give reasonable assurance that public health and safety" would be protected should an emergency occur at the plant.[56] Mr. Petrone added that he believed his agency superiors agreed in general with his conclusion but were pressured by the U.S. Department of Energy, the Nuclear Regulatory Commission (NRC), and the "power lobby."[57] He also stressed that "the Federal Government can no longer have the arrogance to think they can set forth a program and just go with it and say state and local governments be damned."[58]

Similar questions have been raised relative to the February 26, 1986, test of the evacuation procedures at the Seabrook nuclear power plant under construction in New Hampshire. Massachusetts officials withdrew from the two-state exercise because of safety considerations, and seven New Hampshire towns refused to participate. Chairman John Walker, of the Hampton Selectmen, stressed that "[t]here just isn't a highway structure in place to handle the traffic, yet they have known for seven years — since Three Mile Island — that they needed an evacuation plan."[59]

"Regional Director Edward Thomas, of the Federal Emergency Management Agency, concluded that the plan had too many deficiencies and stated that the major problems were evacuation buses (60 percent did not report to their proper locations) and an inadequate backup strategy to compensate for local governments refusing to participate in the exercise.[60] A telephone number broadcast as an emergency information number turned out to be the commercial-loan department of a bank in nearby Portsmouth.[61]

On September 20, 1986, Governor Michael S. Dukakis of Massachusetts announced that he would not submit evacuation plans for the Massachusetts part of the evacuation zone and suggested that consideration should be given to converting the Seabrook facility into a fossil-fuel-burning plant.[62]

On September 26, 1986, Senior Vice President William Derrickson, of New Hampshire Yankee, addressing a meeting of NRC's Advisory Committee on Reactor Safeguards, maintained that "risk from the plant is far, far lower than indicated in the utility's 1983 analysis and the evacuation zone should be reduced from a ten mile radius to a two mile radius."[63]

In 1980, the commission adopted a regulation providing for an emergency evacuation zone of an approximately ten-mile radius from a nuclear power plant.[64] Because of the refusal of certain states and local governments to participate in emergency evacuation tests, the commission, on February 26, 1987, adopted a staff recommendation in the form of a proposed rule allowing the licensing of nuclear power plants in the absence of state and local government participation in emergency plans.[65]

In explaining the proposed rule, the commission referred to the fact that the abandonment of a nuclear power plant completed at the cost of billions of dollars would create serious financial problems for the concerned utility company and added:

Finally, at least in situations where non-cooperation in offsite emergency planning is motivated by safety issues, vesting state or local governments with *de facto* veto authority over full-power operation is inconsistent with the fundamental thrust of the Atomic Energy Act whereby the Commission is given exclusive *de jure* authority to license nuclear power plants and to impose radiological safety requirements for their construction and operation.[66]

On April 22, 1987, the Atomic Safety and Licensing Board of the

Nuclear Regulatory Commission rejected the application of the Public Service Company of New Hampshire for a reduction in the emergency evacuation zone from a ten-miles to a one-mile radius extending from the Seabrook nuclear reactor.[67]

On October 29, 1987, however, the U.S. Nuclear Regulatory Commission unanimously amended its rules relative to the evaluation of the adequacy of off-site emergency planning for nuclear power plants by permitting the operation of such plants in situations where state and/or local governments decline to participate in the off-site emergency planning.[68] The commission justified its action by citing a section of the Nuclear Regulatory Commission Reauthorization Act of 1980 stipulating that the commission may issue operating licenses in the absence of an off-site emergency plan involving the concerned state and local governments, provided there is a "utility plan which provides reasonable assurance that public health and safety are not endangered by operation of the facility concerned."[69]

In 1990, the Nuclear Regulatory Commission voted unanimously to license the Seabrook nuclear power plant, and the U.S. Court of Appeals for the District of Columbia Circuit rejected a petition for a stay of the license pending a ruling in a suit brought by the Massachusetts attorney general and the other plant opponents.[70] Similarly, Chief Justice William H. Rehnquist rejected an appeal for a stay of execution of the license.[71]

The refusal of Massachusetts and a number of general-purpose local governments to participate in the Seabrook evacuation exercises raises the question whether federal preemptive powers are adequate for the task of protecting public safety.

Although Congress can preempt state and local laws relative to ionizing radiation on sites of nuclear facilities and the transportation of nuclear materials, including spent control rods and other radioactive wastes, it is apparent that the federal government lacks the administrative capacity to guarantee public safety. The cooperation of state governments and their political subdivisions is essential when an area within ten miles of a nuclear power plant must be evacuated and/or nuclear materials are being transported. Cooperation and not compulsion is the key. One can advance the premise that conditional federal grants-in-aid would be more successful in eliciting state and local government cooperation than arrogant federal assumption of complete responsibility for regulating ionizing radiation.

Our primary focus has been on the interplane relationships and responsibilities for protecting public health and safety against the hazards associated with the use of ionizing radiation. There also is a great need for a study of the commission's regulatory program to ensure that it guarantees the safe operation of nuclear power plants. Various organizations have issued reports severely criticizing the commission's regulatory activities.

The Subcommittee on General Oversight and Investigations of the House of Representatives in 1987 released a highly critical report of the relationships of the commission to the nuclear industry.

Over the past several years, the Nuclear Regulatory Commission has demonstrated an unhealthy empathy for the needs of the nuclear industry to the detriment of the safety of the American people. The NRC has failed to maintain an arm's length regulatory posture with the commercial nuclear power industry. On a number of occasions, the NRC has acted as if it were the advocate for, and not the regulator of, the nuclear industry. The Subcommittee does not draw these conclusions on the basis of an isolated incident. We arrive at these conclusions based on a pattern of Commission actions taken over a number of years. These actions were by no means trivial; each of them involved important issues of public safety.

Time and again the NRC has afforded the relief sought by industry. In the case of fitness for duty, fire prevention, and backfits, such relief was contrary to previous determination of the Commission itself.[72]

The seriousness of these charges makes it imperative that Congress and the commission initiate the necessary corrective actions and that subnational governments ensure that they are capable of coping adequately with emergencies involving nuclear power plants.

Congress unfortunately failed to respond to the complaints of concerned subnational government officials, even though the latter successfully publicized the problem throughout the nation. The Blackmun thesis is not supported by this case study.

Truck Size and Weight

Confused responsibility for the public's safety is the product of the Surface Transportation Assistance Act of 1982 (STAA) and its provisions allowing heavy trucks, including tandem trailers, to operate on interstate highways, certain federally aided primary routes (designated by the secretary of transportation), and local "access" routes to service stations, motels, restaurants, and terminals.[73] No criteria were provided in the preemptive law for determining whether older interstate highways and federally aided primary routes are capable of accommodating the larger and heavier trucks safely or determining which local roads are bona fide "access" routes. In preempting state and local responsibilities for highway safety, Congress responded to the powerful trucking industry, a major contributor to congressional candidates, without adequate consideration of the safety problems that the states and their political subdivisions would be unable to address because of federal preemption.

Section 311 (a) of the act stipulates:

No State shall establish, maintain, or enforce any regulation of commerce which imposes a vehicle length limitation of less than forty-eight feet on the length of the semitrailer unit operating in a truck tractor-semitrailer-trailer combination, on any segment of the National System of Interstate and Defense Highways and those classes of qualifying Federal-aid Primary System highways as designated by the Secretary.[74]

In addition, section 133 (b) prohibits a state from enacting or enforcing a law prohibiting large trucks to travel "to and from the Interstate Highway System to terminals and facilities for food, fuel, repairs, and rest."[75] Interestingly, section 133 (a) employs federal-highway grants-in-aid, a type of informal preemption, to induce states to allow heavier trucks on interstate highways.

A major advantage of the act, recognized by critics and supporters, is the eliminating of the patchwork quilt of conflicting state truck-size and weight limits. Critics, however, stressed the safety problems that will be produced by STAA. New York State Executive Deputy Commissioner of Transportation John K. Mladinov testified at a public hearing in Albany, New York, on August 9, 1983, that traffic congestion and the substandard condition of New York City metropolitan area highways necessitate the prohibition of tandem trucks in the city and on Long Island because "many of the designated highways have serious geometric, safety, and capacity problems."[76]

Testifying at the same public hearing, Nassau County Police Commissioner Samuel Rozzi maintained that allowing tandem trailers "to utilize our arterial and secondary roadways would be to jeopardize the safety of our motorists, bicyclists, and pedestrians."[77] The New York State Department of Transportation in 1983 identified 884.46 miles of federally designated highways with substandard lane widths for at least a portion of the total length of the routes.[78] Responding to the department's complaint, the Federal Highway Administration, on May 3, 1983, removed several routes from the federally designated system; the removed routes were generally parallel to interstate highways meeting all safety standards.[79] However, fourteen of the non-New York City–Long Island highways classified as substandard

by the New York State Department of Transportation were not removed from the designated system by the Federal Highway Administration.[80]

Adding fuel to the controversy between Congress and the states
over control of highways, Congress enacted an amendment to STAA
in 1983 requiring all states except Hawaii to permit 102-inch-wide
trucks on all federally designated highways if lane widths exceed
twelve feet.[81]

Vermont Attorney General John H. Easton, Jr., maintained that
"it looks like some guy with a Rand McNally map sat in an office here
and drew the whole thing up and he simply forgot that Vermont has
hills."[82] In a similar vein, Dean Tisdale, of the Idaho Transportation
Department, stressed: "We are not against trucks out here—after all,
we allow double trailers and even triple trailers on our interstates and
many other roads. But this plan simply did not put enough emphasis
on the safety factor on mountain roads."[83]

CONGRESSIONAL RESPONSE. The Blackmun thesis is supported by
this case study. The strong protest by officials of various states against
STAA led to congressional responses to state concerns in the form of
the Tandem Truck Safety Act of 1984 and Motor Carrier Safety Act
of 1984.[84]

The former act established a procedure under which the governor
of a state, after consulting concerned local governments, may notify
the secretary of transportation that the governor has determined that
a specific segment(s) "of the national System of Interstate Highways is
not capable of safely accommodating motor vehicles" of the length
permitted by STAA or 102-inch vehicles other than buses.[85]

The act addresses the safety concerns of state officials relative to
local access roads by stipulating that "nothing in this section shall be
construed as preventing any State or local government from imposing
any reasonable restriction, based on safety considerations, on any
truck tractor–semitrailer combination in which the semitrailer has a
length not to exceed 28 1/2 feet and which generally operates as part
of a vehicle combination" as described in the act.[86]

The Motor Carrier Safety Act of 1984 directed the secretary of
transportation, within eighteen months of the enactment date, to issue regulations establishing minimum safety standards for commercial motor vehicles, ensuring that

(1) commercial motor vehicles are safely maintained, equipped, loaded, and
    operated;

(2) the responsibilities imposed upon operators of commercial motor vehicles do not impair their ability to operate such vehicles safely;

(3) the physical condition of operators of commercial motor vehicles is adequate to enable them to operate such vehicles safely; and

(4) the operation of commercial motor vehicles does not have deleterious effects on the physical condition of such operators.[87]

The act also established a Safety Panel to advise the secretary of transportation relative to whether a "state law or regulation is additional to or more stringent than a regulation issued by the Secretary."[88] The state law or regulation may be enforced commencing five years after the enactment date of the act unless the secretary determines that "(A) there is no safety benefit associated with such state law or regulation; (B) such state law or regulation is incompatible with the regulation issued by the Secretary; . . . or (C) enforcement of such state law or regulation would be an undue burden on interstate commerce."[89]

The act authorizes any person, in addition to a state, to petition the secretary of transportation for the issuance of a waiver from a determination of the secretary that a state law or regulation is preempted.[90]

Summary and Conclusions

Our review of Supreme Court decisions reveals that Congress generally has been permitted to exercise broad discretion relative to the partial or total preemption of traditional state and local governmental functional responsibilities, regardless of whether the concerned statutes contain explicit preemption sections.

Our typology of total federal preemption clearly demonstrates that one of the fourteen types requires state and local government assistance if the goals of the preemption statute are to be achieved. The need for such assistance is documented in the case study of emergency evacuation plans for a ten-mile area around nuclear power plants.

The chapter's second case study of total federal preemption — truck size and weights on certain highways — illustrates the concerns initially flowing from the failure of Congress to include criteria in the Surface Transportation Assistance Act of 1982 for determining whether older highways can safely accommodate the larger and heavier trucks. In this instance, Congress responded affirmatively to the complaints of state and local officials. The reason for congressional responsiveness in this case, compared to the emergency-evacuation-plans case, may be due to the fact that the preemptive action affects all states, whereas the evacuation-plans case affects only a limited number of state and local governments.

Chapter 5 presents typologies of *Imperium in Imperio* federalism and partial federal preemption. One of the partial-preemption statutes—the Air Quality Act of 1967—also contains a total-preemption section relative to emissions from new motor vehicles.

V

Imperium in Imperio and Partial Federal Preemption

he framers of the U.S. Constitution recognized the undesirability of a static distribution of political power between the Congress and the states by providing procedures for formally amending the Constitution and authorizing congressional preemption relative to several concurrent powers. Although the Bill of Rights placed explicit limitations upon the powers of Congress, the Constitution was not amended formally to limit the residual powers of the states until the Fourteenth Amendment was ratified in 1868. This amendment laid the basis for enlarged judicial preemption, including judicial receivership, a subject addressed in Chapter 6.

Congressional preemption was not employed on a regular basis until Congress enacted the Water Quality Act of 1965. On occasions, the states have attempted to forestall federal preemptive action by promoting the adoption of uniform state laws and entering into interstate compacts creating agencies with powers to solve problems. An example of an unsuccessful effort of the latter nature is the Mid-Atlantic States Air Pollution Control Compact, which was entered into by Connecticut, New Jersey, and New York subsequent to President Lyndon B. Johnson's message to Congress on air pollution, recommending federal preemption of responsibility for air-pollution abatement.[1] Congress did not grant its consent to the proposed compact.

The sharp post-1965 increase in the exercise of its powers of partial preemption by Congress can be attributed to seven principal factors.

First, interstate cooperation had failed to solve a number of multistate problems such as water-basin problems.

Second, increased industrialization and use of motor vehicles contributed to air-pollution problems; and airsheds are national and international in nature, respecting no state or national boundary, thereby necessitating national corrective action.

Third, many states individually failed to take the required corrective action to solve serious public problems within their boundaries, and pressure built for congressional action. A U.S. representative wrote to me in 1986, attributing the increased preemptive action to "the failure of local governments to do what the Federal Government believes should be done." A western governor wrote to me in 1986 that there is congressional reluctance "to rely on the States due to special interest group influence."

Fourth, manufacturing industries became concerned with individual state laws prescribing standards that varied from state to state, thereby necessitating the manufacture of different models to meet the standards in particular states. The automobile industry, for instance, lobbied Congress to preempt totally responsibility for establishing emission standards for new motor vehicles. A second U.S. representative wrote to me in 1986 that "industry has gradually decided a single standard, though tough, is likely to be better than fifty standards, some loose, some very tough." Another governor wrote that "industry can function more efficiently when state to state differences in product regulation are eliminated."

Fifth, Congress concluded that the carrot of grants-in-aid was insufficient to generate the desired state action—and very expensive. Another governor wrote to me that preemption is employed more frequently because "the federal government does not have the resources to buy compliance with national goals through a grant."

Sixth, the establishment of environmental and other public-interest groups that have lobbied effectively in Washington and concomitant public support for national governmental action to address environmental problems in particular generated pressure upon Congress to employ its powers of preemption.

Seventh, the greater congressional interest in preemption is attributable in part to the election of a new breed of congressional members who lack state and local government experience and an in-depth understanding of the reasons why the drafters of the Constitution provided for a federal system rather than a unitary system with all permitted political power centered in Congress. A U.S. senator in 1986 wrote to me that "Democratic control of the Congress" was the reason for the very significant increase in the enactment of preemptive statutes. A second senator attributed the explosion of preemptive activity to "Congressmen not living up to the spirit of the Constitution."

This chapter focuses upon the exercise of concurrent powers by the states and the Congress under *Imperium in Imperio* and partial federal preemption, and examines the impact of partial federal preemption upon the relationships between the governor and the state legislature in the typical state.

Imperium in Imperio

Imperium in Imperio, an empire within an empire, is the heart of a federal system. Without the exercise of relatively autonomous political power by legislative bodies on at least two planes of government, there would be no federal system; political power would be centralized in the national plane (a unitary system) or in the subnational plane (a confederate system).

Alexander Hamilton, in *The Federalist Number 32,* placed exclusive federal powers in three categories: "where the Constitution in express terms granted an exclusive authority to the Union; where it granted in one instance an authority to the Union, and in another prohibited the States from exercising the like authority; and where it granted an authority to the Union to which a similar authority in the States would be absolutely and totally contradictory and repugnant."[2] The power to establish a uniform rule of naturalization was cited by Hamilton as an example of the third type of exclusive power.

The Founders assumed that Congress would confine its attention and activities almost exclusively to foreign affairs, national defense, major public-works projects such as river and harbor projects, and regulation of interstate commerce. The drafters of the Constitution, of course, recognized that Congress should and would exercise preemptive powers to nullify state action where deemed necessary and included the supremacy-of-the-laws clause in the fundamental document to ensure the prevalence of national law based upon a delegated power in the event of a conflict with a state law.[3]

The interstate commerce clause was specifically placed in the Constitution to enable Congress to deal effectively with restraints placed by the states upon interstate commerce. The Congress under the Articles of Confederation and Perpetual Union had lacked this regulatory power, and trade between the states nearly came to a standstill because of mercantilist actions of state legislatures.[4] In 1949, Mr. Justice Jackson of the Supreme Court described the commerce clause's dormant nature:

The commerce clause is one of the most prolific sources of national power and an equally prolific source of conflict with legislation of the State. While the Constitution vests in Congress the power to regulate commerce among the States, it does not say what the States may or may not do in the absence of congressional action, nor how to draw the line between what is and what is not commerce among the States. Perhaps even more than by interpretation of its written word, this Court has advanced the solidarity and property of this nation by the meaning it has given to these great silences of the Constitution.[5]

The Constitution provides for two types of concurrent powers. The first includes the power to tax, which may be exercised by both Congress and the state legislatures, and the former lacks the authority to preempt formally the taxing powers of the latter unless they are employed to place an undue burden on interstate commerce or discriminate against a person or group in violation of the "equal protection of the laws" clause of the Fourteenth Amendment to the Constitution. Furthermore, adoption of the Constitution in no way restricted the authority of the states to determine the nature of electoral systems and to prescribe voter qualifications, and specifically stipulated that electors of members of the U.S. House of Representatives "shall have the qualifications requisite for electors of the most numerous branch of the State Legislature."[6]

Congress, however, first gained the power to regulate elections under specified conditions in 1870 when the Fifteenth Amendment was declared to be in force. The amendment stipulates that "the right of citizens of the United States to vote shall not be denied or abridged by the United States or by any State on account of race, color, or previous condition of servitude" and authorizes Congress to enforce the guarantee "by appropriate legislation."

In 1870, Congress exercised its new power by enacting a law making private or public obstruction of the right to vote a federal misdemeanor punishable by imprisonment for no less than one month and no longer than one year.[7] Amendments to the law, adopted in 1871, authorized federal oversight of the election of U.S. representatives in every city and town over twenty thousand in population "whenever . . . there shall be two citizens thereof who . . . shall make known, in writing, to the Judge of the Circuit Court of the United States for the Circuit wherein such city or town shall be, their desire to have said registration, or said election, or both, guarded and scrutinized."[8]

The Supreme Court in 1875 ruled that sections of the 1870 act were unconstitutional because the act was not limited solely to the protection of the voting rights of black citizens since the act also provided for the punishment of those who interfered with the voting rights of white citizens.[9]

The most important sections of these two acts were repealed by Congress in 1894, and the states became relatively free of direct supervision of elections by federal officials until Congress enacted the Voting Rights Act of 1965, a suspensive total-preemption law described in Chapter 6.

Six types of *Imperium in Imperio* may be identified and can be contrasted with partial federal preemption, the subject of the latter part of this chapter.

State Powers Not Subject to Preemption

As noted above, the power of the states to tax can not be preempted formally by Congress in the absence of evidence that a state imposed a tax for mercantilistic purposes, thereby placing an inordinate burden on commerce among the several states and Indian tribes. In 1975, for example, the Supreme Court, in *Michelin Tire Corporation v. Wages,* ruled that the prohibition of the levying of "imports or duties on imports" by the states without the consent of Congress does not prohibit the levying of a property tax on imported products.[10] The situation, however, is different if Congress decides to preempt state taxation under the interstate commerce clause. The U.S. District Court for the Northern District of California ruled in 1982 that "as a matter of federal supremacy, the power of the State to discriminate against rail transportation property for purposes of applying tax rates was preempted by the passage of the RRR Act in 1976."[11]

The Supreme Court has not interpreted the Constitution to require the states to secure the consent of Congress for all compacts entered into with other states, although a literal reading of the Constitution reveals a prohibition of such compacts without congressional consent. In *Virginia v. Tennessee* (1893), the Court held that such consent is required only if the states desire to enter into "political" compacts affecting the balance of power between the states and the Union.[12]

Congress lacks the constitutional authority to preempt directly the vast array of powers the states possess to deliver services to their citizens unless the services are provided in a discriminatory manner. And Congress cannot preempt the power of the states to regulate businesses and individuals unless such regulations violate the interstate commerce clause or the equal-protection, due-process, or privileges-and-immunities guarantees of the Fourteenth Amendment. As explained in Chapter 3, Congress has acquired considerable influence over the reserved powers of the states by means of conditional grants-in-aid.

Direct and Positive Conflict between State and Federal Laws

In exercising its delegated power, Congress often includes a section in a law stipulating that a state law on the same subject is valid unless there is a direct and positive conflict between the two laws, in which event the supremacy clause of the Constitution provides for the prevailing of the national law. In enacting the Civil Rights Act of 1964, Congress stipulated: "Nothing in this Act shall be construed as indicating an intent on the part of Congress to occupy the field in which any such title operates to the exclusion of state laws on the same subject matter, nor shall any provision of this Act be construed as invalidating any provision of state law unless such provision is inconsistent with any of the purposes of this Act, or any provision thereof."[13] Similarly, the Gun Control Act of 1968 stresses: "No provision of this chapter shall be construed as indicating an intent on the part of the Congress to occupy the field in which such provision operates to the exclusion of the law of any State on the same matter, unless there is a direct and positive conflict between such provision and the law of the State so that the two can not be reconciled or consistently stand together."[14] An almost identical provision is contained in the Drug Abuse Control Amendments of 1965.[15]

The Federal Railroad Safety Act of 1970 specifically authorizes the states to adopt laws, rules, regulations, orders, and standards relative to railroad safety that are more stringent than the counterpart federal ones "when necessary to eliminate or reduce an essentially local safety hazard, and when not incompatible with any federal law, rule, regulation, order, or standard, and when not creating an undue burden on interstate commerce."[16]

Slightly different wording appears in the Occupational Safety and Health Act of 1970: "Nothing in this Act shall prevent any State agency or court from asserting jurisdiction under State law over any occupational safety or health issues with respect to which no [federal] standard is in effect."[17]

Declaration of Exclusive State Jurisdiction

In enacting statutes regulating marine shipping under the commerce clause, Congress established an *Imperium in Imperio* by an expressed savings clause stipulating that "pilots in the bays, rivers, harbors, and ports of the United States shall be regulated only in conformity with the laws of the States."[18]

The "shipping" statute, however, exempts a pilot of a "coastwide seagoing vessel" licensed by the federal government from state regulation by forbidding states to "impose on a pilot licensed under this subtitle an obligation to procure a State or other license, or adopt any other regulation that will impede the pilot the performance of the pilot's duties under the laws of the United States."[19]

Adoption of a State Standard

The Coast Guard Authorization Act of 1984 directed the secretary of transportation to develop standards for determining whether an individual is intoxicated while operating a marine recreational vessel.[20] In 1987, the Coast Guard, a unit of the Department of Transportation, published a final rule defining operation of a vessel while intoxicated.

The final rule adopts the state blood-alcohol-content (BAC) standards if they exist, but also establishes a federal BAC standard of 0.10 percent in the absence of a state standard.[21] Should a state lacking a BAC standard for the operation of a marine recreational vessel adopt a BAC standard, this standard is automatically adopted by the Coast Guard as the federal standard. The Coast Guard hopes that its establishment of a federal BAC standard of 0.10 percent will encourage states with lower standards to raise their standards to the Coast Guard standard.

Adoption of a State License

Similarly, the Port and Tanker Safety Act of 1978 empowers the secretary of transportation to require federally licensed pilots on all domestic and foreign self-propelled vessels "engaged in foreign trade when operating in the navigable waters of the United States in areas and under circumstances where a pilot is not otherwise required by state law."[22] This requirement, however, is terminated immediately when the state with jurisdiction over the area requires a state-licensed pilot and notifies the secretary.[23]

Administrative or Judicial Ruling Precluding Preemption

As explained in Chapter 4, the Federal Voting Rights Act of 1965 is a total-preemption statute relative to a state or political subdivision if two conditions are met: a voting device such as a literacy test had been employed in 1964 and less than 50 percent of the electorate cast ballots in the preceding presidential election.[24] Whereas the 1965 act was designed to prevent only the abridgment of the voting rights of citizens because of race or color, the 1975 amendments to the act broadened the coverage to include language minorities, defined as "persons who are American Indian, Asian American, Alaskan Natives, or of Spanish heritage," and cited the Fourteenth Amendment as well as the Fifteenth Amendment as the authority for the act.[25] The language-minority "triggers" are pulled if in excess of 5 percent of the citizens of voting age in a state or political subdivision are members of one language group *and* less than 50 percent of all citizens of voting age voted in the 1972 presidential election. The "triggers" are also pulled if in excess of 5 percent of the citizens of voting age in a unit are members of one language minority *and* the illiteracy rate of the group exceeds the national illiteracy rate.

If a subnational unit is covered by the act, no change may be made in its election system unless the attorney general of the United States, within sixty days of submission of a proposed change to him, fails to register an objection or the District Court for the District of Columbia issues a declaratory judgment that the proposed change would not abridge the right to vote of citizens protected by the act.[26]

Whereas the Voting Rights Act provides for either an administrative or judicial ruling precluding federal preemption, the Transportation Safety Act of 1974 provides for only an administrative ruling. The Materials Transportation Bureau of the Department of Transportation can issue administrative rulings addressing the question whether a state law or rule is precluded by federal preemption.[27] To avoid preemption, nonfederal requirements must be consistent with, or afford a greater level of protection than, federal requirements and not unreasonably burden interstate commerce.

In introducing consistency rulings of the Materials Transportation Bureau, the Research and Special Programs Administration of the U.S. Department of Transportation in 1984 wrote that Congress in effect intended to establish a type of *Imperium in Imperio.*

Despite the dominant role that Congress contemplated for departmental standards, there are certain aspects of hazardous materials transportation that are not amenable to exclusive nationwide regulation. One example is traffic control. Although the Federal Government can regulate in order to establish certain national standards promoting the safe, smooth flow of highway traffic, maintaining this in the face of short-term disruptions is necessarily a predominantly local responsibility. Another aspect of hazardous materials transportation that is not amenable to effective nationwide regulation is the problem of safety hazards which are peculiar to a local area. To the extent that nationwide regulations do not adequately address an identified safety hazard because of unique local conditions, State or local governments can regulate narrowly for the purpose of eliminating or reducing the hazard. The mere claim of uniqueness, however, is insufficient to insulate a non-Federal requirement from the preemption provisions of the HMTA.[28]

An example of an administrative ruling is the request of the Nuclear Assurance Corporation for a determination whether the prohibition of the transportation of radioactive materials on the facilities of the New York State Thruway Authority is inconsistent with and thereby preempted by the Hazardous Materials Transportation Safety Act. The key question was whether the corporation could comply with both the Thruway Authority rules and federal rules. The bureau in its administrative ruling held that the authority's "rule is not based upon any finding that transportation of highway route controlled quantity radioactive materials over the Thruway would present an unacceptable safety risk," and hence the "rule thus stands as a repudiation of the Department's rule of national applicability on highway routing of radioactive materials."[29]

Partial Federal Preemption

Partial preemption assumes two general forms. The first form involves Congress enacting a statute assuming complete responsibility for a portion of a regulatory field. The second form is the product of Congress enacting a law and/or federal administrative agencies, as authorized by law, promulgating rules and regulations establishing minimum national standards and authorizing the states to continue to exercise primary responsibility for the partially preempted regulatory function, provided the state standards are at least as high as the national standards and are enforced. The second type of preemption permits a state to tailor regulatory programs to meet special needs and conditions, provided the supervising federal agency certifies the state's programs.

Partial federal preemption permits state regulation at the sufferance of Congress, which at any time may preempt totally the responsibility for a regulatory function. In contrast to the type of *Imperium in Imperio* inherent in the very nature of a federal system, the states under the first type of partial federal preemption may not continue to exercise primary regulatory responsibility in the partially preempted area unless each state has been authorized by the appropriate federal agency to exercise regulatory authority.

In this section, I describe eight types of partial preemption of state and local government authority, place particular emphasis upon the types of powers granted to the governor by the various partial-preemption statutes, and present a short case study of interest-group activities.

Minimum Standards Preemption

This type of partial preemption can be described as "contingent" total preemption based upon the "gun behind the door" theory that states have to be forced to initiate action to meet minimum national standards under the threat of losing primacy in regulating the partially preempted function. To continue to exercise regulatory authority, a state must submit a plan containing standards at least as stringent as federal ones to the appropriate federal agency for approval. In approving a plan, the agency delegates enforcement "primacy" to the state.

By the mid-1960s, Congress decided that a number of area and regional problems—particularly environmental ones—could not be solved by reliance upon state and local governmental action encouraged by fiscal carrots (*i.e.,* conditional grants-in-aid), and direct federal action was essential.

In the absence of mandated minimum national standards, a state was reluctant to initiate corrective action to solve certain problems—air and water pollution—with spillover costs affecting other states and/or nations, for fear that establishment and enforcement of high standards would drive industries out of the state or discourage industry from locating in the state. The states inherently act in a mercantilistic manner if free of national restraints in order to protect their industries, thereby maintaining and perhaps increasing employment opportunities for their citizens. Under minimum standards preemption, a state law supersedes the corresponding national law if state standards are equal to or higher than the national standards.

It is important to recognize that not all state and local governmental officials are opposed to federal preemption. Many subnational officials, as well as a majority of the members of Congress, are convinced that only the establishment of minimum national standards will prevent the development of industrial-haven states that would allow industries to pollute the environment. Another advantage to individual states of partial preemption, according to Connecticut Environmental Protection Commissioner Stanley J. Pac, is that it allows "Connecticut to place pressure on the Environmental Protection Agency to require Massachusetts to clean up rivers flowing into Connecticut."[30] Prior to partial preemption of responsibility for water-pollution abatement, the only recourse Connecticut had against Massachusetts was to sue the Commonwealth in the U.S. Supreme Court.

A New York State official reported that Governor Nelson A. Rockefeller wanted national involvement in water-pollution abatement because federal money would be essential if the state's waters were to be cleaned up.[31] He added that New York State embarrassed the U.S. government by publicizing the pollution caused by federal facilities in the state in order to obtain more federal funds.[32]

Experience with standard partial preemption reveals that the states have initiated socially desirable programs, privately favored by some state legislators and administrators, that probably would not have been implemented in the absence of federal preemption because the programs were too politically explosive on the state plane. An Environmental Protection Agency (EPA) official in 1985 stated that certain state officials "wanted the 'feds' to mandate something and EPA cooperates, thereby taking the heat off the State." An analogy can be drawn with local elected officials who support certain state mandates on local governments because it may not be politically possible for a municipality to initiate a program in the absence of a state directive.[33]

The Water Quality Act of 1965, the first minimum standards partial-preemption statute, directed that each state adopt "water quality standards applicable to interstate waters or portions thereof within such State" as well as an implementation and enforcement plan.[34] The secretary of the interior (now the EPA administrator) is authorized to promulgate interstate water-quality standards which become effective at the end of six months if a state fails to establish adequate standards.

The federal role was subsequently strengthened by other congressional enactments, particularly the Federal Water Pollution Control Act Amendments of 1972.[35] The governor of each state is directed by the amendments to identify areas suffering water-quality-control problems and designate "a single representative organization, including elected officials from local governments or their designees, capable of developing effective areawide waste treatment management plans" for each area. The EPA issued regulations on September 14, 1973, giving governors until March 14, 1974, to designate or non-designate such areas and agencies.[36] A New York State official stated that "the 1972 federal approach is what had been called the 'idiots' approach in the 1960s; *i.e.,* national uniformity. The proper approach was a stream classification approach."[37]

The 1972 law has been amended by subsequent acts, including the Clean Water Act of 1977, which extended the coverage of the Federal Water Pollution Control Act and stated that "it is the policy of Congress that the States manage the construction grant program under this Act and implement the permit programs under sections 402 and 404 of this Act."[38] In 1983, California returned its primacy for the construction-grant program to the EPA "because state officials believed the EPA required more of primacy States than it did of its own regional officials who served as implementors in States that did not accept primacy."[39]

The 1977 act reveals the influence of the farm lobby, which successfully inserted the following provision in the act: "(1)The Administrator shall not require a permit under this section for discharges composed entirely of return flows from irrigated agriculture, nor shall the Administrator directly or indirectly, require any State to require such a permit."[40]

As noted in Chapter 4, the Air Quality Act of 1967 completely preempted the right to establish motor-vehicle exhaust-emission standards for 1968 and subsequent models.[41] The act also partially preempted other air-pollution-abatement activities of subnational governments by following the general procedure embodied in the Water Quality Act of 1965. States were encouraged to assume primary enforcement responsibility. Federal action was authorized in the event of state inaction or inadequate action to combat air pollution.

The Clean Air Amendments of 1970 represented a dramatic break with the earlier approach of relying upon the states to provide the necessary leadership and taking into consideration the economic and technical feasibility of abatement controls.[42] Direct federal action to protect public health was made national policy, and explicit dates for adoption by the states of air-quality standards and abatement plans were specified. The amendments stipulated that 1975-model automobiles must achieve a 90 percent reduction of the 1970 standards for emissions of carbon monoxide, hydrocarbons, and nitrogen oxides.[43] In contrast to earlier ones, the new standards were mandated without considering the economic and technical feasibility of pollution-abatement systems.

The EPA was faced by a major challenge when the Supreme Court in 1973 let stand a district court decision interpreting the Clean Air Act Amendments as forbidding the states to permit significant deterioration of existing air quality.[44] Since the Supreme Court's decision was without opinion and the district court did not elaborate upon its ruling, the EPA was forced to execute a nondegradation policy without judicial guidelines, which posed problems for the states.[45]

The EPA can delegate responsibility for the prevention of significant deterioration (PSD) of air quality to the states. For example, on November 24, 1976, the EPA, at North Carolina's request, granted partial delegation of the PSD to the state and on September 21, 1984, expanded the state's authority by empowering it to modify EPA-issued permits in the state.[46]

In 1981, Idaho "returned its air delegations to the EPA but reaccepted them in 1983 when EPA assured stringent enforcement within Idaho by contracting out supervision to a private firm. This incident illustrates that States will rescind their acceptance of primacy if it suits their political interests."[47]

The Safe Drinking Water Act of 1974, another minimum standards partial-preemption statute, provides that "a State has primary enforcement responsibility for public water systems," provided the EPA administrator determines that the state "has adopted drinking water regulations which . . . are no less stringent than" national standards.[48] Should a state fail to adopt or enforce such standards, the agency applies national standards within that state.

The act's coverage was expanded considerably by the 1986 amendments extending federal standards to underground sources of drinking water.[49] Prior to enactment of the amendments, the EPA had to rely on authority scattered in various federal laws and regulations to take action to protect underground sources of drinking water.

As of 1987, only Indiana, Wyoming, and the District of Columbia had not been granted primacy under the Safe Drinking Water Act.[50] Iowa was granted primacy in 1977 but returned the program to the EPA effective July 1, 1981, because of financial problems. The resolution of the problems led to the return of primacy to the state effective August 1, 1982.[51]

The Surface Mining Control and Reclamation Act of 1977 is also a minimum standards partial-preemption statute. Each state with coal-mined land eligible for reclamation may submit to the secretary of the interior a state reclamation plan and annual projects to be carried out.[52] No federal funds are provided to a state for a reclamation program unless the state program has been approved.

In upholding the act, the Supreme Court in 1981 stressed: "If a State does not wish to submit a proposed permanent program that complies with the Act and implementing regulations, the full regulatory burden will be borned by the federal government. Thus, there can be no suggestion that the Act commandeers the legislative process of the States by directly compelling them to enact and enforce a federal regulatory program."[53]

Currently, nine states—Georgia, Idaho, Massachusetts, Michigan, North Carolina, Oregon, Rhode Island, South Dakota, and Washington—have decided not to develop their own regulatory programs.[54] California is undecided about having a state program, and the federal Office of Surface Mining is planning to propose an additional federal program for the state. The office instituted a full federal regulatory program, effective October 1, 1984, in Tennessee after the state legislature repealed its regulatory program.[55]

Combined Minimum Standards Preemption and Imperium in Imperio

The Occupational Safety and Health Act of 1970 combines minimum standards partial federal preemption with traditional *Imperium in Imperio*.[56] The law specifically stipulates that "nothing in this Act shall prevent any state agency or court from asserting jurisdiction under state law over any occupational safety or health issue with respect to which no standard is in effect under section 6."[57]

The 1970 act also provides that a state agency may submit a plan to the secretary of labor to assume responsibility for the regulatory function but must agree to a condition: State and local government employees must be extended protection equivalent to the protection extended to private employees.[58] If the plan is approved by the secretary, the Occupational Safety and Health Administration (OSHA) will pay up to one-half of the operating costs of the program.

As of 1990, twenty-three states were operating programs covering public-sector and private-sector employees, and Connecticut and New York were operating programs only for public employees. Eight states with federal plan approval subsequently withdrew from participation under the act.[59]

Interestingly, the Ohio Manufacturers' Association brought suit against the city of Akron, Ohio, maintaining that the city's "right-to-know" ordinance was preempted by the Occupational Safety and Health Act. The United States Court of Appeals for the Sixth Circuit, in 1986, upheld the U.S. district court's decision in favor of the city and stressed that "we cannot accept plaintiffs' contention that Congress expressly preempted local regulation by these provisions establishing a national standard. Furthermore, we agree with the trial court to the extent that express preemption, by definition, must be clearly manifested, especially when local health and safety provisions are endangered."[60]

On April 18, 1986, the U.S. Environmental Protection Agency (EPA) made final a proposed rule to protect state and local government employees from the potential hazards of asbestos-abatement work under authority of the Toxic Substances Control Act.[61] OSHA normally is responsible for federal regulations protecting workers, but OSHA lacks authority under the Occupational Safety and Health Act to extend its protection to subnational government employees. However, twenty-two states have established protection standards for their employees that are as strict as or stricter than OSHA's worker-protection rules and regulations, as noted above. OSHA has determined that four additional states — Idaho, Kansas, Oklahoma, and Wisconsin — have regulations comparable to or more stringent (in terms of worker protection) than OSHA's rules and regulations. Hence, the EPA regulation applies only to the remaining states.

There are three principal differences between the OSHA standard and the ERA regulations:

1. The EPA rule includes a provision not in the OSHA rule that generally requires persons to report to the EPA at least ten days prior to beginning an asbestos-abatement project using public employees.

2. The EPA employs a different definition of *asbestos* to make the definition consistent with other EPA regulations. Specifically, the EPA definition does not include nonasbestiform tremolite fibers, while the OSHA standard does.

3. The EPA rule does not include the OSHA provision that indicates a preference for revolving employees in and out of the workplace to meet exposure limits rather than using respirators.

State Transfer of Regulatory Responsibility

Another type of partial federal preemption is illustrated by the Wholesome Meat Act, which grants the secretary of agriculture the authority to inspect meat and transfer responsibility for intrastate meat inspection to a state that has enacted a law requiring meat inspection and reinspection consistent with federal standards.[62] This act also allows the states to transfer responsibility for inspection of meat for intrastate commerce to the U.S. Department of Agriculture. To date, eighteen states have initiated such a transfer.

The Poultry Products Inspection Act contains provisions similar to the provisions in the Wholesome Meat Act, and a total of twenty-six states have shifted responsibility for inspecting intrastate poultry products to the U.S. Department of Agriculture.[63]

Administrative Preemption

The Toxic Substances Control Act of 1976 specifically authorizes states and their political subdivisions to continue to regulate chemical substances or mixtures until the administrator of the U.S. Environmental Protection Agency issues a rule or order applicable to a substance or mixture designed to protect public health.[64]

The act permits a degree of regulatory flexibility subsequent to the issuance of a rule or order by the administrator by providing that the administrator, upon the application of a state or a political subdivision, may issue a rule exempting a chemical substance or mixture from the federal requirements if the subnational requirements provide a higher degree of protection against injury to public health or the environment than the federal requirements and do not "unduly burden interstate commerce."[65]

Stricter State Controls

Two federal preemption statutes allow states to impose controls, provided they are stricter than the federal controls. Relative to bridges and other structures on or in the navigable waters of the United States, the Port and Tanker Safety Act of 1978 provides that "nothing contained in this section, with respect to structures, prohibits a State or political subdivisions thereof from prescribing higher safety equipment requirements or safety standards than those which may be prescribed by regulations hereunder."[66]

A similar provision is contained in the Natural Gas Policy Act of 1978, which stipulates that "nothing in this act shall affect the authority of any State to establish or enforce any maximum lawful price for the first sale of natural gas produced in such State which does not exceed the applicable maximum lawful price, if any, under title I of this act."[67]

These provisions differ from minimum standards partial preemption in that there is no requirement that a state must submit its standards to a federal agency for approval before the standards become effective.

Additional Uses for a Federally Regulated Product

The Federal Environmental Pesticide Control Act of 1972 contains two major provisions relating to the authority of states to regulate pesticides. First, the administrator of the U.S. Environmental Protection Agency may enter into agreements with states providing for state cooperation in the enforcement of the act and making grants to states to cover part of their enforcement costs.[68] This provision is similar to the provision in the Federal Railroad Safety Act of 1970 providing for a limited federal turnback of regulatory authority by allowing for state cooperation in the regulation of railroad safety by means of state inspections of railroad equipment and facilities.[69]

The second provision represents a separate approach to congressional structuring of nation-state relations. A state is authorized by the act to register "pesticides formulated for distribution and use within that State to meet special local needs if that State is certified by the Administrator as capable of exercising adequate controls to assure that such registration will be in accord with the purposes of this act and if registration for such use has not previously been denied, disapproved, or cancelled by the Administrator."[70] Until the Federal Insecticide, Fungicide, and Rodenticide Act of 1947 was amended by the Federal Environmental Pesticide Control Act of 1972, Congress had provided for total federal preemption of the registration of pesticides, and states lacked authority to authorize pesticide uses.[71]

Franchise Renewal Preemption

The Cable Communications Policy Act of 1984 established a new type of federal partial preemption by authorizing subnational governments to issue and renew cable-television franchises, subject to national franchise renewal standards that make denial of a franchise renewal difficult.

The act requires the subnational franchising authority to assess whether

(A) The cable operator has substantially complied with the material terms of the existing franchise and with applicable law;
(B) The quality of the operator's service, including signal quality, response to consumer complaints, and billing practices, but without regard to the mix, quality, or level of cable services or other services provided over the system, has been reasonable in the light of community needs;
(C) The operator has the financial, legal, and technical ability to provide the services, facilities, and equipment as set forth in the operator's proposal; and
(D) The operator's proposal is reasonable to meet the future cable-related community needs and interests, taking into account the cost of meeting such needs and interests.[72]

If a cable operator is denied renewal of the franchise, the operator may seek relief in a state court or the U.S. district court. The court may grant relief if the court finds "that the adverse finding of the franchise authority with respect to each of the factors . . . is not supported by a preponderance of the evidence."[73]

Reverse Preemption

The Coastal Zone Management Act of 1972 declares in its findings that "the key to more effective protection and use of the land and water resources of the coastal zone is to encourage the States to exercise their full authority over the lands and waters in the coastal zone."[74]

To assist the states, the act (1) authorizes grants-in-aid to states for the development of a land and water resources-management program for submission to the secretary of commerce for approval, (2) requires federal agencies to ensure that their development projects in coastal zones are consistent "to the maximum extent practicable" with federally approved state management programs, and (3) forbids federal agencies to issue licenses or permits to a private applicant to undertake "an activity affecting land or water uses in the coastal zone" if the concerned state objects to the application.[75] Should a state fail to act upon the application within six months of its receipt, the federal agency may presume "conclusively" that the state concurs with the application.

A state's objection to the issuance of a license or permit by a federal agency can be overridden by the secretary of commerce if, upon appeal, the secretary determines that "the activity is consistent with the objectives of this title or is otherwise in the interest of national security."[76]

New Roles for the Governor

Federal preemptive laws, and rules, and regulations delegate powers to governors of states that governors have not received from their state constitutions and statutes. In other words, partial federal preemption changes the balance of power between the governor and the state legislatures, has the greatest impact in states where the governor is weak in formal powers, and results in interest groups' bringing increased pressure upon the governor. A governor of an eastern state wrote to me that "I don't think many students of federalism understand how important these changes are, not only in an intergovernmental sense, but to Governors themselves in the expansion of their responsibilities as chief executive within their respective States."

An examination of eleven major federal preemptive acts and one presidential executive order reveals that the governor has been granted new powers, including several of great potential importance. These powers may be placed in twelve general categories.

The first type is specific authorization in the preemption statute for the governor to submit a plan to a federal agency. The Federal Environmental Pesticide Control Act of 1972 provides that if a state desires to assume responsibility for certification of pesticides applicators, the governor must submit a plan for assumption of responsibility to the administrator of the Environmental Protection Agency for approval.[77] A related provision is found in the Clean Air Act Amendments of 1977, whereby the administrator of the Environmental Protection Agency, who is required to review state implementation plans within eighteen months of their submission, must consult the governor before requiring a revision of the plans.[78]

The second category involves the annual certification of state plans. The Federal Water Pollution Control Act Amendments of 1972 requires that the governor or his designee shall annually certify areawide waste-treatment management plans.[79]

The certification of state compliance with a national requirement is a third category of powers granted to governors. The Emergency Highway Energy Conservation Act of 1974 established a state speed limit of fifty-five miles per hour as a condition for the receipt of federal highway funds, and the Federal Highway Administration issued implementing regulations stipulating that "each Governor shall submit to the Federal Highway Administrator . . . a statement that the State" is complying with the speed limit.[80] In 1987, Congress overrode President Ronald Reagan's veto of the Surface Transportation and Relocation Assistance Act of 1987, which authorizes the states to raise the speed limit to a maximum of sixty-five on rural interstate highways without the loss of federal highway grants-in-aid.[81]

Authority to issue temporary permits is a fourth category of powers granted to governors. The Safe Drinking Water Act of 1974 empowers the administrator of the Environmental Protection Agency, upon application of a governor, to issue "one or more temporary permits each of which is applicable to a particular injection well and to the underground injection of a particular fluid."[82]

A fifth category is authority to request the waiver of the single agency requirement. The Federal Metal and Nonmetallic Mine Safety Act of 1966, repealed in 1977, authorized the secretary of labor, "upon request of the Governor, to waive the single state agency provision hereof and approve another state administrative structure or arrangement if the Secretary determines that the objectives of this Act will not be endangered by the use of such other state structure or arrangement."[83]

Authority to request that the state assume responsibility for a federally preempted function is a sixth category of powers granted to governors by federal preemption statutes. Such authority is contained in the Wholesome Meat Act of 1967 and the Poultry Products Inspection Act of 1968.[84]

A category that is of more importance than the preceding categories is the designation of a state agency to be responsible for the preempted function. The National Health Planning and Resources Development Act of 1974 authorizes a governor to designate a state agency as the State Health Planning and Development Agency.[85]

The Federal Water Pollution Control Act Amendments of 1972 contain two provisions authorizing governors to identify areas with "substantial water quality control problems"; define the boundaries of each area; designate "a single representative organization, including elected officials from local governments or their designees, capable of developing effective areawide waste treatment management plans for such" areas; and designate "one or more waste treatment management agencies . . . for each area."[86] The Clean Air Act Amendments of 1977 contain a similar provision authorizing "the Governor (or, in the case of an interstate area, Governors), after consultation with elected officials of local governments in the affected area, or a state agency to prepare such plan."[87] Many conditional grant-in-aid programs also authorize the governor to designate a state agency. To cite one example, the Surface Transportation Assistance Act of 1978 authorizes the governor to designate metropolitan planning organizations.[88]

The eighth category is the authority to appoint members of a state council. The National Health Planning and Resources Development Act of 1974 provides that the Statewide Health Coordinating Council is to be appointed by the governor.[89]

A ninth category is illustrated by the following provision in the Highway Safety Act of 1966: "The Secretary [of Transportation] shall not approve any state highway safety program under this section which does not (A) provide that the Governor of the State shall be responsible for the administration of the program."[90] This provision, of course, means that the legislature cannot decide to place responsibility for state highway-safety programs in an agency independent of the governor. In 1973, for example, Governor Nelson A. Rockefeller of New York established by executive order an Interdepartmental Traffic Safety Committee as the state agency in charge of state highway-safety programs.[91]

Tenth, in the event of a shortage of gasoline, an important power is the authority delegated by the president to the governor "to establish a system of end-used allocation for motor gasoline."[92]

Eleventh, the Tandem Truck Safety Act of 1984 authorizes the governor, after consulting concerned local governments, to notify the secretary of transportation that specific segments of the interstate highway system in the governor's state cannot safely accommodate motor vehicles of the length permitted by the STAA of 1982 or 102-inch vehicles other than buses.[93]

The twelfth and potentially most important category is the powers found in the Clean Air Act Amendments of 1977. As the result of court decisions in 1972 and 1973,[94] the U.S. Environmental Protection Agency was forced to develop and issue regulations forbidding states to permit significant deterioration of existing air quality. To implement the courts' decisions, the agency in 1974 issued final regulations for the prevention of significant deterioration of existing air quality, including the establishment of three classes of air zones.[95] New pollution, measured in terms of sulfur dioxide and total suspended particulate matters, would not be allowed in Class I areas; a limited development would be allowed in Class II areas as such development would not cause "significant deterioration of air quality"; and deterioration up to secondary standards would be allowed in Class III areas. Primary ambient-air-quality standards are national ones designed to protect the health of susceptible citizens. Secondary standards, in general more stringent, are designed to prevent adverse environmental effects, including damage to animals, vegetation, climate, and water quality.

The Clean Air Act was amended by adding a new Part C: Prevention of Significant Deterioration of Air Quality, containing provisions similar to the agency's regulations, with one major exception: Pollutants in Class III areas are limited to 50 percent of the amount allowed by the secondary standards.[96] The governor of each state is allowed to redesignate areas from Class I to Class II with certain specified exceptions, chiefly national parks and wilderness areas, provided the redesignation has been approved

after consultation with the appropriate Committees of the Legislature if it is in session or with the leadership of the Legislature if it is not in session (unless State law provides that such redesignation must be specifically approved by state legislation) and if general purpose units of local government representing a majority of the residents of the area so redesignated enact legislation (including for such units of local government resolutions where appropriate) concurring in the state redesignation; (b) such redesignation will not cause, or contribute to, concentrations or any air pollutant which exceed any maximum allowable increase or maximum allowable concentration permitted under the classification of any other area; and such redesignation otherwise meets the requirements of this part.[97]

The Environmental Protection Agency's administrator may invalidate a redesignation only if procedural requirements were not followed. In effect, the redesignation provision allows the governor to balance the need for economic development with preservation of air quality, provided pollutants emanating from new development do not exceed national standards.

The 1977 amendments also authorize the governor, after a public hearing, to promulgate rules providing "that for purposes of determining compliance with the maximum allowable increases in ambient concentrations of an air pollutant," the concentrations of the pollutant listed below will not be considered:

(A) concentrations of such pollutant attributable to the increase in emissions from stationary sources which have converted from the use of petroleum products, or natural gas, or both, by reason of an order which is in effect under the provisions of sections 2 (a) and (b) of the Energy Supply and Environmental Coordination Act of 1974 (or any subsequent legislation which supersedes such provisions) over emissions from such sources before the effective date of such order.

(B) the concentrations of such pollutant attributable to the increase in emissions from stationary sources which have converted from using natural gas by reasons of a natural gas curtailment pursuant to a natural gas curtailment plan in effect pursuant to the Federal Power Act over emissions from such sources before the effective date of such plan.

(C) concentrations of particulate matter attributable to the increase in emissions from construction or other temporary emission-related activities, and

(D) the increase in concentrations attributable to new sources outside the United States over the concentrations attributable to existing sources which are included in the baseline concentration determined in accordance with section 169 (4).[98]

In addition, the amendments authorize the governor, with the concurrence of the federal land manager, to grant a variance from the maximum allowable increase in sulfur dioxide by a proposed major emitting facility that has been denied certification under the standard certification procedure for a Class I area, with one proviso: The owner or operator must convince the governor, after a public hearing, that although the facility cannot meet the air-quality standard for emissions of sulfur dioxide, a variance "will not adversely affect the air quality related values of the area (including visibility)."[99]

The 1977 amendments also include a provision directing the administrator of the Environmental Protection Agency to delete from a transportation control plan a requirement for the tolling of bridges upon the application of the governor of the concerned state.[100] On October 19, 1977, Governor Hugh L. Carey of New York notified the administration that he desired that the requirement that the East River bridges in New York City be tolled be deleted from the transportation control plan, and the requirement was deleted.[101]

The influence of the coal industry is detectable in another provision of the Clean Air Act Amendments of 1977 authorizing the governor, "with the written consent of the President or his designee," to "prohibit any such major fuel burning stationary source (or class or category thereof) from using fuels other than locally or regionally available coal or coal derivatives to comply with implementation plan requirements."[102] The stated purpose of this provision is "to prevent economic disruption or unemployment," and it applies to existing or new major fuel-burning stationary sources that are not in compliance with the implementation plan.

Summary and Conclusions

Imperium in Imperio is still alive in the United States. The states possess certain powers that are not subject to formal federal preemption; certain federal statutes provide that state laws on specified subjects are nullified only in the event of a direct and positive conflict between the state laws and the federal laws on the same subjects; and national statutes provide for administrative and/or judicial rulings precluding federal preemption.

The most significant development in federal-state relations since 1965 has been the employment of partial federal preemption by Congress under which the states can retain primacy in terms of regulatory responsibilities, provided the states establish standards at least as stringent as national standards and enforce the state standards.

In enacting partial-preemption statutes, Congress clearly recognizes the need for the assistance of subnational governments and hopes that all the states will opt to assume primacy in terms of regulatory responsibilities under the statutes. Congress is also aware that the different conditions in the various states may make it desirable for individual states to transfer certain regulatory responsibilities to federal administrative agencies, and provisions for such transfers have been made in the partial-preemption statutes.

The partial-preemption statutes assign a number of responsibilities to governors that they do not receive from their constitutions or state statutes. These delegations of authority raise the specter of gubernatorial-legislative conflicts, and such conflicts have occurred. Although our description of the new roles for the governor may imply that the state legislatures are unable to influence the performance of these roles, the state legislatures control the "purse strings" in most states and may be able to frustrate the governor's use of powers delegated by federal preemption statutes. On the other hand, voluminous federal rules and regulations make it difficult for the typical state legislature to keep informed about the changing roles of the governor under partial-preemption statutes.

Chapter 6 examines judicial preemption. The federal judiciary plays an important role as an arbitrator of federal-state conflicts and a protector of the civil rights of citizens. Relative to the latter, the U.S. district court assumed complete control of the Boston public-school system in order to ensure that there would be no racial discrimination within the school system.

VI

Preemption and the Courts

he expansion of the preemptive powers of Congress is attributable in part to constitutional amendments authorizing Congress to enforce certain specified guarantees by appropriate legislation and in part to a generally broad judicial interpretation of the scope of the delegated powers of Congress. Although Woodrow Wilson expressed concern in 1885 about the failure of the judiciary to curtail Congress, as noted in Chapter 2 major twentieth-century criticism of the Supreme Court's decisions as preemptive did not occur until the Court in 1954 reversed its "separate but equal" dictum in *Brown v. Board of Education*.[1]

This chapter (1) examines briefly the role of federal courts in protecting U.S. constitutional guarantees by invalidating conflicting state and local laws, (2) focuses primarily on the criteria employed by the federal courts in determining whether Congress intended to exercise its preemptory powers in enacting a statute and the extent of congressional preemptive powers, and (3) highlights the use of judicial forums by interest groups.

The Courts and Constitutional Guarantees

The federal courts, like other courts, are reactors and cannot initiate action. However, once a suit is brought to the U.S. district court to resolve a controversy, the judge can exercise extraordinary powers, including the placement of state and local governmental institutions under judicial receivership. As noted in Chapter 2, the guarantees of the First Amendment were employed by the Supreme Court to invalidate sections of state corrupt-practices laws restricting campaign expenditures by candidates with their own funds and prohibiting corporations from spending funds to advertise their views on a referendum issue.

State and local governments in their employment practices are subject to Supreme Court decisions based upon the First Amendment rights of their employees. In 1976, the Court ruled that patronage dismissal of non-policy-making employees of the Cook County, Illinois, sheriff violated guarantees of the First and Fourteenth amendments on the ground that such dismissals restrict severely the right of association and the political beliefs of the employees.[2]

Similarly, the newly elected mayor of Cohoes, New York, was prevented from dismissing a housing counselor by a state court citing the *Elrod v. Burns* decision. The Appellate Division of the New York State Supreme Court ruled that "Section 10 of the Cohoes City Charter can be applied constitutionally to all appointive officers in policy-making positions, but it can not be applied constitutionally to the petitioner since his position was in a non-policy-making category."[3]

The Supreme Court does not always rule against the state in personnel cases. In 1978, for example, the Court upheld a section of the New York Executive Law providing that appointments of members of the state police be limited to U.S. citizens. The Court pointed out that "it would be as anomalous to conclude that citizens may be subjected to the broad discretionary powers of non-citizen police officers as it would be to say that judicial officers and jurors with power to judge citizens can be aliens."[4] And in 1990 the Court affirmed the operation of a highway sobriety check-point program by the Michigan state police against the argument that such check points violate the Fourth Amendment's guarantee against seizure.[5]

Assistant Attorney General William Bradford Reynolds described the power of federal judges in the following terms:

In order to "remedy" constitutional violations, federal courts have abolished any pretense of state sovereignty by dictating such things as the temperature of the dish water in state hospitals, the appropriate wattage of lamps in state prison cells, and the specific location of a piano in a public school. Federal judges have even informed the local electorate that the court itself will raise taxes to finance its sweeping remedial schemes if the voters continue their churlish refusal to assume the additional fiscal burden voluntarily.[6]

The assistant attorney general was referring to federal court actions constituting judicial receiverships, which can last for a decade or
more. U.S. District Court Judge Joseph Tauro, who placed seven
Massachusetts institutions for the mentally retarded under protection
of his court in 1978, directed Massachusetts officials in 1986 to establish an independent panel to monitor the schools because "the state
government has to run this thing" and "I don't need to be around until
every building is painted and every nail is nailed."[7]

The constitutional rights of taxpayers and the constitutional
rights of pupils in public schools can be in conflict when a U.S.
district court levies a tax or increases the property-tax rate to finance
a program of public-school integration. In 1987, U.S. District Court
Judge Russell G. Clark ordered an approximate doubling of the property-tax levy in Kansas City, Missouri, and levied an income tax surcharge upon individuals working within the Kansas City School District.[8] The income tax surcharge upon nonresidents of the district was
justified by the judge on the theory that many nonresidents had
moved to suburban municipalities to avoid school integration.

In 1990, the U.S. Supreme Court ruled that the direct levy of a
tax by the U.S. district court was an "abuse of discretion" because the
court failed to determine whether the same goal could have been
achieved by another permissible alternative.[9]

The most controversial judicial receivership involved the direct
operation of the Boston school system by U.S. District Court Judge
W. Arthur Garrity, Jr., who assumed jurisdiction in 1974 and relinquished control to the elected Boston School Committee in 1985. In
1982, however, he relinquished day-to-day monitoring of the court's
orders to the Massachusetts Board of Education, which issued progress reports to the court semiannually.[10] In returning control to the
school committee, Judge Garrity issued final orders requiring the
committee to assign students on the basis of prescribed ratios reflecting the racial composition of the student body, to adopt a school-
building rehabilitation plan enhancing desegregation, and to finance
the citywide parents council for a minimum of three years.[11]

Experience has demonstrated that the court-prescribed remedy of
busing to achieve "racial balance" in public schools of large cities is
impossible to accomplish because of the sharply increasing black student population and the great mobility of poor families. Busing black
pupils from a neighborhood populated primarily by black students to
another school where the black percentage is slightly lower in the

name of racial desegregation is not sound public policy. The relatively large cost — money and the time of pupils, administrators, and litigants — of attempting to achieve "racial balance" in schools through busing raises a question of the cost-effectiveness of this approach, relative to other approaches, in constitutionally guaranteeing quality education for all pupils.

The increasing disillusionment of a number of black civil-rights leaders with mandatory school busing may herald the filing of fewer suits in the U.S. district court seeking to promote equality of education through this method, given the reality of "white flight" from the public school system. In addition, the increasing black population of many central cities has resulted in political power passing from whites to blacks. As blacks gain control of the public school system, they will have less interest in federal court intervention to promote the ideal of equality unless such intervention will result in increased financial support for central-city schools.

Congressional Authority and Intent

Opposition to the proposed U.S. Constitution centered on the fear that the national government, Congress in particular, would usurp the powers of the states. Relatively little attention was paid by the opponents of the new document to the role that would be played by the federal judiciary in the federal system. Writing on "the proper extent of the federal judicature" in *The Federalist Number 80,* Alexander Hamilton maintained that controversy should not extend to the types of cases that would be within the jurisdiction of the federal courts under the proposed fundamental document and added relative to its judicial principles:

If some partial inconveniences should appear to be connected with the incorporation of any of them into the plan it ought to be recollected that the national legislature will have ample authority to make such exceptions and to prescribe such regulations as will be calculated to obviate or remove these inconveniences. The possibility of particular mischiefs can never be viewed, by a well-informed mind, as a solid objection to a general principle which is calculated to avoid general mischiefs and to obtain general advantages.[12]

In contrast to the Articles of Confederation and Perpetual Union, the Constitution does not include a provision denying the existence of implied or incidental powers associated with the powers delegated to Congress. The absence of such a provision enabled Chief

Justice John Marshall in *McCulloch v. Maryland* (1819) to develop the doctrine of implied powers, which has expanded tremendously the reach of the expressed or delegated powers of Congress.[13]

While the doctrine of implied powers is of great constitutional significance, the power delegated by the Constitution to Congress "to regulate commerce with foreign Nations, and among the several States, and with the Indian tribes" is considerably more important in terms of the expansion of the preemptive powers of the national legislature.[14] The Supreme Court first gave a sweeping interpretation to this delegated power in *Gibbons v. Ogden* by developing the doctrine of the "continuous journey."[15] The Court held that the commerce power extended to a steamship company operating solely within the boundaries of a state because some of the passengers and merchandise on the company's ships were in transit between states. In effect, the Supreme Court developed a "national-concern" doctrine similar to the later "state-concern" doctrine developed by Judge Benjamin N. Cardozo of the New York Court of Appeals to justify state intervention into matters assigned exclusively by the New York State Constitution to cities.[16]

Writing in 1949, Mr. Justice Robert H. Jackson of the Supreme Court explained the importance of the commerce clause:

The Commerce Clause is one of the most prolific sources of national power and an equally prolific source of conflict with legislation of the State. While the Constitution vests in Congress the power to regulate commerce among the States, it does not say what the States may or may not do in the absence of congressional action, nor how to draw the line between what is and what is not commerce among the States. Perhaps even more than by interpretation of its written word, this Court has advanced the solidarity and prosperity of this Nation by the meaning it has given to these great silences of the Constitution.[17]

Reacting to criticisms of the growing role of the national government in the total political system, President Dwight D. Eisenhower appointed in 1953 the Commission on Intergovernmental Relations to study the federal system and to advance recommendations for changes in the system. In 1955, the commission issued its report and stressed:

And under present judicial interpretations of the Constitution, especially of the spending power and the commerce clause, the boundaries of possible national action are more and more subject to determination by legislative action.

In brief, the policymaking authorities of the national government are for most purposes the arbiters of the federal system.[18]

The commission also developed the following principles to guide governmental regulation:

First, the fact that the National Government has not legislated on a given matter in a field of concurrent power should not bar State action.
Second, national laws should be framed that they will not be construed to preempt any field against State action unless this intent is stated.
Third, exercise of national power on any subject should not bar State action on the same subject unless there is a positive inconsistency.
Fourth, when a national minimum standard is imposed in a field where uniformity is not imperative, the right of States to set more rigorous standards should be carefully preserved.
Fifth, statutes should provide flexible scope for administrative cession of jurisdiction where the objectives of the laws at the two levels are substantially in accord. State legislation need not be identical with the national legislation.[19]

The first principle is nothing more than recognition of a well-established principle of constitutional law that concurrent powers can be exercised by either or both planes of government. The second principle is easy to state but difficult to implement, and questions may be raised whether the principle is workable in all situations.

The third principle is a reinstatement of Article VI of the Constitution—the supremacy-of-law clause. The fourth principle underlies the type of partial preemption exercised by Congress since 1965 and examined in Chapter 5. The fifth principle has been implemented by the Atomic Energy Act of 1959, which authorizes the Nuclear Regulatory Commission to turn over certain regulatory powers to states signing an agreement, provided the state statutes are consistent with the federal statutes, a subject examined in Chapter 4.

Whereas the commission urged Congress to exercise greater care in enacting statutes and did not address harsh criticism of the federal judiciary, U.S. Assistant Attorney General William Bradford Reynolds, reflecting the Reagan administration's "New Federalism" views, referred in 1987 to an activist federal judiciary as follows:

Perhaps the greatest irony of our day is that the judiciary was seen by our Founders as the "least dangerous" branch of all. Yet it is the judicial branch that has done the largest disservice to the Constitution, and the bedrock principles on which it stands. The delicate balance struck in the Constitution's first three articles among legislative, executive, and judicial functions has long since been interpreted virtually out of existence by activist judges who through an overly expansive reading of the commerce and supremacy clauses have nationalized almost every social problem. The core principle of federalism enshrined in the Tenth Amendment—that reserves all power to the States not constitutionally assigned to or reserved for the federal government—was recently removed almost in its entirety by the Supreme Court's pronouncement, in the case of *Garcia v. San Antonio Transit Authority*, that state sovereignty now exists only at the pleasure of Congress. According to *Garcia*, the States have no special status that is constitutionally immune to regulation by the national government.[20]

It is instructive to read this statement by Mr. Reynolds in the light of the views of Mr. Justice William H. Rehnquist in a 1981 Supreme Court decision.

[I]t would be a mistake to conclude that Congress' power to regulate pursuant to the commerce clause is unlimited. Some activities may be so private or local in nature that they simply may not be in commerce. Nor is it sufficient that the person or activity reached have some nexus with interstate commerce. Our cases have consistently held that the regulated activity must have a substantial effect on interstate commerce. . . . In short, unlike the reserved police powers of the States, which are plenary unless challenged as violating some specific provision of the Constitution, the connection with interstate commerce is itself a jurisdictional prerequisite for any substantive legislation by Congress under the commerce clause.[21]

Preemption Criteria

The Supreme Court on various occasions has stressed that there are no precise criteria by which the Court can determine whether Congress intended to exercise its powers of preemption, short of an explicit statement in a statute of an intention to preempt. Although Congress in several statutes has stated that "this Act is intended to supersede any law of any State or political subdivision thereof inconsistent with its provisions,"[22] the bulk of preemption statutes lacks such a clause.

George B. Braden in 1942 noted that a rule stipulating that state laws would remain in force unless specifically prohibited by federal law "would be intolerable. Congress could not be asked to anticipate all possible legislative conflicts, nor could it really solve the problem by blanket prohibition. In some instances a tag end proviso nullifying all state statutes 'conflicting with this act' would only restate the problem. Some leeway must be left."[23] In consequence, the courts are in many instances left with the task of deciding whether a state law or local ordinance is preempted by federal statute.

In 1941, the Supreme Court stressed that each challenge of a state law on the ground of inconsistency with federal law must be determined on the basis of the particular facts of the case.

There is not — and from the very nature of the problem — there can not be any rigid formula or rule which can be used to determine the meaning and purpose of every act of Congress. This Court, in considering the validity of state laws in the light of treaties or federal laws touching on the same subject, has made use of the following expressions: Conflicting; contrary to; occupying the field; repugnance; difference; irreconcilability; violation; curtailment; and interference. But none of these expressions provides an infallible constitutional test or an exclusive constitutional yardstick. In the final analysis, there can be no one crystal clear distinctly marked formula. Our primary function is to determine whether, under the circumstances of this particular case, Pennsylvania's law stands as an obstacle to the accomplishment and execution of the full purposes and objectives of Congress.[24]

In 1947, the Supreme Court explicated two tests of federal preemption: (1) "[T]he question in each case is what the purpose of Congress was." (2) Does the act of Congress involve "a field in which the federal interest is so dominant that the federal system will be assumed to preclude enforcement of state laws on the same subject?"[25] The Court wrote relative to the Noise Control Act of 1972:

Our prior cases on preemption are not precise guidelines in the present controversy, for each case turns on the peculiarities and special features of the federal regulatory scheme in question. . . . Control of noise is of course deep-seated in the police power of the States. Yet the pervasive control vested in EPA [Environmental Protection Agency] and FAA [Federal Aviation Administration] under the 1972 Act seems to us to leave no room for local curfews or other local controls.[26]

In 1979, the Supreme Court ruled that the statute giving federal courts jurisdiction over allegations of violations of constitutional rights does not cover a suit based simply on the fact that a state law conflicts with the federal Social Security Act.[27] Conceding that the conflict between the laws violated the supremacy clause of the Constitution, the Court held that such a violation is not the type of constitutional allegation that confers jurisdiction upon federal courts.

The Court also occasionally voids only the portion of a state or local law held to be preempted. A three-section state of Washington law pertaining to Puget Sound required oil tankers to be guided by state-licensed pilots, specified design standards for oil tankers, and banned all tankers over 125,000 deadweight tons.[28] The Court let stand the first section but ruled that the other two sections had been preempted by Congress.[29]

Building upon its reasoning in *National League of Cities v. Usery,* described in Chapter 4, the Supreme Court in *Hodel v. Virginia Surface Mining and Reclamation Association* (1981) enunciated three tests to determine whether the federal Surface Mining Act preempted state law: "First, there must be a showing that the challenged statute regulates the 'States as States.' . . . second, the federal regulation must address matters that are indisputably 'attributes of state sovereignty.' . . . And, third, it must be apparent that the States' compliance with the federal law would directly impair their ability 'to structure integral operations in areas of traditional functions.' "[30]

In this case, the Court ruled that the plaintiffs had failed to demonstrate that the federal statute regulated the "States as States" and added that states are not mandated to enforce the standards contained in the statute because if a state fails to submit a proposed regulatory program complying with the federal law to the Department of the Interior, the federal government is responsible for "the full regulatory burden."[31] The Court emphasized that "there can be no suggestion that the Act commandeers the legislative processes of the States by directly compelling them to enact and enforce a federal regulatory program."[32]

Ultra Vires Laws

The authority of Congress to preempt totally has been limited occasionally by the Supreme Court. In 1970, Congress lowered the voting age in all elections to eighteen, but the Court ruled that Congress lacked the power to lower the voting age for state and local elections.[33] Justice Hugo L. Black, in delivering the judgment of the Court, wrote that "the Equal Protection of the Laws Clause of the Fourteenth Amendment was never intended to destroy the States' power to govern themselves, making the Nineteenth and Twenty-fourth Amendments superfluous."[34] Justice Black added that the power of Congress to enforce the guarantees of the Fourteenth and Fifteenth Amendments was subject to at least three limitations:

First, Congress may not by legislation repeal other provisions of the Constitution. Second, the power granted to Congress was not intended to strip the States of their power to govern themselves or to convert our national government of enumerated powers into a central government of unrestrained authority over every inch of the whole Nation. Third, Congress may only "enforce" the provisions of the amendments and may do so only by "appropriate legislation."[35]

In 1976, in *National League of Cities,* the Court invalidated the 1974 Fair Labor Standards Act Amendments extending minimum-wage and overtime-pay provisions to nonsupervisory employees of state and local governments on the ground that the extension violated the Tenth Amendment and threatened the "separate and independent existence" of the units.[36] In 1976, the Court held that a written examination for applications to a police department was not unconstitutional simply because a "substantially disproportionate" burden is placed on blacks.[37] The following year, this decision was applied to housing- and school-desegregation cases, with the result that school and housing desegregation can be ordered by the U.S. district court on a metropolitan-wide basis only if there is direct evidence that actions were taken deliberately by suburban governments to prevent housing and school integration in the past.[38]

The Retreat from *National League of Cities*

Many state and local government officials hailed the *National League of Cities* decision as evidence that the Supreme Court was finally recognizing the fact that states were sovereign relative to certain Tenth Amendment matters. This optimism was relatively short-lived. The Supreme Court in 1980 issued two decisions striking at the sovereign immunity of the states and their political subdivisions and illustrating the tendency of the Court to issue expansive interpretations of congressional acts.

The Court, in *Maine v. Thiboutot* and *Owen v. City of Independence,* stripped subnational governments of immunity for actions of their public servants by interpreting broadly section 1983 of the Civil Rights Act of 1871.[39] The section:

Every person who, under color of any statute, ordinance, regulation, custom, or usage, of any State or territory, subjects, or causes to be subjected to, any citizen of the United States or other person within the jurisdiction thereof to the deprivation of any rights, privileges, or immunities secured by the Constitution and laws, shall be liable to the party injured in an action at law, suit in equity, or other proper proceedings for redress.

The Court interpreted the phrase "and laws" to provide a cause of action for deprivation of rights secured by any U.S. law because

Congress had not provided for state and local governmental immunity. Cases brought under the section had previously been limited to infringements of rights protected by the equal protection clause of the Fourteenth Amendment. Under the 1980 rulings, state and local government officials can be held entirely responsible, even though officials of federal administrative agencies have equal administrative responsibility for the relevant programs. In effect, the Supreme Court granted the judiciary unlimited authority to review actions of state and local government officials totally unrelated to civil rights, the subject matter of the 1871 act.

Dissenting in *Thiboutot,* Justice Lewis Powell, Jr., opined that "no one can predict the extent to which litigation from today's decision will harass State and local officials; nor can one foresee the number of new findings in our already overburdened courts. But no one can doubt that these consequences will be substantial."[40] He included in his dissent an appendix listing numerous programs affected by the majority decision.[41]

In his dissent in *Owen,* Justice Powell lamented that

[a]fter today's decision, municipalities will have gone in two short years from absolute immunity under § 1983 to strict liability. As a policy matter, I believe that strict municipal liability unreasonably subjects local governments to damage judgments for actions that were reasonable when performed. It converts municipal governance into a hazardous slalom through constitutional obstacles that often are unknown and unknowable.[42]

In 1982, the Supreme Court interpreted the commerce clause as authorizing Congress to direct state public-utility commissions to consider federally established rate-making standards.[43] Congress included in the Public Utility Regulatory Policies Act of 1978 a provision mandating that "each state regulatory authority (with respect to each electric utility for which it has rate-making authority) and each nonregulated electric utility shall consider each standard established by subsection (d) and make a determination concerning whether or not it is appropriate to implement such standard to carry out the purposes of this title."[44]

The Mississippi Public Service Commission sought a declaratory judgment that sections of the act mandating state action were unconstitutional under both the commerce clause and the Tenth Amendment. The U.S. District Court for the Southern District of Mississippi agreed with the commission, but its decision was reversed by the Supreme Court.

Specifically rejecting *Kentucky v. Dennison,* which suggests that

118 Federal Preemption

Congress and the states are coequal sovereigns, the Court's majority pointed out that "while this Court never has sanctioned explicitly a federal command to the States to promulgate and enforce laws and regulations, . . . there are instances where the Court has upheld federal statutory structures that in effect directed state decision-makers to take or to refrain from taking certain actions."[45] The majority added:

We recognize, of course, that the choice put to the States—that of either abandoning regulation of the field altogether or considering the federal standards—may be a difficult one. And that is particularly true when Congress, as is the case here, has failed to provide an alternative regulatory mechanism to police the area in the event of state default. Yet in other contexts the Court has recognized that valid federal enactments may have an effect on state policy—and may, indeed, be designed to induce state action in areas that otherwise would be beyond Congress' regulatory authority.[46]

The Garcia Decision

While these decisions were viewed as serious federal encroachments upon the sovereignty of state and local officials, the reactions to these decisions were relatively mild compared to reactions to the Court's reversal in 1985, in *Garcia v. San Antonio Metropolitan Transit Authority*, of the Court's 1976 decision in *National League of Cities v. Usery.* In *Garcia*, the Court declared:

Our examination of this "function" standard applied in these and other cases over the last eight years now persuades us that the attempt to draw the boundaries of state regulatory immunity in terms of "traditional governmental function" is not only unworkable but is inconsistent with established principles of federalism and, indeed, with those very federalism principles on which *National League of Cities* purported to rest. That case, accordingly, is overruled.[47]

The rationale underlying the Court's decision is similar to the rationale employed by a number of state supreme courts in striking down the sovereign immunity of municipalities from suits for torts while performing a governmental function as opposed to a proprietary function where they possessed no immunity. The courts concluded that the distinction between a governmental function and a proprietary function was no longer a rational one for determining whether a municipality could be sued.[48]

In angry reaction to this decision, United States Assistant Attorney General William Bradford Reynolds declared: "According to the

Garcia majority, States apparently enjoy no special constitutional autonomy in relation to Congress. They are now held as nothing more sovereign than ordinary private entities when Congress seeks to flex the awesome muscle of its power to regulate commerce."[49]

Reynolds's criticism of the majority decision was echoed in somewhat different words by other federalism experts, including the chairman of the United States Advisory Committee on Intergovernmental Relations, Robert B. Hawkins, Jr.,:

If one strips away all the verbiage in *Garcia,* the Court is saying that the Congress has the right to constrain the authority of state and local governments in any way it sees fit. Or the reverse, that the Congress has the authority to determine the scope of its own power. The principle is clear: What the sovereign giveth, the sovereign can take. Any restraint depends on the benevolence of the Congress and the Executive Branch, and the Court has no constitutional role to protect the rights of state and local governments. If such is true, then let's admit that we have not federalism, but centralized government.[50]

Professor R. Perry Sentell, Jr., of the University of Georgia Law School, after expressing amazement at the Court's majority rationale, concluded that "the Constitution's historical commerce clause now emerges as one of the most potent regulatory weapons at Congress' disposal."[51]

In reading the *Garcia* decision, the reader should bear in mind Justice Rehnquist's caution in 1981 relative to the reach of the commerce power of Congress.

In sum, my difficulty with some of the recent commerce clause jurisprudence is that the Court often seems to forget that legislation enacted by Congress is subject to two different kinds of challenge, while that enacted by the States is subject to only one kind of challenge. Neither Congress nor the States may act in a manner prohibited by any provision of the Constitution. But Congress must bear an additional burden: If challenged as to its authority to act pursuant to the commerce clause, Congress must show that its regulatory activity has a substantial effect on interstate commerce.[52]

We survey briefly in the next section the post-*Garcia* decisions of the Supreme Court and examine in Chapter 7 the political-responsiveness doctrine enunciated by Justice Blackmun by reviewing the congressional response to the pleadings of state and local government officials for relief from the *Garcia* ruling.

Post-*Garcia* Decisions

In *Hillsborough County v. Automated Medical Laboratories* (1985), the Supreme Court ruled that state or local governmental regulation of public health and safety matters is not presumed to be invalidated by the supremacy clause of the Constitution and that regulations of the federal Food and Drug Administration governing the collection of blood plasma from paid blood donors do not preempt local ordinances on the same subject.[53]

The following year, the Supreme Court rejected the contention of landlords that a Berkeley, California, ordinance imposing rent ceilings on residential real property violated the Sherman Anti-trust Act.[54] The Court held that a city ordinance that established rent control lacked the concerted action required for per se violation of the Sherman Anti-Trust Act.

In 1987, the Supreme Court issued several decisions that state laws were not preempted by federal statutes or rules and regulations. In *California Coastal Commission v. Granite Rock Company,* the Court held that the imposition of permit requirements on the operation of an unpatented mining claim in a national forest were not preempted by the Coastal Zone Management Act, federal land-use acts, or Forest Service rules and regulations.[55]

In a similar ruling, the Court held that a Maine severance-pay law for employees terminated by the closing of factories was not preempted by the National Labor Relations Act or the Employee Retirement Income Security Act (ERISA).[56] Specifically,

We hold that a Maine severance pay statute is not preempted by ERISA, since it does not "relate to any employee benefit plan" under the statute. 29 U.S.C. § 1144(a). We hold further that the law is not preempted by the NLRA since its establishment of a minimum labor standard does not impermissibly intrude upon the collective bargaining process.[57]

The Indiana Control Share Acquisition Act, designed to protect shareholders in corporate takeovers, was held in *CTS Corporation v. Dynamics Corporation of America* not to be preempted by the federal Williams Act because the Indiana law did not frustrate the purposes of the Williams Act by conflicting with it.[58]

In another 1987 decision involving the commerce power, the Court upheld the constitutionality of the California Fair Employment and Housing Act, requiring employers to grant leave to and reinstate employees disabled by pregnancy, on the ground that the act was not inconsistent with the purposes of the federal Pregnancy Discrimination Act and did not "require the doing of an act which is unlawful under Title VII" of the federal law.[59]

In 1988, however, the Supreme Court issued two opinions upholding federal preemption. In the first case, the Court ruled that the Federal Communications Commission did not exceed its statutory authority by adopting regulations preempting subnational technical standards for the quality of cable-television signals.[60]

In the second case, the Mississippi Public Service Commission authorized an electric utility to increase its retail rates in order to recover the cost of purchasing power from a nuclear power plant, mandated by the Federal Energy Regulatory Commission. The action was challenged by the Mississippi attorney general and consumer groups. The Court held that the federal commission's proceedings, resulting in the mandated purchase of electricity at rates specified by the commission, were reasonable and just, and preempted the state commission from conducting an inquiry into the question of the prudence of managerial decisions resulting in construction of the nuclear power plant.[61]

In 1990, the Supreme Court affirmed (1) the authority of Oregon to deny claimants unemployment compensation because of their religious use of peyote (a hallucinogenic drug) and (2) North Dakota laws regulating liquor sold to U.S. military bases located within the state.[62]

Although the importance of Supreme Court decisions cannot be underestimated, the bulk of the litigation in the federal judicial system occurs in the district court and the court of appeals. Our focus in the next section is the use of the federal courts by interest groups.

Interest Groups and the Courts

Federal preemptive statutes and implementing regulations have been challenged by certain interest groups and employed by other interest groups in attempts to secure their goals. The increasing number of such statutes and regulations has produced a corresponding increase in judicial litigation.

The high stakes involved with environmental issues have made such issues common subjects of litigation. Environmental protection groups seek court orders mandating enforcement actions by federal and state administrators, and industrial groups often use the courts in attempts to nullify or weaken federal statutes and regulations. The complexity of the latter ensures opportunities for legal challenges and guarantees long delays in the rendering of court opinions.

Environmental or industrial groups challenge nearly every regulation issued by the U.S. Environmental Protection Agency (EPA), thereby delaying implementation of the challenged regulation. The complexity of the administrative problems created by such suits is illustrated by a decision of the U.S. district court, upheld by a split vote of the Supreme Court, in response to a suit initiated by the Sierra Club against the EPA administrator.[63] The district court forbade states to permit significant deterioration of existing air quality. Since the Supreme Court's decision was without opinion and the district court did not elaborate upon its ruling, the EPA was forced to execute a nondegradation policy without judicial guidelines.

To implement the courts' decisions, the EPA in 1974 issued final regulations for the prevention of significant deterioration of existing air quality, including the establishment of three classes of air zones.[64] New pollution, measured in terms of sulfur dioxide and total suspended particulate matters, would not be allowed in Class I areas; limited development would be allowed in Class II areas as such limited development would not cause "significant deterioration of air quality"; and deterioration up to secondary standards would be allowed in Class III area.[65]

Considerable litigation, initiated by the Sierra Club, revolved around these regulations, and it was not until 1976 that the U.S. Court of Appeals for the District of Columbia circuit approved the EPA's air-quality regulations.[66] By this time, Congress was reviewing the issue of air quality and in 1977 enacted the Clean Air Act Amendments.

These amendments added to the Clean Air Act a new Part C: Prevention of Significant Deterioration of Air Quality, containing provisions similar to the EPA's regulations, with one major exception: Pollutants in Class III areas are limited to 50 percent of the amount allowed by the secondary standards.[67] The act also directed the EPA to study four other pollutants—hydrocarbons, carbon monoxide, photo-chemical oxidants, and nitrogen oxides—and promulgate regulations within two years to prevent significant deterioration of air quality by emission of these pollutants.[68]

A particularly undesirable practice associated with certain federal preemption statutes is "forum shopping," whereby each litigant seeks the circuit thought to be the most sympathetic to the claims of the litigant. Congress curtailed this practice relative to four major environmental preemption statutes—Clean Air, Noise Control Act, Safe Drinking Water Act, and Solid Waste Disposal Act—by assigning exclusive jurisdiction over review of the agency's nationally applicable regulations to a single circuit. Congress, however, did not curtail forum shopping relative to other acts until 1988.[69]

Prior to 1988, forum shopping was relatively common under the Clean Water Act. Not unexpectedly, an industrial group considered an agency regulation to be too stringent and an environmental protection group considered the same regulation to be too lax, resulting in a race between the two groups to what each group considered a friendly courthouse. The *United States Code* stipulated until 1988 that in the event suits challenging the same regulation are filed in more than one circuit, the suits will be transferred to the circuit where a suit "was first instituted."[70] Although the recipient circuit can transfer the suits to another circuit "for the convenience of the parties in the interest of justice," the litigant first filing has an advantage.

According to the National Resources Defense Council, racing skills became extremely important.

The process of selecting a judicial review forum often resembles a circus. The time selected to commence a race ordinarily is tied to a physical action or event, such as signing a document, announcing regulations at a press conference, or logging-in a document at the Office of the Federal Register (OFR). In such circumstances, petitioners which have considerable resources have an unfair opportunity to win the race and select their favorite forum. For those who can afford it, the race will involve teams of many people using hand signals, open long-distance telephone lines or two-way radios, and even diversionary tactics.[71]

The technique used by Tenneco to be the first litigant is described in the following terms by Presiding Administrative Law Judge Stephen L. Grossman of the Federal Energy Regulatory Commission:

Tenneco had in position a "human chain" extending from OPI [Office of Public Information] to a public telephone on the second floor of the Commission's Office. Each person in the five-person chain was in line-of-sight of the person behind and ahead. The chain began with counsel for Tenneco proximate to the Commission's Secretary and extended with a member in the open doorway from OPI to the first floor corridor, to a member at the bottom of the staircase to the second floor, to a member on the staircase, and ended with a member at the public telephone on the second floor. An open line to a representative of Tenneco at the Fifth Circuit Clerk's office had been established. Counsel, standing near the Secretary, discerned that the time stamp machine advanced each minute at the time an electric wall clock in OPI indicated nine seconds after the minute. (The wall clock was not calibrated, nor was calibration attempted, with any other time device.) He thus was prepared for the time stamp device to advance to its 3:02 p.m. EDT reading preceded, by from one to five seconds . . . the moment at which the Secretary caused Order No.10-A to be time stamped.[72]

Although Congress and the courts generally have granted wide standing to citizens to bring environmental suits, a 1987 Supreme Court decision in a case initiated by an industrial firm promises to give industrial firms protection against citizen suits for violations that have been corrected prior to initiation of the suits. In *Smithfield v. Chesapeake Bay Foundation,* the Court reversed a decision of the U.S. court of appeals allowing citizens to sue for civil penalties for violations of the Clean Water Act in the past.[73]

Technological developments guarantee that federal preemptive statutes and implementing regulations will be complex. The number of regulations pertaining to pollutants is exceptionally large and growing. Currently, there are approximately 400 wastes regulated under the Resource Conservation and Recovery Act, 126 priority pollutants under the Clean Water Act, numerous chemical products and wastes under the Superfund Act, all new chemicals under the Toxic Substances Control Act, numerous pollutants under the Clean Air Act, and many pollutants under the Safe Drinking Water Act.[74] The number of substances regulated by environmental statutes alone ensures that the courts will be called upon more often in the future than in the past to interpret the extent and nature of federal preemption.

Summary

Federal courts are called on by citizens and interest groups to protect the constitutional guarantees of citizens alleged to be abridged by state and local government laws, to determine whether Congress intended to preempt subnational laws when Congress failed expressly to indicate an intent to preempt, to set the boundaries of preempted activities, and to review administrative actions, rules, and regulations. The great growth in administrative rule making has led to numerous court challenges to rules and regulations implementing preemption statutes and long delays in implementing rules and regulations.

Our review of major Supreme Court decisions reveals that the Court has not developed precise criteria to determine whether state and local laws have been preempted by an act of Congress and that the Court's decisions are made on a case-by-case basis.

In Chapter 7, we examine the arguments in favor of and in opposition to federal preemption, the Blackmun thesis that the congressional political process offers states and their political subdivisions adequate protection against preemptive decisions of the United States Supreme Court, the responsibility problem associated with federal preemption, the fiscal implications of federal mandates, a typology of federal mandates, mandate reimbursement, and the revival of cooperative federalism.

VII

The Silent Revolution

mployment of its powers of partial and total preemption by Congress to restrict the powers of the states has produced what appears to be an infinite variety of intergovernmental relationships. If the drafters of the Constitution were to visit the nation today, they would be able to recognize aspects of the federal system they created, but they would undoubtedly be confounded by the current nature of nation-state interactions and the respective powers of each plane. Who in 1788 would have believed that a bill approved by a state legislature and signed by a governor would require the approval of the U.S. attorney general or the U.S. District Court for the District of Columbia before the law could be implemented? Yet the federal Voting Rights Act contains such a requirement for states and their political subdivisions desiring to make even minor changes in their electoral systems if the units meet the two criteria for triggering the suspensive law.[1]

Our identification of various structuring mechanisms, based upon congressional powers of preemption, clearly reveals the complexities and nuances of federalism in the United States today. With the exceptions of the relatively few instances where Congress has exercised its powers of total preemption with no provision for a limited turnback of authority to the states, confusion generally exists with respect to the extent to which the states may exercise their reserved powers. The Voting Rights Act of 1965 and the Transportation Safety Act of 1974, however, provide for administrative rulings addressing the question whether a state or local law or regulation is precluded by federal preemption and thereby clarifying the authority of the subnational units. As one would anticipate, a product of the confusion produced by federal preemption has been a large expansion in litigation in federal and state courts seeking a definition of the scope of preemption.

Critics of the growth in the powers of the national government have charged that the states and local governments are little more than administrative appendages of the national government and that the states have been deprived of their sovereign reserved powers guaranteed by the Tenth Amendment to the Constitution. In effect, the critics maintain that the federal system has been converted into a monocentric system of government. Many critics attribute the growth in national powers in large measure to expansive rulings of the Supreme Court upholding the exercise of powers of preemption by Congress. In Chapter 1, I referred to Justice Blackmun's comment that the proper forum for the states to receive relief from preemptive federal statutes is Congress and that the federal system has built-in political mechanisms to ensure that Congress will be responsive to the concerns of the states.

If state and local government officials are confused about the scope of their powers under federal preemption statutes, it is not surprising that the citizenry is totally confused about which plane of government is responsible for action or inaction to solve public problems. Is one price to be paid for federal preemption a partial loss of governmental accountability to the citizenry?

Federal preemption statutes directly or indirectly require states and their political subdivisions to initiate actions that cost money. In many instances, Congress has authorized conditional grants-in-aid in the preemption statutes to assist the subnational units in meeting the cost of mandated actions. Subnational governments, not surprisingly, have been seeking federal reimbursement of the costs associated with federal mandates. Assuming that Congress will continue to levy mandates on states and their political subdivisions, the question that needs to be answered is whether all, some, or none of the costs associated with such mandates should be reimbursed by Congress.

In this chapter, we review our findings on the various types of federal-preemption structuring devices employed by Congress and congressional responsiveness to the concerns of the states. In addition, we examine the question of the degree of power possessed and exercised by the states in the period since 1965 when the Congress began to rely heavily upon its preemptive powers to achieve national goals, the responsiveness of Congress to the concerns of the states, and the accountability and responsibility problem under federal preemption.

Total Federal Preemption

In Chapter 4, fourteen distinctive types of complete assumption of regulatory authority by Congress were identified. The first type of total preemption involves regulatory situations where there is no need for state and/or local assistance. Total regulation of bankruptcies by the national government is an example of preemption where the national government needs no outside assistance. Furthermore, strong reasons can be advanced in favor of a nationally uniform system of regulating bankruptcies, a uniform time system, cigarette health labeling, and poison-prevention packaging.

A total-preemption statute often raises more than one preemption issue, and the views of the states toward the various issues may differ. For example, the Poultry Products Inspection Act of 1968 preempts responsibility for inspection of interstate shipments of such products, and states have no objection to this provision. However, controversy swirls around the labeling preemption provision as a number of states believe they should have the power to require that the labels on poultry products indicate the state of origin. In addition, a number of states object to the federal requirement that the net-weight label be based upon the weight at the time of introducing the poultry into the stream of interstate commerce and favor a label indicating the weight at the time of retail sale because of the loss of weight in shipment.

Similarly, total federal preemption can be completely effective if it provides that there shall be no federal or state economic regulation, as illustrated by deregulation of the airline and bus industries or proscription of a mandatory retirement age for employees. Such preemption statutes, of course, generate protests from subnational governments.

The other types of total federal preemption either need or provide for a state and local role in the regulated activity. A case study in Chapter 4 demonstrated that the Nuclear Regulatory Commission is heavily dependent upon subnational governments for assistance in an emergency at a nuclear power plant necessitating evacuation. Nevertheless, the total-preemption statute fails to provide a role for these units and apparently is based on the assumption that these units will provide assistance in the event of an emergency. I argue that the act should be amended to provide specifically for a subnational role relative to emergencies involving nuclear incidents.

While the state-activities exception is an isolated example of a type of total federal preemption, limited regulatory turnbacks authorized by federal laws are of considerable importance. Although only eight states have assumed inspection and weighing functions under the U.S. Grain Standards Act, forty-four states have received a limited turnback of authority from the Environmental Protection Agency under the Resource Conservation and Recovery Act, and thirty-one states participate in the federal railroad-safety inspection program.

The most successful program involving a limited regulatory turnback is the Agreement States Program of the Nuclear Regulatory Commission. All studies reveal that the program is an excellent example of cooperative federalism.

From the standpoint of the states, the most undesirable form of total federal preemption is a statute mandating state law enactment, such as the Equal Employment Opportunity Act of 1972. These acts are viewed as federal encroachments upon the sovereign powers of the states, which may incrementally reduce the states to little more than administrative vassals of Congress. While I disagree about the ultimate fate of the states with the continuation of preemptive actions by the Congress, I am convinced that Congress should refrain from directly mandating states to enact laws. If Congress believes that a particular law should be enacted by all state legislatures, experience reveals that conditional grants-in-aid and tax credits are effective in prodding states to act as desired by Congress.

A similar objection is raised against the one federal contingent total-preemption statute—the Voting Rights Act of 1965, as amended. If a state or local government is subject to the act, the unit may make no change, no matter how small, in its electoral system, broadly defined, without permission from the U.S. attorney general or issuance of a declaratory judgment by the U.S. District Court for the District of Columbia. Experience with the act reveals that officials of the Department of Justice suggest to subnational officials the changes that will be approved by the attorney general and thus mandate the changes de facto.[2] While one can support the objectives of the act, administrative officials should not have the power to dictate in effect to a state or a general-purpose local government the nature of its electoral system.

Although the Nuclear Waste Policy Act of 1982 authorizes a state governor or state legislature to veto a site for a high-level radioactive waste facility selected by the secretary of energy, Congress in 1987 eliminated this innovative procedure by selecting a site for the facility in Nevada. Nevertheless, incorporation of a provision in a total-preemption statute authorizing the exercise of a suspensive veto by a state merits serious consideration. The suspensive veto forces Congress to review a major federal administrative decision to ensure that it is in conformance with congressional intent.

Partial Federal Preemption

In Chapter 5, six distinctive types of *Imperium in Imperio* powers and eight distinctive types of partial-preemption powers were identified. Relative to the former, states are not required to submit plans to federal administrative agencies for approval prior to exercising the powers. With the exceptions of the powers not subject to federal preemption, the other exercisable *Imperium in Imperio* powers are subject to preemption by Congress.

A partial-preemption statute—for example, the Coastal Zone Management Act of 1972—contains a provision for a suspensive veto by a state similar to the one authorized by the Nuclear Waste Policy Act of 1982.

A similar type of regulatory flexibility is authorized by the Toxic Substances Control Act of 1976. States may continue to regulate chemical mixtures and substances until the Environmental Protection Agency administrator issues a rule applicable to the mixture or substance. Upon issuance of such a rule, the administrator may exempt the mixture or substance from the federal requirements if the state requirements do not place an undue burden on interstate commerce and offer a higher degree of protection for the public.

One of the most interesting types of partial preemption was established by the Coastal Zone Management Act of 1972. Once a state has a coastal-zone management program approved by the secretary of commerce, federal agencies may not issue licenses or permits to a private applicant to undertake an activity if the concerned state objects to the application. The reverse preemption, however, may be overridden by the secretary. A similar type of reverse preemption is found in the Port and Tanker Safety Act of 1978, which provides that the requirement for federally licensed pilots is terminated when the state enacts a law requiring a state-licensed pilot and notifies the secretary of transportation.

From a federalism standpoint, the innovative use of its powers of partial preemption by Congress to structure nation-state relations has been highly desirable and has established a new system of cooperative federalism. In many instances, preemptive statutes have made the federal system a more effective decentralized system by pressuring the states to assume greater regulatory responsibilities, thereby preserving the diffusion of political power and simultaneously producing a seminational uniform regulatory scheme. In addition, minimum standards partial preemption has the advantage of decentralization of the responsibility for implementation and enforcement, which to a degree allows the national standards to be applied differentially to varying situations.

One of the least publicized aspects of many preemption statutes is their granting of new roles to the governors of the states. These roles typically involve the exercise of powers that are not granted to the governors by their state constitutions and statutes. In some instances, these federal delegations of authority to governors have produced conflicts between the governor and the state legislature, but in general, the delegations have not generated many conflicts, in part because the voluminous preemption statutes and implementing regulations are beyond the ability of the typical state legislature to understand regarding the significance of the delegations.

Many of the objections raised against conditional grants-in-aid, described in Chapter 3, have been raised against partial preemption. Critics maintain that such preemption reduces the discretionary authority of subnational units, produces federal bureaucratic dominance and distortion of the budgets of subnational units, complicates the governance process by voluminous regulations, fails to provide adequate subnational input into the statute-making and rule-making processes, burdens states with inflexible programmatic requirements, and creates an accountability problem. Although these critics often use polemical terms, it cannot be denied that the criticisms contain a degree of validity.

The Accountability-Responsibility Problem

Federalism is an abstract organizational principle for assigning powers to different planes of government and cannot automatically provide a precise boundary line or lines between the powers of the national and state governments. Hence, the question of exclusive or concurrent jurisdiction is a question necessarily associated with a federal system. Whose authority encompasses a given matter? For the federalist principle to function effectively without generating undue conflict, clearly there must be a delicate balance of powers between the planes of government.

The authors of *The Federalist* were keenly aware that conflicts between national and state powers would be inevitable in a federal system and that a mechanism was necessary to determine responsibility in the event of such conflict. The supremacy clause in the Constitution was designed to resolve any conflict between a federal law based on a delegated power and a state law in favor of Congress. The clause, however, is inadequate today for determining the respective powers and responsibilities of the planes of government. Furthermore, congressional total- and partial-preemption statutes are often nondefinitive relative to the powers of the planes of government in general and the powers of the states at the peripheries of preempted functional areas.

There can be no doubt that the original intent of the drafters of the Constitution was to have "a more perfect union" of the states, capable of dynamically adapting to changing conditions. The framers have left us such a legacy, but it is inconceivable that they could have envisioned the current kaleidoscopic system of federalism with its extreme complexity and interdependence of the three planes.

If the theory of "dual" federalism was implemented fully in a nation, citizens could readily determine the plane of government — national or state — responsible for failures to achieve desired goals or incompetent performance of duties. In the United States, the theory possessed a considerable explanatory value from 1789 until the national economy and society became extremely complex in the twentieth century. Today, the extensive use of total- and partial-preemptive powers by Congress has made it extremely difficult for the electorate in a number of functional areas to determine whether the states or the national government or both should be held responsible for actions taken or not taken, or actions taken incompetently.

Chapter 4 explains that certain federal laws contain a provision expressly providing for total preemption and that other federal laws indicate that Congress does not intend to occupy the field to the exclusion of state regulation. Hence, there are generally fewer jurisdictional problems with these statutes as the intent of Congress is spelled out relatively clearly. The jurisdictional morass is associated with other congressional statutes that are partially preemptive and statutes lacking an express statement of preemption yet held to be preemptive by the federal courts.

In part, the confusion is due to multiple provisions in a single federal statute applicable to a variety of situations or the exercise of preemptive power by Congress *sub silentio* with respect to the reach of the powers.

Democratic theory is premised upon the establishment of responsibility to allow the electorate to hold officials accountable for their failures to achieve mandated goals or to carry out assigned responsibilities. Uncertainty regarding governmental responsibility in a federal system cannot be eliminated completely when *Imperia* exist within an *Imperium*. Nevertheless, Congress can initiate action to clarify the responsibilities of the national and state planes.

The proposals advanced by President Ronald Reagan to have the states and the national government "swap" certain functional responsibilities is a reflection of the dissatisfaction with the existing confused allocation of governmental responsibilities. Implementation of the "swap" proposals, however, would not eliminate all jurisdictional confusion.

Where partial preemption is deemed essential, Congress should enact a "code of restrictions" applicable to state and local activities in the functional areas partially preempted. Such a code would help to remove ambiguity in the law, thereby facilitating the federal and state governments in properly fulfilling their responsibilities.

Total-federal-preemption statutes also could benefit from a "code of restrictions" since the exercise of the police power by the states may be reasonable and not interfere with the achievement of the goals of the preemption statute.

The U.S. Department of Transportation has in effect issued a "code of restrictions" in the form of administrative regulations relative to the routing of motor carriers transporting radioactive materials.

A state routing rule is preempted if

1. It prohibits transportation of highway route controlled quantity radioactive materials by highway between any two points without providing an alternative route for the duration of the prohibition; or
2. It does not meet all of the following criteria:
   (a) The rule is established by a State routing agency as defined in 171.8 of this subchapter.
   (b) The rule is based on a comparative radiological risk assessment process at least as sensitive as that outlined in the "DOT Guidelines";
   (c) The rule is based on evaluation of radiological risk wherever it may occur, and on a solicitation and substantive consideration of views from each affected jurisdiction, including local jurisdictions and other States; and
   (d) The rule ensures reasonable continuity of routes between jurisdictions.[3]

The department's regulations also address local-routing rules, quantities of radioactive materials required to be placarded, and radioactive materials for which placarding is not required. Any other state or local transportation rule is preempted if it

A. Conflicts with physical security requirements which the Nuclear Regulatory Commission has established in 10 CFR Part 73 or requirements approved by the Department of Transportation under § 173.22(c) of this subchapter;
B. Requires additional or special personnel, equipment, or escort;
C. Requires additional or different shipping paper entries, placards, or other hazard warning devices;
D. Requires filing route plans or other documents containing information that is specific to individual shipments;
E. Requires prenotification;
F. Requires accident or incident reporting other than as immediately necessary for emergency assistance; or
G. Unnecessarily delays transportation.[4]

Since fluidity will continue to characterize nation-state relations and adjustments in the assignments of responsibilities will be made, these statutory changes should be reflected in the "code of restrictions."

Unfortunately, federal preemption generally provides few opportunities for citizen participation in the governance process, though not curtailing the role of special-interest groups in influencing the nature of federal preemption statutes and administrative regulations. As noted in Chapter 2, the Supreme Court has contributed to the problem by its decisions nullifying key provisions of state corrupt-practices acts regulating campaign finance, thereby increasing the political power of pressure groups promoting their special interests.[5] Although preemption statutes may necessitate holding public hearings, critics are convinced that this approach is generally ineffective because citizens lack detailed technical information and staff support similar to those possessed by special-interest groups and governmental officers.

Citizens have the greatest opportunity to play an important role in the governance system on the local-government plane since most public services are delivered by units on this plane and the relatively small geographic scale of local governments facilitates citizen involvement. To the extent that federal preemption directly, or indirectly through the states, limits the authority of general-purpose local governments, participatory democracy will suffer because citizens will have fewer opportunities to play significant roles in the governance process.

Federal Preemption and Goal Achievement

A major reason for federal preemptive activity has been the belief of the majority in Congress that conditional grants-in-aid failed to induce adequate subnational governmental action to solve many major public problems viewed as national by Congress. In general, Congress has not exercised its powers of total preemption because of the diversity of conditions in a nation with a large geographic area and the limited capacity of the executive branch of the national government to assume complete responsibility for the preempted functions.

Drawing conclusions about the effectiveness of total and partial federal preemption in solving problems is limited by three facts. First, Congress often employs the grant-in-aid approach, in conjunction with the preemption approach, and the contribution of each to solving a problem is difficult to disaggregate.

Second, the basic preemptive approach to solving a problem may be an effective one, but the established standards may be incapable of achievement with existing or future technology, or the time frame mandated by Congress for goal achievement may be too short. The latter situation has been common with respect to air-pollution abatement and has necessitated Congress to grant extensions of time for the achievement of mandated air-quality goals.

Third, a preemptive statute may be effective in achieving a stated goal but create other problems in the process. For example, total preemption of the regulation of nuclear power plants promoted the development of such plants in the 1970s during the energy shortage associated with the Organization of Petroleum Exporting Countries' (OPEC) oil embargo but created other problems in the area of public safety. Similarly, federal preemption of truck weights and sizes in the Surface Transportation Assistance Act of 1982 facilitates the transport of goods across state lines but creates safety problems on certain highways.

In 1984, the U.S. Advisory Commission on Intergovernmental Relations (ACIR) released a major report, *Regulatory Federalism,* that examined the growth of intergovernmental regulation, legal foundations, legislative origins, implementation, and impact of federal intergovernmental regulation, and also advanced recommendations for reforming the system of intergovernmental regulation.[6] The commission identified enforcement as "the weakest link" in intergovernmental regulation and added:

As a general rule, then, federal intergovernmental regulations have proven difficult to enforce, statutory deadlines have been repeatedly extended or ignored, and compliance — though probably better than one would anticipate, given the generally haphazard character of federal supervision — has fallen short of official expectations. Such shortcomings in performance account for the Doctor Jekyll and Mr. Hyde reputation of the Office of Civil Rights (OCR) and many other federal regulatory agencies. OCR has been regarded as a hotbed of regulatory zealots by one set of critics and as a timid, lumbering bureaucracy by another. Both are correct — but each is looking at a different aspect of the process.[7]

ACIR attributes the enforcement problems to "administrative and technical problems, a lack of adequate resources, and political obstacles to the imposition of sanctions."[8] This assessment is accurate. The federal bureaucratic behemoth has major administrative and technical problems, and lacks adequate resources to supervise state performance under minimum standards partial preemption. In addition, Congress has been responsive to the requests of subnational governments for extensions of time to meet federal standards, particularly in the environmental field.

Air-Pollution Abatement

In 1967, Dr. John Middleton, director of the National Center for Air Pollution Control of the Public Health Service, testified before the U.S. Senate Subcommittee on Air and Water Pollution that "there are severe limitations on the technology now available for controlling many important sources of air pollution."[9] Nevertheless, the Clean Air Amendments of 1970 mandated achievement of air-quality goals by specified dates without consideration of the economic and technical feasibility of the abatement controls. To cite one example of a specific goal, 1975-model automobiles were required to achieve a 90 percent reduction of the 1970 standards for the emissions of carbon monoxide, hydrocarbons, and nitrogen oxides.[10]

Why did Congress adopt this approach? The evidence is clear that Congress followed the lead of Senator Edmund S. Muskie of Maine, chairman of the Subcommittee an Air and Water Pollution. He was convinced that continuous pressure must be brought to bear upon the major polluters if air quality was to be improved.[11]

Relative to the attainment of ambient-air-quality standards throughout the United States, the Council on Environmental Quality in 1978 reported that only Honolulu of the 105 metropolitan areas with populations exceeding 200,000 had "recorded eight consecutive quarters without a violation" of the oxidant standard which is "the criterion for attainment designation."[12]

In 1979, the comptroller general of the United States issued a report stressing that the Environmental Protection Agency's (EPA) "methods of reporting and determining compliance of stationary sources have not been reliable. Consequently, the actual compliance status of major stationary sources is still unknown, and the severity of the Nation's air pollution problems have not been put into the proper perspective."[13] The report noted that the agency included in its compliance data all sources on cleanup schedules and that half of the major sources considered by the agency to be in compliance were violating the agency's schedule.[14]

In the Clean Air Act Amendments of 1977, Congress weakened the air-pollution-abatement program, and the EPA administrator also initiated action weakening the program. Senator Muskie, one of the architects of the federal air-pollution-abatement program, stated that some individuals maintained that agency Administrator Douglas M. Costle "has opened Pandora's Box. Why, they argue, should any environmental law be implemented when standards might be lessened at a later date?"[15]

Congressman Barry Goldwater, Jr., of California, referring to the Clean Air Act Amendments of 1970, stated in 1979 that "we are wallowing in bureaucratic haze as thick as the smog in Los Angeles on a hot summer day. . . . I have come to the conclusion that our messy concoction of regulations, procedures, guidelines, and mandates are creating more aggravation than they are worth."[16] Goldwater also stressed that the failure of the majority of air-quality-control regions to meet ambient-air-quality standards as late as one year after the original deadline should have led to questioning of the approach and added:

The 1977 amendments . . . have revised the timetable again,but in talking with officials at the Environmental Protection Agency, and with agency heads in California at the state and local level, I am convinced that this standard of procrastination has become par for the course. Let us face it — we are bogged down in a cesspool of government rules which have already impacted on our economic growth and program to achieve energy self-sufficiency at a time when the economy and our energy situation are both very uncertain.[17]

In 1979, the EPA extended the compliance deadline for refiners to reduce the amount of lead in gasoline and also relaxed pollution standards for individual power plants such as two operated by the Cleveland Electric Illuminating Company that produce more air pollution than all Consolidated Edison Company power plants in New York State.[18]

A decade later, air quality had improved, but the December 31, 1987, deadlines were not met in most areas of the nation. Under provisions of the Clean Air Act, the agency can penalize areas failing to meet the air-quality standards by banning the construction of new major sources, or modifications of existing sources, of air pollutants — electric utilities, industrial boilers, petroleum refiners — and restricting federal highway funding and clean-air grants.

Responding to pressure from state and local governments, Congress in the closing days of 1987 enacted a law extending the deadline for attainment of Clean Air Act goals to August 1, 1988.[19] This short extension of seven months did not permit the nonattainment areas to achieve the goals but afforded Congress more time to address the problem. As of late October 1990, Congress had failed to amend and extend the Clean Air Act.

Water-Pollution Abatement

Relative to water-pollution abatement, the Council on Environmental Quality in December 1978 reported that "members of Congress expressed serious concern over the direction the grants program had taken — whether it had been used more to promote growth than to control pollution" and that after thirteen years of partial federal preemption, "water quality is gradually improving."[20]

Addressing the national convention of the Water Pollution Control Federation on October 9, 1979, EPA Administrator Douglas M. Costle reported that monitoring by his agency and the U.S. Geological Survey revealed "no substantial change in the concentration of conventional pollutants in our water for the nation as a whole between 1974 and 1978" and added: "We've made mistakes in the water program, no doubt about it. We've learned to analyze grant applications to make sure that they address genuine community needs rather than subsidizing community growth."[21]

The agency reported that 80 percent of the industrial-discharge sources met the congressionally mandated July 1, 1977, deadline for water-pollution abatement, but that approximately 60 per cent of the seventeen thousand municipal sewerage plants failed to meet the deadline, even though the federal government had made sewerage grants totaling approximately $28 billion to the municipalities.

Complaints from industry that the removal of all nontoxic discharges into waterways would cost more than industry already had spent to remove up to 98 percent of such discharges were heard sympathetically by the agency, which on August 29, 1979, relaxed the water-quality standards for sixty-four subcategories of discharges on the ground that the 1977 amendments to the Clean Water Act require the nontoxic standards to be "reasonably" economic.[22]

Municipalities were originally required to meet secondary treatment standards by 1977, but Congress extended the deadline to 1983 and subsequently to March 31, 1989.[23] Nevertheless, approximately fifteen hundred major treatment facilities and approximately one thousand minor treatment facilities were not in compliance with the standards in 1988.[24]

Municipalities complain that they have been hindered in achieving the secondary treatment standards by reductions in federal grants for sewerage facilities and the EPA's decision to seek court fines for municipalities failing to meet the standards. The financial problem is particularly serious for economically depressed municipalities.

In 1988, the U.S. Department of Justice filed a proposed consent decree under which the consolidated government of Baton Rouge and East Baton Rouge Parish in Louisiana would pay a $750,000 penalty for violations of the Clean Water Act, the largest amount any municipality has paid for violating the act.[25]

Similar problems have plagued the safe drinking water program. The U.S. Environmental Protection Agency in 1989 had only forty-three enforcement agents who took action on only eight hundred of approximately eighty thousand complaints.[26]

Critics of time extensions for the achievement of air- and water-quality standards maintain that the compliance burden is shifted from older facilities to new facilities that are required to meet the standards immediately.[27] In effect, municipalities that are not "good neighbors" and cause problems for other municipalities escape some of the economic burden carried by good-neighbor municipalities that conscientiously initiated action over the years to prevent or reduce environmental pollution.

Congressional Responsiveness

In Chapter 1, we referred to the statement of Justice Harry A. Blackmun about states' receiving relief from preemptive judicial rulings by employing the built-in provisions of the Constitution to bring political pressure to bear upon Congress. The preemptive role of the courts was analyzed in Chapter 6, and emphasis was placed upon the fact that many judicial decisions clearly intrude significantly upon the reserved powers of the states, yet the states retain significant powers.

Is Justice Blackmun's view of congressional responsiveness to the concerns of the states an accurate one? The evidence is mixed. Chapter 6 contains case studies involving total preemption of the power of states to regulate nuclear power plants and truck size and weights. Relative to the former case study, Congress has not responded to the concern of states by amending the Atomic Energy Act of 1946 to allow the states a formal role in emergency evacuation plans around nuclear power plants. On the other hand, Congress enacted two laws to provide relief from the provisions of the Surface Transportation Assistance Act of 1982, which preempted responsibility for establishing maximum truck size and weights on interstate highways, sections of the national highway system designated by the secretary of transportation, and access roads. It appears that the failure of Congress to respond to state concerns relative to nuclear power plants is due to the fact that relatively few states were affected by the total preemption, in contrast to the Surface Transportation Assistance Act, which affected every state.

Chapter 4 also examined the federal statute invalidating state mandatory-retirement-age laws and reported that Congress in 1986 amended the Age Discrimination in Employment Act to exempt firemen and policemen until the year 1993.

As noted in an earlier section of this chapter, Congress responded to the problems states and municipalities were experiencing in complying with deadlines for the achievement of mandated air- and water-quality standards by granting extensions of time. In this section, we examine the response of Congress to the request of Mayor Abraham Beame of New York City for changes in air-pollution-control requirements in his city; the *Boulder* decision of the Supreme Court, extending the Clayton Antitrust Act to municipalities; and the *Garcia* decision of the Court, bringing subnational units under coverage of the Fair Labor Standards Act.

New York City Air-Pollution-Abatement Plan

The federal Clean Air Amendments of 1970, described in Chapter 5, represent a sharp break with the earlier federal approach to air-pollution abatement, which relied upon state and local governments to provide the necessary leadership and took into consideration the economic and technical feasibility of abatement controls.[28] Direct federal action to protect public health was made national policy, and explicit dates for adoption of standards and abatement plans by states were specified. In contrast to earlier ones, the new standards were mandated without considering the economic or technical feasibility of pollution abatement systems.

The administrator of the Environmental Protection Agency was directed to publish, within 90 days, in the *Federal Register* a list of categories of stationary sources of air pollution subject to performance standards established under the amendments. He was given an additional 120 days following publication of the list to include in the *Federal Register* proposed regulations establishing federal standards for new sources of air pollution. Each state was authorized to submit to the administrator a proposed procedure for implementing and enforcing standards of performance for new sources located in the state, and the administrator was empowered to delegate authority to each state to implement and enforce the standards for other than new United States–owned sources. On February 24, 1974, the administrator published final regulations for reviewing the air-quality impact prior to construction of new facilities — labeled indirect sources — that may generate significant automobile traffic.[29]

If stationary-source controls, combined with motor-vehicle emission controls, cannot guarantee the attainment of statutory ambient-air-quality standards within an air-quality-control region, transportation controls must be adopted, and such controls will force significant changes in the lifestyles of many residents of the region.

Governor Nelson A. Rockefeller, in April 1973, transmitted a plan, developed in cooperation with Mayor John V. Lindsay of New York City, to the EPA administrator.[30] The air-quality implementation plan for the New York City metropolitan area, approved by the agency in June 1973, provided for the imposition of transportation controls, including mandatory vehicle-emission inspection, tolling of East River and Harlem River bridges in New York City, staggering of work hours, a sharp reduction in the number of midtown Manhattan parking spaces, improved traffic management, designation of exclusive bus lanes, and a selective ban on taxicab cruising in midtown Manhattan. In 1974, the U.S. Court of Appeals for the Second Circuit upheld the validity of the plan.[31]

Abraham Beame, the newly elected mayor, sought in 1975 to have the transportation-control plan amended to eliminate the requirements for tolling of the bridges and vehicle-emission inspection. Unsuccessful in his attempt to have the plan amended, Mayor Beame and other officials mobilized the New York State congressional delegation to work for the inclusion of a provision—the Moynihan-Holtzman Amendment—in the Clean Air Act Amendments of 1977, directing the EPA administrator to delete from a transportation-control plan a requirement for the tolling of bridges upon application of the governor of the concerned state. The provision was incorporated into the act, and Governor Hugh L. Carey, on October 19, 1977, notified the administrator, and the requirement was deleted from the plan on November 28, 1977.[32]

Municipal Antitrust Immunity

In *Parker v. Brown* (1945), the Supreme Court ruled that in accordance with the basic principles of federalism, Congress did not intend to apply its antitrust laws to state governments if a state made a deliberate decision to exclude competition by private firms in the conduct of state economic affairs.[33] The case involved a California-sponsored raisin cartel. Congress did not overturn this decision, and until 1978 the presumption was made that the immunity of states from federal antitrust laws extended to political subdivisions.

In 1978 and 1982, the Supreme Court issued decisions making clear that the extension of immunity to municipal corporations was not automatic. In the first decision, the Court revealed its intention to scrutinize carefully the application of the antitrust laws to political subdivisions.[34]

While the first decision disturbed a number of municipal officials, the second decision, *Community Communications Corp. v. City of Boulder,* caused great anxiety in municipal halls.[35] The Court held that anticompetitive conduct by a municipality based upon a municipal home-rule power was subject to the antitrust laws. The Court rejected the claim that a general state "home-rule" authorization automatically provided a "state-action" exemption from the federal antitrust laws and ruled that there must be a clearly expressed state policy to displace competition with municipal monopolization or regulation if the exemption is to apply. The Court specifically ruled that a policy under which a state allows "its municipalities to do as they please can hardly be said to have 'contemplated' the specific anticompetitive actions for which municipal liability is sought. Nor can those actions be truly described as 'comprehended within the powers grants,' since the term, 'granted,' necessarily implies an affirmative addressing of the subject by the State."[36]

In 1984, Congress responded to the pleas of local governments and states for relief from these two decisions by enacting the Local Government Antitrust Act of 1984, providing that damages, interest on damages, and plaintiffs' legal fees may not be recovered from municipal defendants in the damage phase of a Clayton Act lawsuit but that plaintiffs can be awarded legal fees for costs incurred in their efforts to obtain the issuance of a writ of injunction.[37] In addition, the 1984 act exempts from liability municipal officials and their employees acting in an "official capacity" and private parties following directions of municipal officials. While the act does not apply retroactively, federal courts have the discretion to exempt municipal defendants from damages if they prove that damages should not be assessed. The provision stipulating that plaintiffs may not collect the costs of their legal fees from municipal governments is designed to prevent the filing of frivolous suits.

Interestingly, a number of state officials recommended that Congress not grant municipal governments complete immunity from the antitrust laws because such action would be a congressional intrusion upon the reserved powers of the states to control their political subdivisions.[38]

Fair Labor Standards
Chapter 6 examined the decisions of the Supreme Court in *National League of Cities* (1976) and *Garcia* (1985), dealing with the question whether the federal fair labor standards apply to subnational governments.[39] The Congressional Budget Office released in 1985 a preliminary estimate that the states and their subdivisions would experience "initial annual compliance costs totaling between $0.5 billion and $1.5 billion nationwide."[40] Much of the compliance costs would result from the requirement that employees be paid for overtime work instead of receiving compensatory time off.

Responding to the requests for relief from *Garcia*, Congress enacted the Fair Labor Standards Amendments of 1985, authorizing subnational governments to offer their employees compensatory time off at a rate of one and one-half hours for each hour of overtime work in lieu of overtime compensation, making clear that the federal labor standards do not apply to volunteers, and granting state and local legislative employees the same exemptions from the standards as those for employees of Congress.[41]

Reagan Administration Responsiveness

President Ronald Reagan's New Federalism program was a direct response to the criticisms of the intergovernmental regulatory role of the national government at the time he was inaugurated in 1981. One of the first actions initiated by the president to implement his program was the appointment of the Presidential Task Force on Regulatory Relief, which issued its report in 1983.[42] In addition, in 1981 the president issued an executive order (no. 12291) requiring that all proposed and final regulations must be submitted for review by the Office of Management and Budget prior to publication in the *Federal Register*, and a second executive order (no. 12372) providing for intergovernmental review of federal programs and affording subnational governments greater opportunities to influence the federal decision-making process.

A major action taken by the Environmental Protection Agency was granting states greater regulatory discretion on the issuance of regulations allowing a state to employ the "bubble" concept in determining whether a change in a stationary source within a plant met the requirements of the Clean Air Act.[43] In 1984, the Supreme Court issued a memorandum decision upholding the agency's regulations as in compliance with the Clean Air Act Amendments.[44]

The Reagan Administration also sped up the process of delegating "primacy" to the states under various partial-preemption statutes, reduced federal oversight of state regulatory activities under partial-preemption statutes, and relaxed federal regulatory standards.[45]

In 1985, the president transmitted a message on the regulatory program of the national government and stressed that the objectives of the program are to

—Create a coordinated process for developing on an annual basis the Administration's Regulatory Program;
—Establish Administration regulatory priorities;
—Increase the accountability of agency heads for the regulatory actions of their agencies;
—Provide for presidential oversight of the regulatory process;
—Reduce the burdens of existing and future regulations;
—Minimize duplication and conflict of regulations; and
—Enhance public and congressional understanding of the Administration's regulatory objectives.[46]

In 1981, the president proposed and Congress enacted a law consolidating fifty-seven categorical grant-in-aid programs into nine new or revised grant programs, according the states greater flexibility in the use of the grant funds.[47] In implementing the nine block-grant programs, the responsible federal agencies replaced 905 pages of detailed regulations in the *Code of Federal Regulations* with 31 pages.

Federalism Theory

Our review of the use of partial and total preemptive powers by Congress to structure nation-state relations makes it evident that the terms *dual federalism* and *cooperative federalism* lack sufficient explanatory value. A transformation of a fundamental nature has occurred in the American federal system that today bears relatively little resemblance to the federal system in 1788. A theory with sufficient explanatory value is exceedingly difficult to formulate because of the constantly changing intertwining of the three planes of government in the administration of many functions and functional components. Developing a prescriptive theory of federalism is also hampered by the fact that the optimal degree of centralization or noncentralization of power varies by function and functional component.

The theory of *dual federalism* is a simple one, premised upon the national government and the states each possessing a number of sovereign powers. A true "independence" model of national and state powers, however, never existed, although the model was approximated at the beginning of the federal system. The early relationship was largely "symbiotic," the two planes of government coexisting in close proximity yet having little contact, with the result that one plane did not harm or injure the other. The concept of dual federalism is useful as a general descriptor for the essential stable feature of a federal system—two or more planes of government, each with significant powers, within the same territory.

The theory of *cooperative federalism* is also a relatively simple one, suggesting that each plane cooperates freely with the other to promote the common good. While the current federal system exhibits elements of cooperation based upon comity, Congress has clearly been innovative in structuring nation-state relations by employing both incentives and coercion to involve the states in national programs.

No theory of American federalism has a great explanatory value unless its elements include informal federal preemption—conditional grants-in-aid and tax credits—and formal federal preemption, total and partial. Informal and formal federal preemption have produced significant changes in the American federal system. Congress has provided incentives (conditional grants-in-aid and tax credits) and prescriptions (minimum national standards) to induce states to play a fuller regulatory role.

Change must be the key word in a new theory of federalism that explains fluctuating relationships on a continuing basis. Adequate recognition has generally not been given to the fact that the drafters of the Constitution were aware of the importance of "building-in" flexible national powers in the Constitution to enable it to become a living document responding to a metamorphic environment. The framers of the fundamental document deliberately decided not to establish procrustean spheres of congressional and state powers.

The fact that Congress did not use its latent powers of total preemption until 1898 (bankruptcy) and 1946 (atomic energy) or its powers of standard partial preemption until the sixth decade of this century (environmental regulation) should not blind the reader to the fact that these powers were potentially exercisable during an earlier period. Politically, however, Congress probably would have been unable to exercise its powers of complete supersession of state laws in certain areas if external conditions had been otherwise. The cold war not only facilitated but almost mandated Congress's preempting completely the regulation of atomic energy.

When Congress exercises its powers of total preemption with no provision for a limited turnback of regulatory authority to the states, it is apparent that no element of nation-state cooperation is involved. The total preemption may include forbidding the states to engage in the economic regulation of an industry — such as the airline, bus, and truck industries — that Congress freed from federal economic regulation. In these instances, total federal preemption assumes the form of an absolute restraint on the exercise of economic regulatory powers by the states. Or the total federal preemption may assume the form of a complete prohibition of state regulation and total federal regulation, as with nuclear power plants.

The total preemptive action may be "total" only initially. For example, the federal government regulates emissions from new motor vehicles but relies upon states in many areas to conduct periodic inspections to ensure that motor vehicles are not exceeding allowable emissions of specified pollutants. The emission-inspection programs are based on the exercise of the police power of the states in a new manner, thereby resulting in the exercise of a power for the first time.

Discussions of the changes in the powers exercised by Congress and the states, respectively, over the decades are typically premised on the belief that the changes are related to a "zero-sum" model, an increase in the powers exercised by Congress automatically producing a corresponding decrease in the powers of the states.

Since the powers of the states are unlisted in the Constitution, with the exception of the Twenty-first Amendment, and the delegated powers of Congress are described in broad terms, it is impossible to measure precisely the totality of powers capable of being exercised by each plane. Exercisable powers on each plane, however, are considerably greater than the powers exercised to date. Hence, the first exercise of a partial-preemption power by Congress usually results in the first exercise of certain powers by some or all states. In other words, the states possessed the power potential to act but failed to initiate a regulatory program until pressured to do so by Congress.

A Mutuality Model

Standard partial preemption and informal preemption have produced a dynamic *reliance,* or *mutuality,* model of nation-state relations, reflecting the interdependence of the actors and the reliance of the actors on each plane upon actors on the other plane for the performance of certain functions or functional components (such as monitoring and inspection of pollution-emitting facilities by the states and technical assistance provided to the states by the federal government). Minimum standards partial preemption helps to retain the diffusion of political power to a large extent, thereby preventing the overcentralization of political power that would result from total federal preemption.

Some observers may view the use of partial preemption as the "commandeering" of the states' resources by Congress. Such a view is overly simplistic; states often wish to initiate action but fear that strong regulation of industry to eliminate or reduce pollution will drive industry out of the state or that such a regulatory action will give the state an "antibusiness" image, thereby injuring industry-recruitment efforts. It is true, of course, that partial preemption affects the ability of subnational units to address problems independently in preempted and nonpreempted areas. Employment of resources for preempted regulatory programs reduces the resources available for employment in the attack on problems in nonpreempted areas.

The American federal system, in addition to being based upon a reliance model, is also kaleidoscopic in nature, with interplane relationships changing constantly as the result of new federal structuring statutes, new federal implementing regulations, and decisions by state policymakers to refuse to apply for, accept, or return regulatory primacy under federal partial-preemption statutes. The types of structuring mechanisms that can be employed by Congress appear to be limited only by the innovative ability of Congress.

The drafters of the Constitution sought "a more perfect union" of the states by allowing for additional unifying actions as conditions changed and a consensus built in Congress for a stronger national role in the assault upon public problems, thereby producing "a more perfect union" of the states with the national government.

Although the federal government today directly administers few programs that it did not administer prior to 1965, it plays a much greater role in state-administered programs primarily designed to reduce negative externalities. Minimum national environmental standards, for example, ensure that there will be no industrial-polluter-haven states.

Until 1965, national regulatory policies were generally administered by federal departments and agencies. The Water Quality Act of 1965 represents the start of a new national regulatory system, the states administering regulations at least as stringent as minimum national standards and the federal government administering the regulatory program only if a state returns or does not apply for primacy.

It would be a mistake to conclude that the federal government has complete control, even in the functional areas where it has exercised its powers of total preemption. The controversy surrounding the plans for the emergency evacuation of residents near nuclear power plants, described in Chapter 4, reveals the dependence of the Nuclear Regulatory Commission upon the states and local governments for emergency assistance.

Congress and Federalism Theory

In 1959, Congress recognized that the fluidity of the federal system, which had accelerated in the post–World War II period, necessitated a substantial continuing research program on the relations of governments in the American system, and created the U.S. Advisory Commission on Intergovernmental Relations to carry out such research. Unfortunately, there is relatively little evidence that the Congress employs its preemptive powers on the basis of commission recommendations or on the basis of a concept of federalism. Prior to the expanded uses of congressional powers of preemption, Henry M. Hart, Jr., wrote in 1954, relative to nation-state relations, that "the opportunity for long-range and systematic thinking lies with the courts and the legal profession, with such help as political science can muster."[48]

It appears that congressional restructuring actions are simply ad hoc responses to particular problems that result in a comprehensive and unplanned restructuring of nation-state relations. The preemption problems created for subnational units stem in part from the fact that an increasing number of the members of Congress have had no previous state or local government experience and the growth of national interest groups that contribute funds to congressional election campaigns.

The failure of many members of Congress to appreciate the impact of preemption statutes on the subnational governance systems is illustrated by the following statement by Mayor Edward I. Koch of New York City, a former member of the U.S. House of Representatives:

As a member of Congress I voted for many of the laws, . . . and did so with every confidence that we were enacting sensible permanent solutions to critical problems. It took a plunge into the Mayor's job to drive home how misguided my congressional outlook had been. The bills I voted for in Washington came to the floor in a form that compelled approval. After all, who can vote against clean air and water, or better access and education for the handicapped. But as I look back it is hard to believe I could have been taken in by the simplicity of what the Congress was doing and by the flimsy empirical support — often no more than a carefully orchestrated hearing record or a single consultant's report — offered to persuade the members that the proposed solution could work throughout the country.[49]

A 1986 survey by the author of members of Congress produced a number of interesting comments about the reasons for the growth in preemption activity. A California representative responded that "preemptory powers have become necessary because of the growth of the executive branch and the activist roles of recent Presidents." A second California representative responded "Don't know" to the question. A third representative attributed the increased use of preemptory powers to "television."

A representative who had served as a state senator for eight years attributed the expansive activities of Congress to "weak state governments; ineptness, corruption, power bullying, and insensitivity to the problems of those who have no political powers has made the state decision-making process less objective and less generous than the national process."

A Republican senator answered the question with "Democratic control of the Congress," and a second senator replied, "Congressmen not living up to the spirit of the Constitution."

In employing preemption powers, Congress must examine the broader federalism implications of many bills prior to enacting them into law and exercise caution to ensure that the innovative capacities of the states are not eliminated or reduced. Achievement of national goals should be the objective of each preemption statute rather than the precise mechanism to be employed. There are decided advantages in having many loci of decision-making power. With such loci, jurisdictional issues will continue to arise, and in the event of an impasse, the federal judiciary will have to continue to play its arbiter role.

The importance of clarity in preemption statutes was emphasized by Senator Howard H. Baker, Jr., of Tennessee as early as 1967: "But I respectfully suggest that we ought to give very close attention to the language that we adopt so that this question of preemption or nonpreemption or even personal legislative preemption is clearly spelled out, so that we do not hinder the efforts of local authorities to respond to local circumstances."[50]

To achieve national goals in the most effective manner, Congress should review the types of structuring devices it has employed in terms of their cost-effectiveness and ability to achieve national goals. It is unrealistic to expect the entire Congress to conduct such a study. I suggest that each house direct its Subcommittee on Intergovernmental Relations to act as a preemption-review body that will prepare a federalism assessment and advance recommendations for legislative structuring of nation-state relations, thereby ensuring that powers of preemption will not be employed by Congress de novo without consideration of alternative structuring approaches. Alternatively, each house could create a new committee for this purpose, or the two houses could establish a joint preemption-review committee.

Fiscal Implications of Federal Mandates

Federal mandates commanding action by the states and their subdivisions must be distinguished from federal restraints restricting or prohibiting certain actions by these units and from conditional grants-in-aid. Subnational officials often describe conditions attached to federal grants-in-aid as "mandates," but these conditions are not true mandates since a subnational unit can avoid the conditions by not applying for or accepting federal funds. As described in Chapter 3, conditional grants-in-aid should be viewed as informal federal preemption since the action leading to the imposition of the conditions was initiated by the subnational units and the conditions are not based upon the preemptive powers delegated to Congress by the Constitution. However, compliance costs are involved with such grants. In common with grants, states and local governments can avoid some of the compliance costs associated with partial preemption by refusing to accept regulatory primacy from the national government.

We define a federal *mandate* as a legal requirement—constitutional provision, statutory provision, or administrative regulation— that states and local governments must undertake a specific activity or provide a service meeting minimum national standards. A mandate can also be defined in marginal-cost terms as the difference between what a subnational government would spend on the same activity in the absence of the mandate and what a unit is required to spend by the mandate.

Congress has responded to the concerns of the states and their subdivisions by requiring that cost estimates be attached to any bill imposing expenses on these units but, with one exception, has not responded to the calls from subnational officials for reimbursement of the expenses by the federal government.

The Fiscal Note Process

Officials of the states and local governments often attribute mandates in part to members of Congress who are unaware of the compliance costs imposed on subnational governments by the mandates. Whereas genuine federal mandates are relatively recent in origin, state mandates on local governments have a long history, and in many states fiscal notes are attached to all bills introduced in the state legislature.

In 1977, the U.S. Advisory Commission on Intergovernmental Relations surveyed the fifty states and reported that fiscal notes were employed in twenty-two states — by both houses of the legislature in nineteen states, by the senate in Alabama, and by the governor's office in Minnesota and Washington.[51] Subsequently, other states — including Maine, New Hampshire, and New York — have adopted fiscal-impact requirements for bills affecting local governments. The states believe that their cost estimates are relatively accurate, and no major attempt has been made in recent years to repeal the requirement in any state. Nevertheless, many local officials believe that fiscal notes give their units little protection against mandated costs. The Association of County Commissioners of Georgia commented in 1986 on the Georgia Fiscal Note Act by observing that "in practice the Act has been ignored more often than observed."[52]

The federal deficit problem induced Congress in 1974 to authorize the Congressional Budget Office (CBO) to prepare fiscal notes indicating the cost to the federal government of all bills introduced in Congress.[53] Responding to state and local complaints about mandated compliance costs, Congress in 1981 enacted the State and Local Government Cost Estimate Act, directing the CBO to prepare "an estimate of the cost which would be incurred by State and local governments in carrying out or complying with any significant bill or resolution in the fiscal year in which it is to become effective and in each of the four fiscal years following such fiscal year, together with the basis for each such estimate."[54] The requirement pertains only to bills resulting in an average annual cost to subnational units of $200 billion.[55]

Sponsors of the act were convinced that national lawmakers lacked adequate cost data that could influence the action of Congress in legislating national policy. Although the objectives of a bill may be highly desirable, sponsors of the cost-impact law believed that Congress might not enact or might amend a bill if the costs imposed on state and local governments would be high.

Testifying before the U.S. Senate Subcommittee on Intergovernmental Relations in 1985, CBO Assistant Director James Blum stated relative to the Ninety-eighth Congress:

Our records indicate that only 30 bill cost estimates exceeded the $200 million threshold. Many of these were for different versions of the same legislation.

While I believe our cost estimates provide useful information to the Congress for gauging the potential cost of its legislation, I don't think they are precise enough or detailed enough to be used as a basis for actually reimbursing State and local governments for the costs they might incur.[56]

Mr. Blum also reported that the CBO examined 1,214 bills and prepared cost estimates indicating that 1,080 (89 percent) of the bills would have no cost impact upon state and local governments.[57]

In 1987, Associate Director J. William Gadsby, of the Human Resources Division of the U.S. General Accounting Office, testified before another Senate subcommittee that "the cost estimate process alone can not be generally expected to deter mandates on States and localities. The actual reduction of mandates seem to be more a function of commitment by legislators as well as the interest groups representing State and local governments."[58]

The Federal Mandate Problem

As noted in an earlier section, the term *federal mandate* must be distinguished from a federal restraint, which is difficult to avoid if it is specific in nature. In Chapter 4, we described examples of specific federal restraints, including prohibition of state regulation of bankruptcy, buses and airlines, emissions from new motor vehicles (with the exception of California), and transportation of radioactive materials.

The fiscal impact of federal mandates upon subnational governments is difficult to measure, in part due to problems of determining the precise total cost of each mandate or the marginal cost of a mandate. While a single federal mandate may not add significantly to expenditures of subnational units, a series of federal mandates may have a burdensome cumulative effect. It is apparent that federal mandates imposing major costs upon subnational governments reduce their discretionary authority and make the units less responsive to the needs of their citizenry unless the mandated costs are reimbursed by the federal government or federal financial assistance is provided.

Although there have been studies identifying federal mandates, there have been few attempts to calculate with precision the costs imposed by such mandates on state and local governments. States with state mandate reimbursements, such as California and Massachusetts, have demonstrated that it is possible to determine the cost of mandates.[59]

U.S. Senator David F. Durenberger of Minnesota, Senator Pete Wilson of California, and other senators have introduced for several years an Intergovernmental Regulatory Relief Act, requiring the federal government to reimburse subnational units for additional direct costs imposed by federal regulations promulgated after the enactment of the act by Congress.[60] The bill defines additional direct costs as

the amount of costs incurred by a State or local government solely in complying with an intergovernmental regulation promulgated pursuant to a Federal law concerning a particular activity which is in excess of the amount that such State or local government would be required to expend in carrying out such activity in the absence of such law, except that such term does not include any amount which a State or local government is required by law to contribute as non-Federal share under a Federal assistance program.[61]

Recognizing that certain local governments are experiencing severe fiscal problems because of the reduction in federal financial assistance, Senator Durenberger and Senator Charles E. Grassley introduced in 1987 a bill — S. 660, entitled the Targeted Fiscal Assistance Act — that provides special federal financial assistance to needy local governments. In introducing the bill, Senator Durenberger stressed that "wealthy communities, defined as those whose average per capita income is 25 percent or more above the State average, will not be eligible to receive funds. Communities with low fiscal capacity but high tax-effort can receive up to three times the United States average per capita grant."[62]

Justifying the proposed Targeted Fiscal Assistance Act is an easier task than justifying the proposed Intergovernmental Regulatory Relief Act's provision for federal reimbursement of direct costs imposed upon states and their subdivisions by federal regulations promulgated after enactment of the act by Congress.

The latter proposed law would reimburse subnational units for all direct costs resulting from any federal regulation, including conditions attached to grants-in-aid, with the exception of the condition specifying the nonfederal share of individual grants-in-aid programs. If there is to be federal reimbursement, a stronger case can be made for reimbursing state and local governments for added costs associated with partial- or total-preemption mandates.

A Typology of Federal Mandates

A typology of federal mandates on subnational governments will promote rational analysis of the question whether all such mandates should be reimbursed in full or in part. Listed below are nine types of federal mandates.

CIVIL RIGHTS. These mandates are designed to ensure that there is no discrimination practiced by state and local governments. Many of these mandates are contained in court orders relative to school busing and hiring of minority persons by police and fire departments. School busing to prevent racial discrimination obviously can be expensive.

GOOD NEIGHBOR. These seek to prevent individual state or local governments from spilling problems and resulting costs over their boundary lines to neighboring jurisdictions. Air pollution and water pollution are obviously expensive problems to eradicate.

PERSONNEL. These mandates relate to equal-employment opportunities and fair labor standards, including working conditions and pay.

PUBLIC HEALTH. These requirements are designed to ensure that grains, meat, and poultry are safe for human consumption and that drinking water is potable.

PUBLIC SAFETY. These provisions are designed to ensure that states initiate action to ensure that the public is properly protected. The Low Level Radioactive Policy Act of 1980, for example, makes states responsible for disposing of the low-level radioactive wastes generated within their boundaries.

SERVICE LEVEL. Such mandates require state and/or local governments to provide specified services meeting minimum national standards. The Safe Drinking Water Act applies to all suppliers of drinking water to the general public.

TAX. These mandates are designed to ensure that federal tax resources are protected. The Tax Equity and Fiscal Responsibility Act of 1982, for example, requires that subnational governments making income tax refunds to their taxpayers report the refunds to the Internal Revenue Service.

WORKER SAFETY. Such mandates seek to protect workers from injuries and the deleterious effects of materials they employ in their productive activities. The Occupational Health and Safety Administration's mandates, the EPA's banning of asbestos, and mine safety and health standards are examples of worker-safety mandates.

VOTING RIGHTS. These mandates specifically protect the electoral privileges of blacks and certain foreign-language minority individuals.

It must be recognized that several types of federal mandates overlap each other, as illustrated by certain good-neighbor and certain public-health mandates. The above types are suggestive, and other types can be developed.

A strong case can be made that the following mandates should not be subject to federal reimbursement for added costs imposed upon subnational governments: civil rights, good neighbor, personnel, worker safety, and voting rights. These mandates ensure that state and local governments do not discriminate on the basis of race, religion, or national origin, do not cause problems for their neighbors or deny the voting rights of citizens, and ensure that employees are treated fairly in terms of pay and working conditions and that working conditions are safe.

Good-neighbor mandates present a problem in that municipalities responsible for major air and water pollution may be fiscally weak. The proposed Targeted Fiscal Assistance Act would be the preferable approach for providing federal financial aid to these units to enable them to become good neighbors. One must acknowledge, however, that the municipalities that have been good neighbors will not benefit from the act and that the "free riders" will benefit.

Added costs to subnational governments resulting from public-safety mandates should be reimbursed. The tax mandates in particular directly benefit the national government, and mandated costs should be reimbursed. States administering regulatory programs under agreements with the Nuclear Regulatory Commission should be compensated for costs incurred since the costs could be avoided if a state withdrew from its agreement with the commission.

My review of the fiscal condition of subnational governments reveals that the termination of the general revenue-sharing program by Congress and the reduction in federal grants-in-aid have caused serious fiscal problems for a number of general-purpose local governments. To date, federal mandates have had the greatest fiscal impact upon local governments because these units must meet minimum national standards in such areas as air quality and water quality.

Currently, the Comprehensive Environmental Response, Compensation, and Liability Act of 1980 is the only preemptive statute authorizing federal reimbursement of a state or subdivision for "reasonable response costs."[63] The reimbursement relates to the release of a hazardous substance or pollutant into the environment.

In general, it is difficult to justify reimbursing all states and all local governments for added costs associated with most mandates. The serious financial problems of certain general-purpose local governments represent a strong reason for the enactment by Congress of the proposed Target Fiscal Assistance Act. Without the fiscal assistance provided by this law, it is apparent that these general-purpose local governments will probably be unable to meet their good-neighbor responsibilities and ensure a healthy environment for their citizens.

Concluding Comments

It is difficult to argue against Congress's playing a larger role in the domestic governance system as the economy and society become more national and international in nature. Nevertheless, the federal role should be delimited, primarily on a partnership basis with the states, and the general-purpose political subdivisions more directly involved in shaping the nature of the attack upon major societal problems.

A strong case can be made for consultation with governors and leaders of state legislatures by Congress prior to acting upon preemptive bills. Such consultation could be the responsibility of a preemption-review committee in each house or a joint committee that would also prepare and attach a regulatory-impact note to each preemptive bill. States have detailed knowledge of problems within their borders, and congressional use of this knowledge will result in the most expeditious and complete solution of the problems addressed by the preemptive bills. Furthermore, an active state role in solving problems promotes citizen interest in the governance system and helps to educate the public about attacks upon major societal problems.

In particular, Congress should exercise great care when employing its powers of preemption to ensure that impediments are not created that impose major restrictions upon the ability of the states to develop and implement innovative regulatory programs. I recommend that preemptive statutes provide the states with multiple avenues for securing relief from burdensome preemption short of congressional amendment of a statute and Congress should serve as a court of last resort to grant the requested relief. To the extent practicable, each partial-preemption statute should contain two or more structuring mechanisms to afford the states a choice relative to the mechanisms that would be most effective in achieving national goals within individual states.

When the Congress determines that enactment of a preemption statute is essential, the Congress should enact a "code of restrictions" applicable to state and local activities in the preempted functional areas. Relative to ionizing radiation, for example, the code could specify clearly the areas where subnational governments would be prohibited from banning the shipment of radioactive materials through tunnels and over bridges. The fluid nature of the federal system should be reflected in amendments to the "codes of restrictions."

Past experience with preemption statutes suggests that it is improbable that the Congress will enact "codes of restrictions" in the future. Congressional practice, with a few exceptions, has been to enact statutes with broad preemption provisions and authorize the administering agencies to develop and promulgate implementing rules and regulations. Consequently, should the Congress be sympathetic to the concept of a "code of restrictions," it is more probable that administering agencies will be directed to include such codes in their rules and regulations.

Coordination problems abound when the Congress exercises its powers of partial preemption. States concerned with a resource such as water, for example, have to consult and negotiate with numerous federal administrative agencies — with the Environmental Protection Agency relative to water quality, flood control with the U.S. Army Corps of Engineers, flood insurance with the Federal Emergency Management Agency, and drainage with a gamut of agencies.

Congress's response to coordination problems has been piece-meal to date, perhaps reflecting uncertainty as to the desirability of establishing a new permanent, formal coordinating mechanism. A modest proposal to help ensure that programs are planned and implemented in a cooperative manner is the employment of interagency committees, composed of officials from each plane of government, to minimize operating problems. Interagency agreements can facilitate coordination if the responsibilities of the signatory parties are spelled out clearly and procedures are established to maintain continuing communications and joint oversight of programs.

Regardless of the initial justification for preemptive action, Congress should periodically review preemptive statutes to determine whether changes are needed to meet new conditions. In the absence of congressional action, the burden of reviewing and adjusting the statutes to new conditions falls upon the unelected federal judiciary. The solution to this problem is the incorporation of a "sunset" provision in each preemptive statute.

States have historically played important roles in the governance system as experimental laboratories inventing solutions for public problems that are subsequently adopted by other states and Congress. Unfortunately, I am unable to determine the extent to which the inventiveness of the states and their subdivisions has been stifled by total and partial federal preemption. To encourage innovation by the states, Congress should rely primarily upon partial preemption and authorize the states to develop their own regulatory programs, provided they are consistent (rather than identical) with the federal program.

In deciding upon the best method(s) for achieving national goals, Congress should give special consideration to equity in the financing of subnational regulatory activities and achievement of federal standards, effectiveness and efficiency of subnational governments in achieving preemptive goals, and governmental responsiveness to the citizenry. In other words, the concern of Congress should extend beyond the act of approving preemptive statutes.

In an earlier section, it was noted that power within a federal system is not a zero-sum game and that partial federal preemption has promoted an expansion of the exercise of powers by the states. The power expansion in certain states may be potential rather than actual since state administrative agencies may lack the resources to exercise the powers fully. The problem of adequate resources, of course, will be accentuated if the national economy experiences a recession. In several states, the tax revolt of the late 1970s and early 1980s, involving the use of the initiative and referendum, made it impossible for many local governments to raise additional funds and in some cases required the municipalities to lower their property-tax rates. Local governments needing to borrow funds for major projects, such as sewerage plants, may also encounter taxpayer resistance in required bond referenda.

In terms of federalism theory, I argue for the acceptance by Congress of a true concept of cooperative federalism based upon a "mutuality" model of nation-state relations, reflecting the reliance of each plane of government upon the other planes for the performance of certain functions and functional components, and investment of funds to achieve national goals.

The restructuring of nation-state relations resulting from the employment of preemptive powers by Congress can be viewed as based in part upon a "leadership-feedback" model of decision making, with Congress providing leadership in solving a public problem by enacting a preemptive statute, receiving negative and positive feedback from the states and general-purpose local governments, and amending the statute if need be to make it more palatable to subnational units and more effective in achieving national policy goals. The Blackmun thesis is related to this model in that Justice Blackmun suggested that negative feedback from the states to Congress on a Supreme Court decision will result in corrective statutory action if sufficient political pressures are brought to bear on Congress.

One prediction can be made safely with respect to the future of the American federal system: The balance of power between Congress and the states will continue to change, and efforts will be made to reassign functional responsibilities to establish a system more closely approximating a dual federalism model. As Congress continues its policy of neutralizing completely or partially certain powers of the states and their subdivisions, the most important controversies will continue to involve the jurisdictional confusion at the periphery of the regulatory area preempted by Congress.

In sum, federal preemption has been successful in solving completely or partially a number of major public problems but has not reached its full potential in several functional areas because of the failure of Congress to base its decisions to preempt upon a mutuality theory of federalism.

Notes

Chapter I

1. Mr. Gerry's letter of October 18, 1787, was published in *New Hampshire Spy,* November 6, 1787, and is quoted in Charles E. Clark, "New Hampshire's First Look at Anti-ratification Arguments," *The Keene Sentinel,* November 18, 1987, p. 5.

2. Luther Gulick, "Reorganization of the State," *Civil Engineering* (August 1933): 421.

3. Harold J. Laski, "The Obsolescence of Federalism," *New Republic,* May 3, 1939, pp. 362–69, and Harold J. Laski, *The American Democracy: A Commentary and an Interpretation* (New York: Viking, 1948), p. 139.

4. Felix Morley, *Freedom and Federalism* (Chicago: Henry Regnery, 1959), p. 209.

5. *The Federalist Papers* (New York: New American Library, 1961), p. 119.

6. D. W. Brogan, *Politics in America* (Garden City, N.Y.: Anchor Books, 1960), p. 228.

7. *The Commission on Intergovernmental Relations: A Report to the President for Transmittal to the Congress* (Washington, D.C.: GPO, 1955), pp. 63–64.

8. *Regulatory Federalism: Policy, Process, Impact, and Reform* (Washington, D.C.: U.S. Advisory Commission on Intergovernmental Relations, 1984), p. 259.

9. Ronald Reagan, "Federalism: Executive Order 12612, October 26, 1987," *Weekly Compilation of Presidential Documents,* November 2, 1987, p. 1231.

10. Garcia v. San Antonio Metropolitan Transit Authority, 469 U.S. 556 (1985).

11. Jackson Pemberton, "A New Message: On Amendment XVII," *The Freeman* (November 1976): 657.

12. Gibbons v. Ogden, 9 Wheaton 1 at 197 (1824).

13. Garcia, 469 U.S. 556 (1985).

14. William H. Steward, *Concepts of Federalism* (Lanham, Md.: University Press of America, 1984), p. 4.

15. Daniel J. Elazar, *Exploring Federalism* (Tuscaloosa: Univ. of Alabama Press, 1987), p. 225.

16. For details, see Joseph F. Zimmerman, "The State Mandate Problem," *State and Local Government Review* (Spring 1987): 78–84.

17. S. 2387, 1987, § 201.

Chapter II

1. Water Quality Act of 1965, 79 Stat. 903, 33 U.S.C. 1151 (1965 Supp.).

2. William F. Swindler, "Our First Constitution: The Articles of Confederation,' *American Bar Association Journal* (February 1981): 166–69.

3. Articles of Confederation and Perpetual Union, Art. II.

4. Thomas A. Bailey, *The American Pageant: A History of the Republic,* 3d ed. (Boston: D.C. Heath, 1967), p. 136.

5. Ibid., p. 137.

6. Richard Hofstadter, William Miller, and Daniel Aaron, *The American Republic* (Englewood Cliffs, N.J.: Prentice-Hall, 1959), p. 223.

7. U.S. Constitution, Art. I, §§ 8, 10.

8. Ibid., §§ 9, 10.

9. Ibid., § 9.

10. Ibid., § 10.

11. Ibid., § 8.

12. Constitution, Art. VI, § 2.

13. Ibid., Art. I, § 10.

14. Virginia v. Tennessee, 148 U.S. 503 (1893); Michelin Tire Corporation v. Wages, 423 U.S. 276 at 286 (1975).

15. R.J. Reynolds Tobacco Company v. Durham County, 107 S. Ct. 499 (1986).

16. Constitution, Art. VII. For details on the views of the Anti-Federalists, see Herbert J. Storing, *What the Anti-Federalist Were For* (Chicago: Univ. of Chicago Press, 1981).

17. *The Federalist Papers* (New York: New American Library, 1961), p. 292.

18. Ibid., p. 119.

19. Ibid., p. 296.

20. Robert H. Walker, ed., *The Reform Spirit in America: A Documentation of Reform in the American Republic* (New York: Putnam, 1976), pp. 25–26.

21. Ibid., pp. 26–27.

22. Alan V. Briceland, "Virginia's Ratification of the U.S. Constitution," *Newsletter* (Institute of Government, University of Virginia) (October 1984): 2.

23. For the historical development of cooperative federalism, see Daniel J. Elazar, *American Federalism: A View from the States,* 3d ed. (New York: Harper & Row, 1984), and Morton Grodzins, *The American Systems* (Chicago: Rand McNally, 1967).

24. Paul L. Ford, ed., *The Writings of Thomas Jefferson,* vol. 9 (New York: Putnam, 1898), p. 452.

25. *A Catalog of Federal Grant-in-Aid Programs to State and Local Governments: Grants Funded FY 1978* (Washington, D.C.: U.S. Advisory Commission on Intergovernmental Relations, 1979), p. 1.

26. Atomic Energy Act of 1946, 60 Stat. 755, 42 U.S.C. § 2011 (1947 Supp.); Atomic Energy Act of 1959, 73 Stat. 688, 42 U.S.C. § 2021 (1960 Supp.).

27. Uniform Time Act of 1966, 80 Stat. 107, 15 U.S.C. § 260 (1967 Supp.).

28. Water Quality Act of 1965, 79 Stat. 903, 33 U.S.C. § 1151 (1966 Supp.); Air Quality Act of 1967, 81 Stat. 485, 42 U.S.C. § 1857 (1968 Supp.).

29. Federal Water Pollution Control Amendments of 1972, 70 Stat. 498, 33 U.S.C. § 1151 (1973 Supp.).

30. Air Quality Act of 1967, 81 Stat. 485, 42 U.S.C. § 1857 (1968 Supp.).

31. McCulloch v. Maryland, 4 Wheaton 316 (1819); Gibbons v. Ogden, 9 Wheaton 1 (1824).

32. Woodrow Wilson, *Congressional Government: A Study in American Politics* (Boston: Houghton Mifflin, 1925), pp. 36–37.

33. Buckley v. Valeo, 424 U.S. 1 at 143 (1976).

34. Ibid., at 52.

35. Ibid., at 52–53.

36. First National Bank of Boston et al. v. Bellotti, 435 U.S. 765 (1978). In 1981, the Court struck down a Berkeley, California, ordinance placing a limit of $250 on contributions to committees supporting or opposing referendum issues on the ground that the ordinance contravened the rights of association and expression guaranteed by the First Amendment. United States Constitution. See Citizens Against Rent Control v. City of Berkeley, 454 U.S. 290 (1981).

37. Edwin Meese III, "The Attorney General's View of the Supreme Court: Toward a Jurisprudence of Original Intention," *Public Administration Review* (November 1985): 704.

38. William J. Brennan, Jr., "The Constitution of the United States: Contemporary Ratification," (paper presented at a text and teaching symposium, Georgetown University, Washington, D.C., October 12, 1985), p. 4.

39. Robert H. Bork, "The Constitution, Original Intent, and Economic Rights" (address presented at the University of San Diego Law School, November 18, 1985), p. 8.

40. H. Jefferson Powell, "The Original Understanding of Original Intent," *Harvard Law Review* (March 1985): 948.

Chapter III

1. "Án Ordinance for Ascertaining the Mode of Disposing of Lands in the Western Territory," *Journals of the American Congress, from 1774 to 1788* (Washington, D.C., 1823), pp. 395–400. See p. 398.

2. Morrill Act of 1862, 12 Stat. 503, 7 U.S.C. §§ 301 *et seq.* (1982). In 1850, the Congress granted swamp lands to the states. See 9 Stat. 519.

3. McGee v. Mathias, 4 Wall. 143, 71 U.S. 314 (1866).

4. Sheppard-Towner Act, 42 Stat. 224 (1921); Massachusetts v. Mellon, 262 U.S. 447 (1922).

5. Hatch Act of 1887, 24 Stat. 440, 7 U.S.C. § 362. In 1808, Congress appropriated $200,000 to the states for arming and equipping the militia. See 2 Stat. 490.

6. Carey Act of 1894, 28 Stat. 422, 43 U.S.C. § 641.

7. Weeks Act of 1911 36 Stat. 961, 16 U.S.C. § 552. The Smith-Lever Act of 1914 contained a formula for apportioning funds to the various states for agricultural cooperative extension programs and stipulated that no more than 10 percent of the funds could be allotted to any one state. See 38 Stat. 372, 7 U.S.C. § 347d.

8. Federal Road Aid Act of 1916, 39 Stat. 355.

9. Federal Road Aid Act of 1921, 42 Stat. 212.

10. For details of a case involving Florida, see *The Federal Influence on State and Local Roles in the Federal System* (Washington, D.C.: U.S. Advisory Commission on Intergovernmental Relations, 1981), p. 43.

11. Social Security Act of 1935, 49 Stat. 620, 42 U.S.C. §§ 301 *et seq.* (1982).

12. Hatch Act of 1939, 53 Stat. 1147, 5 U.S.C. §§ 118i *et seq.* (1964); Hatch Act of 1940, 43 Stat. 767, 5 U.S.C. §§ 118i *et seq.* (1964).

13. United States Housing Act of 1937, 50 Stat. 888, 12 U.S.C. § 1701 *et seq.* (1982).

14. Joseph F. Harris, "The Future of Federal Grants-in-Aid," in W. Brooke Graves, ed., "Intergovernmental Relations in the United States," *The Annals* (January 1940): 14.

15. *Fiscal Balance in the American Federal System* (Washington, D.C.: U.S. Advisory Commission on Intergovernmental Relations, 1967), pp. 139, 145.

16. *Federal Aid to States Fiscal Year 1980* (Washington, D.C.: U.S. Department of the Treasury, 1981), p. 1.

17. *Fiscal Balance,* p. 145.

18. Ibid., p. 145.

19. Ibid.

20. Carl W. Stenberg, "Federal-Local Relations in a Cutback Environment: Issues and Future Directions" (paper presented at the Annual Conference of the American Politics Group of the United Kingdom Political Studies Association, Manchester, England, January 4, 1980), p. 5.

21. Harris, "Future of Federal Grants-in-Aid," 17.

22. The Commission on Intergovernmental Relations, *A Report to the President for Transmittal to the Congress* (Washington, D.C.: GPO, 1955), p. 59.

23. Harris, "Future of Federal Grants-in-Aid," 17.

24. For an excellent description and analysis of the overloading of the federal system through the proliferation of categorical grant-in-aid programs, see David B. Walker, *Toward a Functioning Federalism* (Cambridge: Winthrop, 1981).

25. *Categorical Grants: Their Role and Design* (Washington, D.C.: U.S. Advisory Commission on Intergovernmental Relations, 1978), p. 42.

26. Ibid., pp. 52–53.

27. The best work on state and local government officials' actions and attitudes toward federal grants-in-aid is Deil S. Wright, *Understanding Intergovernmental Relations* (North Scituate, Mass.: Duxbury Press, 1978).

28. Charles L. Schultze, "Federal Spending: Past, Present, and Future," in Henry Owen and Charles L. Schultze, eds., *Setting National Priorities: The Next Ten Years* (Washington, D.C.: The Brookings Institution, 1976), p. 367.

29. James L. Buckley, "The Trouble with Federalism: It Isn't Being Tried," *Commonsense* (Summer 1978): 13.

30. Ibid., 14.

31. *Categorical Grants,* p. 281.

32. MacManus v. Love, 499 P.2d 609 (1972); Sego v. Kirkpatrick, 524 P.2d 975 (1974).

33. Anderson v. Regan, 53 N.Y.2d 356 at 366 (1981). See also Anderson v. Regan, 197 Misc.2d 335 (1981).

34. Wheeler v. Barrera, 417 U.S. 402 at 416–19 (1972).

35. Shapp v. Casey, 99 S. Ct. 717 (1979); Shapp v. Sloan, 391 A.2d 595 (1978).

36. G. Homer Durham, "Politics and Administration in Intergovernmental Relations," *The Annals* (January 1940): 5.

37. *Proposed Changes in Federal Matching and Maintenance of Effort Require-*

ments for State and Local Governments (Washington, D.C.: U.S. General Accounting Office, 1980), p. 61.

38. V. O. Key, Jr., "State Legislation Facilitative of Federal Action," *The Annals* (January 1940): 24.

39. *Fiscal Balance,* p. 153.

40. *State and Local Roles in the Federal System* (Washington, D.C.: U.S. Advisory Commission on Intergovernmental Relations, 1982), p. 412.

41. Florida Department of Health v. Califano, 499 F. Supp. 274, 585 F.2d 150 (5th Cir.), cert. denied, 99 S. Ct. 2051 (1979).

42. South Dakota v. Dole, 107 S. Ct. 2793 at 2799 (1987).

43. Stenberg, "Federal-Local Relations," 13.

44. United States Housing Act of 1937, 50 Stat. 888, 12 U.S.C. §§ 1701 *et seq.* (1982). See also *A State Response to Urban Programs: Recent Experience Under the "Buying In" Approach* (Washington, D.C.: U.S. Advisory Commission on Intergovernmental Relations, 1970).

45. Intergovernmental Cooperation Act of 1968, 82 Stat. 1098, 42 U.S.C. §§ 531–35, 4201 *et. seq.*

46. Revenue Act of 1926, 44 Stat. 9, 48 U.S.C. § 845.

47. Social Security Act of 1935, 49 Stat. 620, 42 U.S.C. § 301. (1935).

48. Economic Recovery Tax Act of 1981, 95 Stat. 399, 26 U.S.C. § 103 (1981 Supp.).

49. The Commission on the Organization of the Executive Branch of Government, *Overseas Administration, Federal-State Relations, Federal Research* (Washington, D.C.: GPO 1949), p. 36. See also Comprehensive Health Planning and Public Health Services Amendments of 1966, 80 Stat. 1180, 42 U.S.C. §§ 243, 246.

50. *The Partnership for Health Act: Lessons from a Pioneering Block Grant* (Washington, D.C: U.S. Advisory Commission on Intergovernmental Relations, 1977), pp. 4–5.

51. Michael D. Reagan and John G. Sanzone, *The New Federalism,* 2d ed. (New York: Oxford University Press, 1981), pp. 129–30.

52. Housing and Community Development Act of 1974, 88 Stat. 633, 42 U.S.C. § 5301.

53. Omnibus Budget Reconciliation Act of 1981, 95 Stat. 357, 31 U.S.C. § 1331.

54. Richard S. Williamson, "Block Grants—A Federalist Tool," *State Government* (no. 4, 1981): 115.

55. *Maternal and Child Health Block Grant: Program Changes Emerging Under State Administration* (Washington, D.C.: U.S. General Accounting Office, 1984); *States Use Added Flexibility Offered by the Preventive Health and Health Services Block Grant* (Washington, D.C.: U.S. General Accounting Office, 1984); *Education Block Grant Alters State Role and Provides Greater Local Discretion* (Washington, D.C.: U.S. General Accounting Office, 1984), p. 37.

56. Michael S. Knapp and Craig H. Blakely, *The Education Block Grant at the Local Level: The Implementation of Chapter 2 of the Education Consolidation and Improvement Act in Districts and Schools* (Menlo Park, Calif.: SRI International, 1986), p. iii.

57. State and Local Fiscal Assistance Act of 1972, 86 Stat. 919, 33 U.S.C. § 1221.

58. Richard P. Nathan, "The New Federalism Versus the Emerging New Structuralism," *Publius* (Summer 1985): 112.

59. "Text of Reagan's Speech Accepting the Republican Nomination," *The New York Times,* 18 July 1980, p. A8.

60. *Reagan Administration Regulatory Achievements* (Washington, D.C.: Presidential Task Force on Regulatory Relief, 1983). For an excellent insider's view of the administration's regulatory relief program, see Richard S. Williamson, "Reagan Federalism: Goals and Achievements," in Lewis G. Bender and James A. Stever, eds., *Administering the New Federalism* (Boulder, Colo.: Westview Press, 1986), pp. 47–50.

61. Charles A. Bowsher, "Federal Cutbacks Strengthen State Role," *State Government News* (February 1986): 19.

62. Single Audit Act of 1984, 98 Stat. 2327, 31 U.S.C. § 7501. See also *Circular A-128* (Washington D.C.: U.S. Office of Management and Budget, 1985) and *Single Audit* (Washington, D.C.: Arthur Andersen & Co., 1985).

63. "The Reagan Record," *The Urban Institute Policy and Research Report,* (August, 1984): 11.

64. Ronald Reagan, "America's Agenda for the Future," *Congressional Record,* 6 February 1986, p. S 1142.

65. Gerald M. Boyd, "Mayors' Study Says Recovery Does Not Help Poor," *The New York Times,* 25 September 1984, p. A22.

66. Ibid.

67. Victor Atiyeh, "Unreasonable and Inflexible Federal Mandates," *Western Report* (Western Governors' Association), 19 December 1986, p. 2.

68. Balanced Budget and Emergency Deficit Control Act of 1985, 99 Stat. 1037, 2 U.S.C. §§ 602 *et seq.*

69. Robert L. McCurely, Jr., *Federally Mandated State Legislation* (Washington, D.C.: National Conference of State Legislatures, 1986), p. 3.

70. *Fiscal Survey of the States* (Washington, D.C.: National Governors' Association and National Association of State Budget Officers, 1986), p. 1.

71. For details, see Joseph F. Zimmerman, *State-Local Relations: A Partnership Approach* (New York: Praeger, 1983), pp. 49–62.

72. See Joseph F. Zimmerman, *Participatory Democracy: Populism Revived* (New York: Praeger, 1986), pp. 26–28, 85–87.

73. See S. 585 of 1987.

74. David Durenberger, "Intergovernmental Regulatory Relief Act," *Congressional Record,* 26 February 1987, p. S 2508.

75. Ibid.

76. Pete Wilson, "Intergovernmental Regulatory Relief Act," *Congressional Record,* 26 February 1987, p. S2511.

77. Ibid., p. S2512.

Chapter IV

1. I define *formal preemption* as the authority granted to Congress by the Constitution to assume partial or total responsibility for a governmental function.

2. W. Brooke Graves, ed., "Intergovernmental Relations in the United States," *The Annals* (January 1940): 1–218.

3. Richard H. Leach, ed., "Intergovernmental Relations in America Today," *The Annals* (November 1974): 1–169. See, in particular, Deil S. Wright, "Intergovernmental Relations: An Analytical Overview," 1–16; Brevard Crihfield and H. Clyde Reeves,

"Intergovernmental Relations: A View from the States," 99–107; and Joseph F. Zimmerman, "The Metropolitan Area Problem," 133–47.

4. *Policy Positions: 1980–81* (Washington, D.C.: National Governors' Association, 1980).

5. *Goals for State-Federal Action: 1984–1986* (Washington, D.C.: National Conference of State Legislatures, n.d.), p. 48.

6. Flammable Fabrics Act, 81 Stat. 574, 15 U.S.C. § 1191 (1967 Supp.).

7. United States Grain Standards Act, 82 Stat. 769, 7 U.S.C. § 71 (1968 Supp.).

8. Radiation Control for Health and Safety Act of 1968, 82 Stat. 1186, 42 U.S.C. § 162 (1968).

9. Gun Control Act of 1968, 82 Stat. 1226, 18 U.S.C. § 921 (1968 Supp.).

10. Drug Abuse Control Amendments of 1965, 79 Stat. 235, 21 U.S.C. § 321 (1965 Supp.).

11. Garcia v. San Antonio Metropolitan Transit Authority, 469 U.S. 556 (1985).

12. An Act to Establish a Uniform System of Bankruptcy, 30 Stat. 544, 11 U.S.C. §§ 1 *et seq.* See also the Bankruptcy Act of 1933, 47 Stat. 1467, 11 U.S.C. § 101 (1933).

13. Bankruptcy Act of 1933, 47 Stat. 1467, 11 U.S.C. § 101 (1933).

14. Air Quality Act of 1967, 81 Stat. 485, 42 U.S.C. §§ 1857 *et seq.* (1968 Supp.).

15. Clean Air Amendments of 1970, 84 Stat. 1676, 42 U.S.C. §§ 1857 *et seq.* and 49 U.S.C. §§ 1421, 1430 (1971 Supp.).

16. Airline Deregulation Act of 1978, 92 Stat. 1708, 49 U.S.C. §§ 1305, 1371.

17. Motor Carrier Act of 1980, 94 Stat. 793, 49 U.S.C. § 1101, and Bus Regulatory Reform Act of 1982, 96 Stat. 1104, 49 U.S.C. § 10521.

18. Robinson-Patman Act of 1936, 49 Stat. 1526, 15 U.S.C. § 13a.

19. Age Discrimination in Employment Act of 1967, 81 Stat. 381, 29 U.S.C. § 623.

20. Tax Equity and Fiscal Responsibility Act of 1982, 96 Stat. 324, 26 U.S.C. § 1.

21. Age Discrimination in Employment Amendments of 1986, 100 Stat. 3342, 29 U.S.C. § 623.

22. "Emergency Plans," 10 C.F.R. § 50.47 (1986).

23. Safe Drinking Water Act Amendments of 1986, 100 Stat. 651, 42 U.S.C. § 300g.

24. Ibid., 100 Stat. 652, 42 U.S.C. § 300g.

25. National Traffic and Motor Vehicle Safety Act of 1966, 80 Stat. 719, 15 U.S.C. § 1392(d).

26. United States Grain Standards Act, 82 Stat. 769, 7 U.S.C. § 71.

27. Ibid.

28. Hazardous and Solid Waste Amendments of 1984, 98 Stat. 3256, 42 U.S.C. §§ 6297–6928, 6901–6991.

29. Resource Conservation and Recovery Act of 1976, 90 Stat. 2809, 42 U.S.C. § 6926.

30. Letter to author from Director Marcia E. Williams of the Office of Solid Waste, United States Environmental Protection Agency, dated April 17, 1987.

31. Federal Railroad Safety Act of 1970, 84 Stat. 971, 45 U.S.C. §§ 431 *et seq.*

32. *Rail Safety: State's Reaction to Proposed Elimination of Inspection Funding* (Washington, D.C.: U.S. General Accounting Office, 1987), p. 1.

33. Atomic Energy Act of 1946, 60 Stat. 755, 42 U.S.C. § 2011 (1947 Supp.); Atomic Energy Act of 1959, 73 Stat. 688, 42 U.S.C. § 2021 (1960 Supp.).

34. Committee on Energy and Environment, *The Agreement State Program: A*

State Perspective (Washington, D.C.: National Governors' Association, 1983), p. 3.

35. Memorandum dated March 19, 1986, to New Mexico Governor Toney Anaya from Director Denise Fort of the Environmental Improvement Division, pp. 4–5. See also Uranium Mill Tailings Radiation Control Act of 1978, 92 Stat. 3021, 42 U.S.C. §§ 2014 *et seq.*

36. Equal Employment Opportunity Act of 1972, 86 Stat. 104, 42 U.S.C. § 2000 (e)(5).

37. Fair Labor Standards Act of 1938, 52 Stat. 1060, 29 U.S.C. §§ 201 *et seq.*

38. Federal Mine Safety and Health Act of 1977, 83 Stat. 803, 30 U.S.C. §§ 801 *et seq.*

39. Tax Equity and Fiscal Responsibility Act of 1982, 96 Stat. 603, 26 U.S.C. § 6050E.

40. Low-Level Radioactive Waste Policy Act of 1980, 94 Stat. 3347, 42 U.S.C. § 2021d (1981 Supp.). For the origin of the act, see Richard C. Kearney and John J. Stucker, "Interstate Compacts and the Management of Low Level Radioactive Wastes," *Public Administration Review* (January/February 1985): 210–20.

41. Ibid., 94 Stat. 3348, 42 U.S.C. § 202ld.

42. Letter to Chairman Strom Thurmond of the United States Senate Committee on the Judiciary dated September 19, 1984, from Assistant Attorney General Robert A. McConnell, p. 6.

43. Low-Level Radioactive Waste Policy Act of 1980, 94 Stat. 3347, 42 U.S.C. § 2021d.

44. Department of Transportation and Related Agencies Appropriation Act of 1986, 100 Stat. 1288.

45. Nuclear Waste Policy Act of 1982, 96 Stat. 2217, 42 U.S.C. § 10125.

46. George Lobsenz, "Lawmakers Pick Nevada to Host Nuke Waste Dump," *The Union Leader* (Manchester, New Hampshire), 18 December 1987, p. 16, and "Nevada's Radioactive Jackpot," *The New York Times,* 5 January 1988, p. A18.

47. Voting Rights Act of 1965, 79 Stat. 437, 42 U.S.C. § 1973. Subsequent amendments changed the wording of the reference to the presidential election to refer to the most recent election. For details on the act, see Joseph F. Zimmerman, "The Federal Voting Rights Act and Alternative Election Systems," *William and Mary Law Review* (Summer 1978) 621–60.

48. Abandoned Shipwreck Act of 1987, 102 Stat. 432, 43 U.S.C. § 2101.

49. Atlantic Striped Bass Conservation Act Amendments of 1986, 100 Stat. 989, 16 U.S.C. § 1851 note.

50. Age Discrimination in Employment Amendments of 1986, 100 Stat. 3342, 29 U.S.C. § 623.

51. *Congressional Record,* 25 May 1983, pp. S 7556–57.

52. Letter from Governor Mario M. Cuomo of New York to U.S. Secretary of Energy John S. Herrington dated March 29, 1985. Available from the Executive Chamber, Albany, New York 12224. For the discussion of the problems in the period 1979 to 1984, see Richard T. Syles, "Nuclear Power Plants and Emergency Planning: An Intergovernmental Nightmare," *Public Administration Review* (September/October 1984): 393–401.

53. Ibid.

54. "Shoreham Drill Gets Positive Initial Appraisal," *The New York Times,* 16 February 1986, p. 48.

55. Ibid.

56. Jane Perlex, "U.S. Aide Quits, Charging Pressure on LILCO Drill," *The New York Times,* 15 April 1986, p. B1.

57. Ibid., p. B5.

58. Clifford D. May, "Shoreham Dispute Centers on Policy," *The New York Times,* 16 April 1986, p. B2.

59. Brad Pokorny and Ray Richard, "Seabrook Tests Evacuation Plans," *The Boston Globe,* 27 February 1986, p. 23.

60. Richard March, "Seabrook Drill Called A Failure," *The Keene Sentinel* (New Hampshire), 1 March 1986, pp. 1–2.

61. "Full participation in Seabrook Drill is Critical to Plan, Critics Assert," *The Keene Sentinel* (New Hampshire), 3 March 1986, p. 6.

62. "Massachusetts Governor Seeks to Stop Nuclear Plant Opening," *The New York Times,* 21 September 1986, p. 24.

63. "Public Service Argues for 2-Mile Safety Zone," *The Keene Sentinel* (New Hampshire), 27 September 1986, p. 3.

64. *Federal Register,* 8 August 1980, p. 55409, and 10 C.F.R. § 50.47 (1986).

65. "Nuclear Regulatory Commissioners Vote to Seek Public Comment on Proposed Rule Change in Emergency Planning Rule," *United States Nuclear Regulatory Commission News Releases,* 3 March 1987, p. 1.

66. "Licensing of Nuclear Power Plants Where State and/or Local Governments Decline to Cooperate in Offsite Emergency Planning," *United States Nuclear Regulatory Commission News Releases,* 10 March 1987, p. 2.

67. Ben A. Franklin, "Nuclear Panel Denies Waiver on New Hampshire Reactor," *The New York Times,* 23 April 1987, p. A24.

68. *Federal Register,* 3 November 1987, pp. 42078–87 and 10 C.F.R. Part 50. See also John Distaso, "NRC Adopts New Nuke Evac Rule," *The Union Leader* (Manchester, New Hampshire), 30 October 1987, pp. 1, 9.

69. Nuclear Regulatory Commission Reauthorization Act of 1980, 94 Stat. 783, 42 U.S.C. §§ 2133–134 (1981 Supp.).

70. Larry Tye, "NRC Approves Licensing of Seabrook," *The Boston Globe,* 2 March 1990, pp. 1 and 12, and James L. Franklin, "Court Denies License Delay at Seabrook," *The Boston Globe,* 15 March 1990, pp. 1 and 22.

71. "Supreme Court Okays Seabrook," *The Keene (New Hampshire) Sentinel,* 27 April 1990, p. 1.

72. *NRC Coziness with Industry: An Investigation Report* (Washington, D.C.: Subcommittee on General Oversight and Investigations, U.S. House of Representatives, 1987), p. 41.

73. Surface Transportation Assistance Act of 1982, 96 Stat. 2097, 23 U.S.C. § 101.

74. Ibid., 96 Stat. 2159, 49 U.S.C. § 2311.

75. Ibid., 96 Stat. 2124, 23 U.S.C. § 101.

76. *Implementing Nationally Uniform Truck Laws* (Albany: New York State Legislative Commission on Critical Transportation Choices, August 1983), p. 8.

77. Ibid.

78. Ibid, p 9.

79. *Federal Register,* 3 May 1983, pp. 22028–29.

80. *Implementing Nationally Uniform Truck Laws,* p. 9.

81. Motor Vehicle Width Regulations, 97 Stat. 59, 49 U.S.C. § 2316.

82. Ernest Holsendolph, "State Officials Gather to Plan Resistance to Big Truck Rules," *The New York Times,* 15 April 1983, p. B10.

83. Ernest Holsendolph, "Double-Trailer Plan Stirs Outcry in Some Unexpected Quarters," *The New York Times,* 11 April 1983, p. A14.
84. Tandem Truck Safety Act of 1984, 98 Stat. 2829–830, 42 U.S.C. § 2301; Motor Carrier Safety Act of 1984, 98 Stat. 2832, 42 U.S.C. § 2501.
85. Tandem Truck Safety Act of 1984, 98 Stat. 2829–830, 42 U.S.C. §§ 2301–302.
86. Ibid., 98 Stat. 2832, 42 U.S.C. § 2312.
87. Motor Carrier Safety Act of 1984, 98 Stat. 2834, 42 U.S.C. § 2502.
88. Ibid., 98 Stat. 2837, 49 U.S.C. § 2508.
89. Ibid.
90. Ibid.

Chapter V

1. Connecticut General Statutes Annotated, §§ 19–523, 19–524 (1967 Supp.); New Jersey Statutes Annotated, §§ 32-29-1 to 32-29-39 (1968); and New York Public Health Law, § 1299-m (McKinney 1967 Supp.). See also "Air Pollution: Message from the President of the United States," *Congressional Record,* 30 January 1967, p. H737. For details on other compacts, see Weldon V. Barton, *Interstate Compacts in the Political Process* (Chapel Hill: Univ. of North Carolina Press, 1967), and Frederick L. Zimmermann and Mitchell Wendell, *The Law and Use of Interstate Compacts* (Lexington, Ky.: The Council of State Governments, 1976).
2. *The Federalist Papers* (New York: New American Library, 1961), p. 198.
3. U.S. Constitution, art. VI.
4. Ibid., art. I, § 8.
5. H. P. Hood & Sons, Incorporated v. DuMond, 336 U.S. 525 at 534–35 (1949).
6. Constitution, art. I, § 2 (1).
7. 16 Stat. 140 (1870).
8. 16 Stat. 433 (1871).
9. United States v. Reese, 92 U.S. 214 (1875).
10. Michelin Tire Corporation v. Wages, 423 U.S. 276 at 286 (1975).
11. Trailer Train Co. v. State Board of Equalization, 538 F. Supp. 509 at 599 (1981).
12. Virginia v. Tennessee, 148 U.S. 503 (1893).
13. Civil Rights Act of 1964, 78 Stat. 268, 2 U.S.C. § 206.
14. Gun Control Act of 1968, 82 Stat. 1226, 18 U.S.C. § 921.
15. Drug Abuse Control Amendments of 1965, 79 Stat. 235, 21 U.S.C. § 321.
16. Federal Railroad Safety Act of 1970, 84 Stat. 972, 45 U.S.C. § 151.
17. Occupational Safety and Health Act of 1970, 84 Stat. 1608, 29 U.S.C. § 667.
18. Shipping, 97 Stat. 553, 46 U.S.C. § 8501 (a) (1984 Supp.).
19. Ibid., 46 U.S.C. § 8502(c).
20. Coast Guard Authorization Act of 1984, 98 Stat. 2862, 46 U.S.C. § 2302 (c).
21. 33 CRF § 95.025 (1987). For an explanation of the standard, see the *Federal Register,* 4 December 1987, pp. 47526–32.
22. Port and Tanker Safety Act of 1978, 92 Stat. 1475–76, 33 U.S.C. § 1226 (1979 Supp.).
23. Ibid.
24. Voting Rights Act of 1965, 79 Stat. 437, 42 U.S.C. § 1973.

25. Voting Rights Act Amendments of 1975, 89 Stat. 438, 42 U.S.C. §§ 1973a, 1973d, 1973l.

26. Voting Rights Act of 1965, 79 Stat. 438, 42 U.S.C. § 1973c. For a discussion of the impact of this act upon local governments, see Joseph F. Zimmerman, "Local Representation: Designing a Fair System," *National Civic Review* (June 1980): 307–12.

27. Transportation Safety Act of 1974, 88 Stat. 2156, 49 U.S.C. §§ 1801 *et seq.* See also 49 C.F.R. §§ 170–79.

28. Department of Transportation, "Hazardous Materials: Inconsistency Rulings IR-7 through IR-15," *Federal Register,* 27 November 1984, p. 46633.

29. Ibid., p. 46646.

30. Interview with Connecticut Commissioner of Environmental Protection Stanley J. Pac, Hartford, Connecticut, November 8, 1985.

31. Interview with Richard Wiebe, a former Assistant Program Secretary to Governor Nelson A. Rockefeller, Albany, New York, February 26, 1982. (hereinafter referred to as "Wiebe interview").

32. Ibid.

33. See Joseph F. Zimmerman, "Mandating in New York State" in *State Mandating of Local Expenditures* (Washington, D.C.: U.S. Advisory Commission on Intergovermental Relations, 1978), p. 76.

34. Water Quality Act of 1965, 79 Stat. 903, 33 U.S.C. §§ 1151 *et seq.*

35. Federal Water Pollution Control Act Amendments of 1972, 86 Stat. 498, 33 U.S.C. §§ 1151 *et seq.*

36. *Federal Register,* 14 September 1983, pp. 25681 *et seq.*

37. Wiebe interview.

38. Clean Water Act of 1977, 91 Stat. 1575, 33 U.S.C. § 1251.

39. Patricia M. Crotty, "The New Federalism Game: Options for the States," A paper presented at the annual meeting of the Northeastern Political Science Association, Philadelphia, November 14–16, 1985.

40. Clean Water Act of 1977, 91 Stat. 1577, 33 U.S.C. § 1342.

41. Air Quality Act of 1967, 81 Stat. 485, 42 U.S.C. §§ 18570–571.

42. Clean Air Amendments of 1970, 84 Stat. 1676, 42 U.S.C. §§ 1857 *et seq.,* 49 U.S.C. §§ 1421, 1430 (1970).

43. Ibid., §§ 1421, 1430.

44. Fri v. Sierra Club, 412 U.S. 541 (1973).

45. Sierra Club v. Ruckelshaus, 344 F. Supp. 253 (D. D.C. 1972). For a description and analysis of how the EPA complied with the court's order, see Albert C. Hyde, "The Politics of Environmental Decision Making: The Non-Decision Issue," unpublished Ph.D. dissertation, State University of New York at Albany, 1980. See also R. Shep Melnick, *Regulation and the Courts: The Case of the Clean Air Act* (Washington, D.C.: The Brookings Institution, 1983).

46. "Prevention of Significant Deterioration (PSD) of Air Quality; Supplemental Delegation of Authority to North Carolina," 49 *Federal Register,* 21 September 1984, p. 37064. See also 40 C.F.R. § 52.

47. Crotty, "The New Federalism Game," p. 13. See also Joseph F. Zimmerman, "The Role of the State Legislature in Air Pollution Abatement," *Suffolk University Law Review* (Spring 1971): 850–77.

48. Safe Drinking Water Act, 88 Stat. 1665, 42 U.S.C. § 201.

49. Safe Drinking Water Act Amendments of 1986, 100 Stat. 642, 42 U.S.C. § 300g-1.

50. Letter to author from Director Michael B. Cook, of EPA's Office of Drinking Water, dated March 13, 1987.

51. Ibid.

52. Surface Mining Control and Reclamation Act, 91 Stat. 445, 30 U.S.C. §§ 1201 *et seq.*

53. Hodel v. Virginia Surface Mining and Reclamation Association, 452 U.S. 264 at 287.

54. Letter to the author from Chief Annello L. Cheek, of the Division of Permit and Environmental Analysis of the U.S. Department of the Interior, dated February 13, 1987.

55. Ibid.

56. Occupational Safety and Health Act of 1970, 84 Stat. 1590, 5 U.S.C. § 5108.

57. Ibid., 84 Stat. 1608, 29 U.S.C. § 667.

58. Ibid.

59. Letter to author from Bruce Hillenbrand, director of Federal-State Operations of the Occupational Safety and Health Administration, dated August 5, 1988. See also *State Programs: Background* (Washington, D.C.: Occupational Safety and Health Administration, August 1985), p. 1.

60. Ohio Manufacturers Association v. City of Akron, 801 F.2d 824 at 831 (6th Cir. 1986).

61. *Federal Register,* 12 July 1985, pp. 28530 *et seq.* See also the Toxic Substance Control Act, 90 Stat. 2003, 15 U.S.C. §§ 2601 *et seq.*

62. Wholesome Meat Act, 81 Stat. 595, 21 U.S.C. § 71.

63. Poultry Products Inspection Act, 82 Stat. 791, 21 U.S.C. § 451. For an analysis of the quality of state inspection programs under this act and the Wholesome Meat Act, see *USDA's Oversight of State Meat and Poultry Inspection Programs Could Be Strengthened* (Washington, D.C.: U.S. General Accounting Office, 1983).

64. Toxic Substances Control Act of 1976, 90 Stat. 2038, 15 U.S.C. § 2617.

65. Ibid., 90 Stat. 2039, 15 U.S.C. § 2617.

66. Port and Tanker Safety Act of 1978, 92 Stat. 1475, 33 U.S.C. § 1225.

67. Natural Gas Policy Act of 1978, 92 Stat. 3409, 15 U.S.C. § 3431.

68. Federal Environmental Pesticide Control Act of 1972, 86 Stat. 996–97, 7 U.S.C. §§ 136u–136v.

69. Federal Railroad Safety Act of 1970, 84 Stat. 971, 45 U.S.C. §§ 431 *et seq.*

70. Federal Environmental Pesticide Control Act of 1972, 86 Stat. 996–97, 7 U.S.C. §§ 136u–136v.

71. Federal Insecticide, Fungicide, and Rodenticide Act of 1947, 61 Stat. 163, 7 U.S.C. §§ 136 *et seq.*

72. Cable Communications Policy Act of 1984, 98 Stat. 2792, 47 U.S.C. § 546.

73. Ibid., 98 Stat. 2779 at 2800, 47 U.S.C. § 555.

74. Coastal Zone Management Act of 1972, 86 Stat. 1280, 16 U.S.C. §§ 1451–64.

75. Ibid., 86 Stat. 1282, 16 U.S.C. § 1454.

76. Ibid., 86 Stat. 1286, 16 U.S.C. § 1456(d).

77. Federal Environmental Pesticide Control Act of 1972, 86 Stat. 983. 7 U.S.C. § 136b(2). See also the Emergency Energy Conservation Act of 1979, 93 Stat. 759, 42 U.S.C. § 8512.

78. Clean Air Act Amendments of 1977, 91 Stat. 722, 42 U.S.C. § 7424.

79. Federal Water Pollution Control Act Amendments of 1972, 86 Stat. 841, 33 U.S.C. § 1151.

80. Emergency Highway Energy Conservation Act of 1974, 88 Stat. 1046, 23 U.S.C. § 154, 23 C.F.R. § 658.6.

81. R. W. Apple, Jr., "Senate Rejects Reagan Plea and Votes 67–33 to Override His Veto of Highway Funds," *The New York Times,* 3 April 1987, pp. 1, A25.

82. Safe Drinking Water Act of 1974, 88 Stat. 1676, 42 U.S.C. § 300h.

83. Federal Metal and Nonmetallic Mine Safety Act of 1966, 80 Stat. 783, 42 U.S.C. § 2011. This act was replaced by the Federal Mine Safety and Health Act of 1977, 91 Stat. 1290, 30 U.S.C. §§ 801 *et seq.*

84. Wholesome Meat Act of 1967, 81 Stat. 596, 21 U.S.C. § 71.; Poultry Products Inspection Act of 1968, 82 Stat. 797, 21 U.S.C. § 451.

85. National Health Planning and Resources Development Act of 1974, 88 Stat. 2242, 42 U.S.C. § 300m.

86. Federal Water Pollution Control Act Amendments of 1972, 86 Stat. 840, 842, 33 U.S.C. § 1151.

87. Clean Air Act Amendments of 1977, 91 Stat. 749, 42 U.S.C. § 7504 (1977 Supp.). See also the Federal Environmental Pesticide Control Act of 1972, 86 Stat. 983, 7 U.S.C. § 136b(2).

88. Surface Transportation Assistance Act of 1978, 92 Stat. 2724, 23 U.S.C. § 134.

89. National Health Planning and Resources Development Act of 1974, 88 Stat. 2247, 42 U.S.C. § 300m-3.

90. Highway Safety Act of 1966, 80 Stat. 731, 23 U.S.C. § 402(b)(1).

91. State of New York Executive Order No. 75, April 3, 1973. The executive order is published in *Public Papers of Nelson A. Rockefeller: Fifty-Third Governor of the State of New York, 1973,* (Albany: State of New York, n.d.), pp. 811–12.

92. "Executive Order 12140 of May 29, 1979," *Federal Register,* 31 May 1979, p. 31159. The delegation is based upon authority vested in the president by the Emergency Petroleum Allocation Act of 1973 and his inherent powers.

93. Tandem Truck Safety Act of 1984, 98 Stat. 2834, 42 U.S.C. § 2312.

94. Sierra Club v. Ruckelshaus, 344 F. Supp. 253 (D. D.C. 1972), and Fri v. Sierra Club, 412 U.S. 541 (1973).

95. *Federal Register,* 5 December 1984, pp. 42510 *et seq.*

96. Clean Air Act Amendments of 1977, 91 Stat. 731, 42 U.S.C. § 7470.

97. Ibid., 91 Stat. 734, 42 U.S.C. § 7474.

98. Ibid., 91 Stat. 733, 42 U.S.C. § 7473.

99. Ibid., 91 Stat. 737, 42 U.S.C. § 7475.

100. Ibid., 91 Stat. 695, 42 U.S.C. § 7410.

101. *Federal Register,* 5 December 1977, p. 61543. See also *New York State Air Quality Implementation Plan: The Moynihan/Holtzman Amendment Submission: Transit Improvements in the New York City Metropolitan Area* (Albany: New York State Department of Environmental Conservation and Department of Transportation, May 1979).

102. Clean Air Act Amendments of 1977, 91 Stat. 723, 42 U.S.C. § 7425.

Chapter VI

1. Brown v. Board of Education, 347 U.S. 483 (1954).

2. Elrod v. Burns, 427 U.S. 347 (1976). In 1990, the Court held that promotions, recalls, and transfers of state employees based on political affiliation or support infringes upon public employees' First Amendment rights. See Rutan et al. v. Republican Party of Illinois et al., 110 S. Ct. 2729 (1990).

3. Corbeil v. Canestrari, 47 A.D.2d 153 (1977). Section 10 of the charter provides that "where the term of an appointive officer is not specifically fixed by statute, it shall be deemed to continue only during the pleasure of the officer, officers, board, or body authorized to make the appointment."

4. Foley v. Connelie, 435 U.S. 291 at 299–300 (1978). See also New York Executive Law, § 215(3) (McKinney 1972).

5. Michigan Department of State Police v. Sitz, 110 S. Ct. 2481 (1990).

6. William Bradford Reynolds, "The Bicentennial: A Constitutional Restoration," a paper presented at the University of Texas, 19 February 1987, p. 8.

7. "Federal Judge Orders a Panel to Monitor State Schools for Retarded," *The Boston Globe,* 15 March 1986, p. 16.

8. Lynn Bycznski, "Judge Raises Taxes to Pay for School Bias Remedy," *The National Law Journal,* 5 October 1987, p. 25.

9. Missouri v. Jenkins, 110 S. Ct. 1651 (1990).

10. Peggy Hernandez, "Garrity Expected to Yield Control of Schools Today," *The Boston Globe,* 3 September 1985, p. 15.

11. *Memorandum Regarding Final Orders: Civil Action No. 72–911–G* (Boston: United States District Court, November 1, 1985). See also *Viewpoints and Guidelines on Court Appointed Citizens Monitoring Commissions in School Desegregation* (Washington, D.C.: U.S. Department of Justice, 1978). For a critical review of Judge Garrity's judicial receivership of the Boston school system, see Elizabeth A. Marek, "Education by Decree," *New Perspectives* (Summer 1985): 36–41. Letters objecting to the author's views and the author's reply appear in "Busing in Boston," *New Perspectives* (Fall 1985): 36–37.

12. Alexander Hamilton, "The Federalist Number 80," in Clinton Rossiter, ed., *The Federalist Papers* (New York: New American Library, 1961), p. 481.

13. McCulloch v. Maryland, 4 Wheaton 316 (1819).

14. United States Constitution, art. I, § 8.

15. Gibbons v. Ogden, 9 Wheaton 1 (1824).

16. Adler v. Deegan, 251 N.Y. 467 at 491, 167 N.E. 705 at 714 (1929).

17. H. P. Hood & Sons v. DuMond, 336 U.S. 525 at 534–35 (1949).

18. The Commission on Intergovernmental Relations, *A Report to the President for Transmittal to the Congress* (Washington, D.C.: GPO, 1955), p. 59.

19. Ibid., p. 70.

20. Address of William Bradford Reynolds, Assistant Attorney General, Civil Rights Division, Counselor to the Attorney General, United States Department of Justice before the Conservative Law Students — A Federalist Society Chapter, Washington University, St. Louis, Missouri, October 28, 1987, p. 5.

21. Hodel v. Virginia Surface Mining and Reclamation Association, 452 U.S. 264 at 311 (1981).

22. Flammable Fabrics Act, 81 Stat. 574, 15 U.S.C. § 1191 (1967 Supp.).

23. George D. Braden, "Umpire to the Federal System," *The University of Chicago Law Review* (October 1942): 45.

24. Hines v. Davidowitz, 312 U.S. 52 at 67 (1941).

25. Rice v. Santa Fe Elevator, 331 U.S. 218 (1947).

26. City of Burbank v. Lockheed Air Terminal, 411 U.S. 624 at 632 (1973).

27. Chapman v. Houston Welfare Rights Organization, 441 U.S. 600 (1979).

28. Washington Revised Code, §§ 88.1670–88.1690 (1975 Supp.).

29. Ray v. Atlantic Richfield Company, 435 U.S. 151 (1978).

30. Hodel v. Virginia Surface Mining and Reclamation Association, 452 U.S. 264 at 287 (1981).

31. Ibid.

32. Ibid.

33. Oregon v. Mitchell, 400 U.S. 112 (1970).

34. Ibid. at 126.

35. Ibid. at 128.

36. National League of Cities v. Usery, 426 U.S. 833 (1976).

37. Washington v. Davis, 426 U.S. 299 (1976).

38. Village of Arlington Heights v. Metropolitan Housing Development, 429 U.S. 252 (1977). For a housing decision based upon the *Arlington Heights* dictum, see, Silken v. Toledo, 558 F.2d 350 (1977).

39. Maine v. Thiboutot, 448 U.S. 1 (1980); Owen v. City of Independence, 445 U.S. 622 (1980); Civil Rights Act of 1871, 42 U.S.C. § 1983.

40. Maine v. Thiboutot, 448 U.S. 1 at 22.

41. Ibid. at 34–37.

42. Owen v. City of Independence, 445 U.S. 622 (1980). See also City of Newport v. Fact Concerts, 453 U.S. 247 (1981).

43. Federal Energy Regulatory Commission v. Mississippi, 456 U.S. 742 (1982).

44. Public Utility Regulatory Policies Act of 1978, 92 Stat. 3121, 16 U.S.C. § 2621 (1979 Supp.).

45. Federal Energy Regulatory Commission v. Mississippi, 456 U.S. 742 at 760.

46. Ibid. at 763–67.

47. Garcia v. San Antonio Metropolitan Transit Authority, 469 U.S. 528 at 531 (1985).

48. The Florida Supreme Court's lead in striking down the distinction has been followed by many other state supreme courts. See Hargrove v. Cocoa Beach, 96 So.2d 139 (Fla. 1957).

49. Statement of William Bradford Reynolds, Assistant Attorney General, Civil Rights Division before the Committee on Labor and Human Resources, Subcommittee on Labor, U.S. Senate Concerning Impact of *Garcia v. San Antonio Metropolitan Transit Authority* on September 10, 1985, p. 2.

50. Robert B. Hawkins, Jr., "The Chairman's View," *Intergovernmental Perspective* (Spring/Summer 1985: 22.

51. R. Perry Sentell, Jr., "Gesticulations of Garcia," *Urban Georgia* (October 1985): 34–35.

52. Hodel v. Virginia Surface Mining and Reclamation Association, 452 U.S. 264 at 312 (1981).

53. Hillsborough County, Florida v. Automated Medical Laboratories, 471 U.S. 707 (1985). See also 21 C.F.R. §§ 640.60–640.76 (1984).

54. Fisher v. City of Berkeley, California, 106 S. Ct. 1045 at 1053 (1986). See also Ordinance 5261-N.S., Rent Stabilization and Eviction for Good Cause Ordinance, City of Berkeley, California, 1980.

55. California Coastal Commission v. Granite Rock Company, 107 S. Ct. 1419 (1987).

56. Fort Halifax Packing Company v. Coyne, 107 S. Ct. 2211 (1987).

57. Ibid. at 2223.

58. CTS Corporation v. Dynamics Corporation of America, 107 S. Ct. 1637 at 1652 (1987).

59. California Federal Savings and Loan Ass'n v. Guerra, 107 S. Ct. 683 at 695 (1987).

60. City of New York v. Federal Communications Commission, 108 S. Ct. 1637 (1988).

61. Mississippi Power & Light Co. v. Mississippi, 108 S. Ct. 2428 (1988).

62. Employment Division, Department of Human Resources of Oregon v. Smith, 110 S. Ct. 1595 (1990) and North Dakota v. United States, 110 S. Ct. 1986 (1990).

63. Sierra Club v. Ruckelshaus, 344 F. Supp. 253 (D. D.C. 1972), and Fri v. Sierra Club, 412 U.S. 541 (1973).

64. 39 *Federal Register,* 5 December 1984, p. 42510 *et seq.*

65. Primary ambient-air-quality standards are national ones designed to protect the health of susceptible citizens. Secondary standards, which in general are more stringent, are designed to prevent adverse environmental effects, including damage to animals, climate, vegetation, and water quality.

66. Sierra Club v. EPA, 540 F2d 114 (D.C. Cir. 1976). For an excellent analysis of this controversy, see Albert C. Hyde, *The Politics of Environmental Decision-making: The Non-Decision Issue,* unpublished Ph.D. dissertation, State University of New York at Albany, 1980.

67. Clean Air Act Amendments of 1977, 91 Stat. 731, 42 U.S.C. § 7470 (1977 Supp.).

68. Ibid., 91 Stat. 739, 42 U.S.C. § 7476.

69. 101 Stat. 1731, 28 U.S.C. § 2112(a) (1988 Supp.). See also Marcia Coyle, "Ban OK'd on Agency-Review Forum Shopping," *The National Law Journal,* 25 January 1988, p. 9.

70. 28 U.S.C. § 2112(a) (1985 Supp.).

71. 44 *Federal Register,* 4 June 1979, p. 32008.

72. Ibid., p. 32009–10.

73. Smithfield v. Chesapeake Bay Found., 108 S. Ct. (1987).

74. *The Hazardous Waste System* (Washington, D.C.: U.S. Environmental Protection Agency, 1987), pp. 1–2, 1–3.

Chapter VII

1. Voting Rights Act of 1965, 79 Stat. 437, 42 U.S.C. § 1973 (1966 Supp.). For an analysis of the act, see Joseph F. Zimmerman, "The Federal Voting Rights Act and Alternative Election Systems," *William & Mary Law Review* (Summer 1978): 621–60. See also the dissent by Justice Hugo L. Black in Perkins v. Matthews, 499 U.S. 379 at 404 (1971).

2. Zimmerman, "Federal Voting Rights Act," 627.

3. 49 C.F.R. § 177, App. A.

4. Ibid.

5. For a broad view of citizen participation, see Joseph F. Zimmerman, *Participatory Democracy: Populism Revived* (New York: Praeger, 1986).

6. *Regulatory Federalism: Policy, Impact, and Reform* (Washington, D.C.: U.S. Advisory Commission on Intergovernmental Relations, 1984).

7. Ibid., p. 139.

8. Ibid., pp. 139–44.

9. *Hearings before the Subcommittee on Air and Water Pollution of the Committee on Public Works, United States Senate, on S. 780* (Washington, D.C.: GPO, 1967), p. 2514.

10. Clean Air Amendments of 1970, 84 Stat. 485, 42 U.S.C. §§ 1857 *et seq.*, 49 U.S.C. §§ 1421, 1430.

11. R. Shep Melnick, *Regulation and the Courts: The Case of the Clean Air Act* (Washington, D.C.: The Brookings Institution, 1983), p. 254.

12. *Environmental Quality: The Ninth Annual Report of the Council on Environmental Quality* (Washington, D.C.: GPO, 1978), pp. 63, 66.

13. *Improvements Needed in Controlling Major Air Pollution Sources* (Washington, D.C.: Comptroller General of the United States, 1979), p. 5.

14. Ibid., pp. 9–10.

15. "Muskie Defends Environmental Requirements," *Congressional Record,* 5 March 1979, p. S2097.

16. "Smog in the Clean Air Act," *Congressional Record,* 5, April 1979, p. H2054.

17. Ibid.

18. "Ohio Told to Meet Clean-Air Deadline," *The New York Times,* 18, October 1979, p. A16.

19. 100 Stat. 1329–199, 42 U.S.C. § 7503. See also Matthew L. Wald, "Clean Air Deadline is History," The New York Times, 3 January 1988, p. E9.

20. *Environmental Quality: The Ninth Annual Report of the Council on Environmental Quality* (Washington, D.C.: GPO, 1978), pp. 110, 113.

21. Gladwin Hill, "E.P.A. Head, Conceding Errors, Reports Gain on Water Pollution," *The New York Times,* 10 October 1979, p. A24. See also Douglas M. Costle, "Toward a Quiet Victory: A Report-Card on the Clean Water Program," a paper presented at the fifty-second Annual Conference of the Water Pollution Control Federation, Houston, Texas, October 9, 1979 (mimeographed).

22. *Federal Register,* 29 August 1979, pp. 5073–76. See also Gladwin Hill, "E.P.A. Plans a Drive on Sewage Cleanup," *The New York Times,* 11 October 1979, p. A17, and *National Municipal Policy and Strategy for Construction Grants, NPDES Permits, and Enforcement Under the Clean Water Act* (Washington, D.C.: U.S. Environmental Protection Agency, 1979).

23. Clean Water Act of 1977, 91 Stat. 1582–83, 33 U.S.C. § 1311, and Water Quality Act of 1987, 101 Stat. 29–30, 33 U.S.C. §§ 1311, 1314.

24. Rob Gurwitt, "The Tap Has Run Dry on EPA Extensions to the Clean Water Act," *Governing* (January 1988): 16. See also Philip Shabecoff, "Most Sewage Plants Meeting Latest Goal of Clean Water Act," *The New York Times,* 28 July 1988, pp. 1, A18.

25. United States Department of Justice News Release 88-073 dated March 3, 1988, pp. 1–3.

26. "U.S. is Faulted for Role in Water Quality," *The New York Times,* 8 October 1990, p. A9.

27. Melnick, *Regulation and the Courts,* p. 385.

28. Clean Air Amendments of 1970, 84 Stat. 1676, 42 U.S.C. §§ 1857 *et seq.,* 49 U.S.C. § 1421, § 1430 (1970 Supp.).

29. *Federal Register,* 24 February 1974, pp. 7271 *et seq.*

30. 40 C.F.R. § 52.1670 (1973). For the amended version of this plan, see *New York State Air Quality Implementation Plan: Transportation Element, New York City Metropolitan Area* (Albany: New York State Department of Environmental Conservation, 1978).

31. Friends of the Earth v. EPA, 499 F.2d 1118 (2d Cir. 1974).

32. Clean Air Act Amendments of 1977, 91 Stat. 695, 42 U.S.C. § 7410 (1977 Supp.), *Federal Register,* 5 December 1977, p. 61453.

33. Parker v. Brown, 317 U.S. 341 (1945).

34. Lafayette v. Louisiana Power and Light Co., 434 U.S. 389 (1978).

35. Community Communications Corp. v. City of Boulder, 475 U.S. 40 (1982).

36. Ibid., at 56–57.

37. Local Government Antitrust Act of 1984, 98 Stat. 2750, 15 U.S.C. §§ 34–36.

38. "Localities Get Antitrust Cost Relief," *Intergovernmental Perspective* (Fall 1984): 4.

39. National League of Cities v. Usery, 426 U.S. 833 (1976), and Garcia v. San Antonio Metropolitan Transit Authority, 469 U.S. 528 (1985).

40. *Report to Accompany H.R. 3530* (Washington, D.C.: Committee on Education and Labor, U.S. House of Representatives, 1985), p. 30.

41. Fair Labor Standards Amendments of 1985, 99 Stat. 787, 29 U.S.C. §§ 201 *et seq.*

42. *Reagan Administration Regulatory Achievements* (Washington, D.C.: Presidential Task Force on Regulatory Relief, 1983).

43. 40 C.F.R. §§ 51.18(j)(1)(i), (ii).

44. Chevron, U.S.A. v. Natural Resources Defense Council, 464 U.S. 975 (1984).

45. Michael Fix, "Regulatory Relief: The Real New Federalism?" *State Government News* (January 1985): pp. 7–8.

46. Ronald Reagan, "Regulatory Program of the U.S. Government—Message from the President Received During the Adjournment—PM 73," *Congressional Record,* 14 August 1985, pp. S11023–24.

47. Omnibus Budget Reconciliation Act of 1981, 95 Stat. 357, 31 U.S.C. § 1331.

48. Henry M. Hart, Jr., "The Relations Between State and Federal Law," *Columbia Law Review* (April 1954): 541.

49. Edward I. Koch, "The Mandate Millstone," *The Public Interest* 61 (Fall 1980): 42–57.

50. *Hearings before the Subcommittee on Air and Water Pollution of the Committee on Public Works, United States Senate on "Problems and Progress Associated with Control of Automobile Exhaust Emissions"* (Washington, D.C.: GPO, 1967), p. 116.

51. *State Mandating of Local Expenditures* (Washington, D.C.: U.S. Advisory Commission on Intergovernmental Relations, 1978), p. 32.

52. Association of County Commissioners of Georgia, "Majority of States Address their Unfunded Mandates," *Georgia County Government* (February 1986): 98.

53. Congressional Budget Act of 1974, 88 Stat. 320, 2 U.S.C. § 653.

54. State and Local Government Cost Estimate Act of 1981, 95 Stat. 1510, 31 U.S.C. §§ 1301, 1353.

55. Ibid., 95 Stat. 1510, 42 U.S.C. § 4201.

56. *Intergovernmental Regulatory Relief Act of 1985: Hearings before the Subcommittee on Intergovernmental Relations, United States Senate on S.483* (Washington, D.C.: GPO, 1986), p. 9.

57. Ibid., p. 12.

58. "Reauthorization of the State and Local Cost Estimate Act: Statement of J. William Gadsby before the Subcommittee on Government Efficiency, Federalism, and the District of Columbia, United States Senate." Available from the U.S. General Accounting Office, Washington, D.C. Report GAO/T-HRD-87-20, July 30, 1987.

59. For details, see Joseph F. Zimmerman, "The State Mandate Problem," *State and Local Government Review* (Spring 1987): 78–84.

60. See S. 2387 of 1987, § 201, U.S. Senate.

61. Ibid., § 2.

62. David F. Durenberger, "Targeted Fiscal Assistance Act," *Congressional Record,* 6 March 1987, p. S2822.

63. Comprehensive Environmental Response, Compensation, and Liability Act of 1980, 94 Stat. 2767, 42 U.S.C. §§ 9601–57.

Bibliography

Books and Monographs

Ackerman, Bruce A., and Hassler, William T. *Clean Coal/Dirty Air,* New Haven: Yale University Press, 1981.

The Agreement State Program: A State Perspective. Washington, D.C.: National Governors' Association, 1983.

Allen, J. B. *Enhancing Decentralization for Development.* The Hague: International Union of Local Authorities, 1985.

Anderson, William. *Intergovernmental Relations in Review.* Minneapolis: University of Minnesota Press, 1960.

_____. *The Nation and the States: Rivals or Partners?* Minneapolis: University of Minnesota Press, 1955.

Antieu, Chester J. *States Rights Under Federal Constitutions.* Dobbs Ferry, N.Y.: Oceana, 1984.

Archer, Jules. *Washington vs. Main Street: The Power Struggle Between Federal and Local Power.* New York: Crowell, 1975.

Bailey, Thomas A. *The American Pageant: A History of the Republic.* 3d ed. Boston: Heath, 1967.

Barton, Weldon V. *Interstate Compacts in the Political Process.* Chapel Hill: University of North Carolina Press, 1967.

Benker, Karen M., Wortley, Jay, and Felde, Jon. *Issues Raised for States by Federal Tax Reform.* Washington, D.C. National Association of State Budget Officers and National Conference of State Legislatures, 1986.

Brogan, D. W. *Politics in America.* Garden City: Anchor Books, 1960.

Brown, Lawrence D., Fossett, James W., and Palmer, Kenneth T. *The Changing Politics of Federal Grants.* Washington, D.C.: Brookings Institution, 1984.

Bryce, James. *The American Commonwealth.* New York: Macmillan, 1900.

Cain, Bruce. *The Reapportionment Puzzle.* Berkeley: University of California Press, 1984.

Calhoun, John C. *Disquisition on Government.* New York: Political Science Classics, 1947.

City Fiscal Conditions in 1986. Washington, D.C.: National League of Cities, 1986.

The Civil Rights Division — Enforcing the Law, January 20, 1981, to January 31, 1987. Washington, D.C.: U.S. Department of Justice, 1987.

Clark, Jane P. *The Rise of the New Federalism: Federal-State Cooperation in the United States.* New York: Columbia University Press, 1938.

Colglazier, E. William, Jr., ed. *The Politics of Nuclear Waste.* New York: Pergamon, 1982.

Commission on Intergovernmental Relations. *A Report to the President for Transmittal to the Congress.* Washington, D.C.: Government Printing Office, 1955.

Coping with Federal Requirements. Washington, D.C.: National Association of Towns and Townships, 1985.

Cortner, Richard C. *The Supreme Court and the Second Bill of Rights: The Fourteenth Amendment or the Nationalization of Civil Liberties.* Madison: University of Wisconsin Press, 1981.

Corwin, Edward S. *The Commerce Power Versus States' Rights.* Princeton: Princeton University Press, 1936.

_____. *National Supremacy: Treaty Power vs. State Power.* New York: Henry Holt, 1913.

Currie, David P. *The Constitution in the Supreme Court.* Chicago: University of Chicago Press, 1985.

Dahl, Robert A. *Dilemmas of Pluralist Democracy: Autonomy vs. Control.* New Haven: Yale University Press, 1982.

Derthick, Martha, and Quirk, Paul J. *The Politics of Deregulation.* Washington, D.C.: Brookings Institution, 1985.

Dilger, Robert J., ed. *American Intergovernmental Relations Today: Perspectives and Controversies.* Englewood Cliffs, N.J.: Prentice-Hall, 1986.

Elazar, Daniel J. *American Federalism: A View from the States.* 3d ed. New York: Harper & Row, 1984.

_____. *The American Partnership.* Chicago: University of Chicago Press, 1962.

_____. *Exploring Federalism.* Tuscaloosa: University of Alabama Press, 1986.

Epstein, David F. *The Political Theory of the Federalist.* Chicago: University of Chicago Press, 1984.

Failed Oversight: A Report on the Failure of the Office of Surface Mining to Enforce the Federal Surface Mining Control and Reclamation Act. Washington, D.C.: National Wildlife Federation, 1985.

Farrand, Max. *The Fathers of the Constitution.* New Haven: Yale University Press, 1921.

The Federalist Papers. New York: New American Library, 1961.

Federal-State Environmental Programs — The State Perspective: A Compilation of Questionnaire Responses. Washington, D.C.: U.S. General Accounting Office, 1980.

Fiscal Survey of the States. Washington, D.C.: National Governors' Association and National Association of State Budget Officers, 1986.

Friedrich, Carl J. *Trends of Federalism in Theory and Practice.* New York: Praeger, 1968.

Glendening, Parris N., and Reeves, Marvis Mann. *Pragmatic Federalism.* 2d ed. Pacific Palisades: Palisades, 1984.

Goals for State-Federal Action: 1984–1986. Denver: National Conference of State Legislatures, n.d.

Goldwin, Robert A., ed. *A Nation of States: Essays on the American Federal System.* 2d ed. Chicago: Rand McNally, 1974.

Graves, W. Brooke. *American Intergovernmental Relations: Their Origins, Historical Development, and Current Status.* New York: Scribner's, 1964.

Green, Robert L., ed. *Metropolitan Desegregation.* New York: Plenum Press, 1985.

Grodzins, Morton. *The American System: A New View of Government in the United States.* Chicago: Rand McNally, 1966.

Haider, Donald. *When Governments Come to Washington: Governors, Mayors and Intergovernmental Lobbying.* Riverside, N.J.: Free Press, 1974.

Hand, Learned. *The Bill of Rights.* New York: Atheneum, 1964.

Hanus, Jerome, ed. *The Nationalization of State Government.* Lexington, Mass.: Lexington, 1981.

Hawkins, Robert B., Jr., ed. *American Federalism: New Partnership for the Republic.* San Francisco: Institute for Contemporary Studies, 1982.

Hofstadter, Richard, Miller, William, and Aaron, Daniel. *The American Republic.* Englewood Cliffs, N.J.: Prentice-Hall, 1959.

Inman, Robert P. *Does Deductibility Influence Local Taxation?* Philadelphia: Federal Reserve Bank of Philadelphia, 1985.

Jensen, Merrill. *The Making of the American Constitution.* Princeton, N.J.: Van Nostrand, 1964.

Jones, Charles O. *Clean Air: The Policies and Politics of Pollution Control.* Pittsburgh: University of Pittsburgh Press, 1975.

Kee, James E., and Diehl, William. *Assessing the Costs of Federal Mandates on State and Local Governments.* Washington, D.C.: Academy for State and Local Government, 1988.

Ketcham, Ralph, ed. *The Anti-Federalist Papers and Constitutional Convention Debates.* New York: New American Library, 1986.

Kettl, Donald F. *The Regulation of American Federalism.* Baton Rouge: Louisiana State University Press, 1983.

Keys to Successful Funding. Washington, D.C.: National Association of Towns and Townships, 1985.

Knapp, Michael S., and Blakely, Craig H. *The Education Block Grant at the Local Level: The Implementation of Chapter 2 of the Education Consolidation and Improvement Act in Districts and Schools.* Menlo Park, Calif.: SRI International, 1986.

Kneese, Allen V., and Bower, Blair T. *Managing Water Quality: Economics, Technology, Institutions.* Baltimore: Johns Hopkins University Press, 1984.

Laski, Harold J. *The American Democracy: A Commentary and an Interpretation.* New York: Viking Press, 1948.

Leach, Richard H. *American Federalism.* New York: Norton, 1970.

_____, ed. *Intergovernmental Relations in the 1980s.* New York: Marcel Dekker, 1983.

Leadership for Dynamic State Economies. New York: Committee for Economic Development, 1986.

Lindblom, Charles E. *The Intelligence of Democracy: Decision Making Through Mutual Adjustment.* New York: Free Press, 1965.

Lovell, Catherine, et al. *Federal and State Mandating on Local Governments: An Exploration of Issues and Impacts.* Riverside: University of California, 1979.

Lowi, Theodore J. *The End of Liberalism: The Second Republic of the United States.* 2d ed. New York: Norton, 1979.

Lufkin, Dan W. *Many Sovereign States: A Case for Strengthening State Government.* New York: McKay, 1975.

McCurley, Robert L., Jr. *Federally Mandated State Legislation.* Washington, D.C.: National Conference of State Legislatures, 1986.

MacMahon, Arthur W. *Administering Federalism in a Democracy.* New York: Oxford University Press, 1972.

_____, ed. *Federalism: Mature and Emergent.* Garden City, N.Y.: Doubleday, 1955.

Martin, Roscoe C. *The Cities and the Federal System.* New York: Atherton Press, 1965.

Mason, Alpheus T., and Beaney, William M. *American Constitutional Law.* New York: Prentice-Hall, 1959.

Mass, Arthur, ed. *Area and Power.* Glencoe, Ill.: Free Press, 1959.

Maxwell, James A. *Tax Credits and Intergovernmental Fiscal Relations.* Washington, D.C.: Brookings Institution, 1962.

Melnick, R. Shep. *Regulation and the Courts: The Case of the Clean Air Act.* Washington, D.C.: Brookings Institution, 1983.

Monti, Daniel J. *A Semblance of Justice: St. Louis School Desegregation and Order in Urban America.* Columbia: University of Missouri Press, 1985.

Morrison, Steven, and Winston, Clifford. *The Economic Effects of Airline Deregulation.* Washington, D.C.: Brookings Institution, 1986.

Nathan, Richard, P., Adams, Charles F., Jr., et al. *Revenue Sharing: The Second Round.* Washington, D.C.: Brookings Institution, 1977.

Nathan, Richard P., Doolitle, Fred C., et al. *Reagan and the States.* Princeton: Princeton University Press, 1987.

Nathan, Richard P., Navel, Allen D., and Calkins, Susannah E. *Monitoring Revenue Sharing.* Washington, D.C.: Brookings Institution, 1975.

National Commission on Urban Problems. *Building the American City.*

Washington, D.C.: Government Printing Office, 1968.

NCSL Supreme Court Amicus Briefs: The Impact of the State and Local Legal Center. Washington, D.C.: National Conference of State Legislatures, 1986.

Oates, Wallace E. *Fiscal Federalism.* New York: Harcourt, Brace, Jovanovich, 1972.

————, ed. *The Political Economy of Fiscal Federalism.* Lexington, Mass.: Lexington, 1977.

Ostrom, Vincent. *The Intellectual Crisis in American Public Administration.* University: University of Alabama Press, 1973.

Owen, Henry, and Schultze, Charles L., eds. *Setting National Priorities: The Next Ten Years.* Washington, D.C.: Brookings Institution, 1976.

Palmer, John L., and Sawhill, Isabel V., eds. *The Reagan Experiment: An Examination of Economic and Social Practices under the Reagan Administration.* Washington, D.C.: Urban Institute, 1982.

Peterson, George E., and Lewis, Carol W. *Reagan and the Cities.* Washington, D.C.: Urban Institute, 1986.

Phillips, Barbara Y. *How to Use Section 5 of the Voting Rights Act.* 3d ed. Washington, D.C.: Joint Center for Political Studies, 1983.

Preemption: Drawing the Line: A State and Local Government Report on Federal Preemption and Mandates. Washington, D.C.: Academy for State and Local Government, 1986.

Pressman, Jeffrey L. *Federal Programs and City Politics.* Berkeley: University of California Press, 1975.

Pride, Richard A., and Woodard, J. David. *The Burden of Busing: The Politics of Desegregation in Nashville, Tennessee.* Knoxville: University of Tennessee Press, 1985.

Reagan, Michael D. *Regulation: The Politics of Policy.* Boston: Little, Brown, 1987.

Reagan, Michael D., and Sanzone, John G. *The New Federalism.* 2d ed. New York: Oxford University Press, 1981.

Rebell, Michael A., and Block, Arthur R. *Equality and Education: Federal Civil Rights Enforcement in the New York City School System.* Princeton: Princeton University Press, 1985.

Regulatory Federalism: Policy, Process, Impact, and Reform. Washington, D.C.: U.S. Advisory Commission on Intergovernmental Relations, 1983.

Roberts, Owen J. *The Court and the Constitution.* Cambridge: Harvard University Press, 1951.

Robinson, Donald L., ed. *Reforming American Government: The Bicentennial Papers of the Committee on the Constitutional System.* Boulder, Colo.: Westview Press, 1985.

Rockefeller, Nelson A. *The Future of Federalism.* New York: Atheneum,1964.

Rossum, Ralph A., and McDowell, Gary L., eds. *The American Founding:*

Politics, Statesmanship, and the Constitution. Port Washington, N.Y.: Kennikat Press, 1981.

Russell, Clifford S., Harrington, Winston, and Vaughan, William J. *Enforcing Pollution Control Laws.* Baltimore: Johns Hopkins University Press, 1986.

Savitch, H. V. *Urban Policy and the Exterior City: Federal, State, and Corporate Impacts Upon Major Cities.* New York: Pergamon, 1979.

Seklecki, Mark. *Gramm-Rudman-Hollings: Impact on the States.* Washington, D.C.: National Conference of State Legislatures, 1986.

Single Audit. Washington, D.C.: Arthur Andersen, 1986.

Smallwood, Frank, ed. *The New Federalism.* Hanover, N.H.: The Public Affairs Center, Dartmouth College, 1967.

Smith, T. V., and Lindeman, Eduard C. *The Democratic Way of Life.* New York: Mentor Books, 1951.

Sokolow, Alvin D. *Small Governments and the Federal Budget.* Washington, D.C.: National Association of Towns and Townships, 1986.

STAPPA's Recommendations for Revising the Clean Air Act. Washington, D.C.: State and Territorial Air Pollution Program Administrators, 1985.

State and Local Roles in the Federal System. Washington, D.C.: U.S. Advisory Commission on Intergovernmental Relations, 1982.

Stewart, William H. *Concepts of Federalism.* Lanham, Md.: University Press of America, 1984.

Storing, Herbert J. *What the Anti-Federalists Were For.* Chicago: University of Chicago Press, 1981.

Sundquist, James L. *Constitutional Reform and Effective Government.* Washington, D.C.: Brookings Institution, 1986.

Sundquist, James L., and Davis, David W. *Making Federalism Work.* Washington, D.C.: Brookings Institution, 1969.

Tietenberg, T. H. *Emissions Trading: An Exercise in Reforming Pollution Policy.* Baltimore: Johns Hopkins University Press, 1985.

Tipton, Diane. *Nullification and Interposition in American Political Thought.* Albuquerque: Division of Research, Institute for Social Research and Development, The University of New Mexico, 1969.

Tocqueville, Alexis de. *Democracy in America.* New York: Vintage Books, 1954.

To Form a More Perfect Union: The Report of the Committee on Federalism and National Purpose. Washington, D.C.: National Conference on Social Welfare, 1985.

Truman, David B. *Administrative Decentralization: A Study of the Chicago Field Office of the United States Department of Agriculture.* Chicago: University of Chicago Press, 1940.

Van Doren, Carl. *The Great Rehearsal.* New York: Viking Press, 1948.

Walker, David B. *Towards a Functioning Federalism.* Cambridge, Mass.: Winthrop, 1981.

Walker, Robert H., ed. *The Reform Spirit in America: A Documentation of Reform in the American Republic.* New York: G.P. Putnam 1976.

Wasby, Stephen. *The Supreme Court in the Federal Judicial System.* 3d ed. Chicago: Nelson-Hall, 1988.

Where Will the Money Come From? Finding Reliable Revenue for State and Local Governments in a Changing Economy. Washington, D.C.: Academy for State and Local Government, 1986.

White, Leonard D. *The States and the Nation.* Baton Rouge: Louisiana State University Press, 1953.

White, Morton. *Philosophy, "The Federalist," and the Constitution.* New York: Oxford University Press, 1987.

Wilson, Woodrow. *Congressional Government: A Study in American Politics.* Boston: Houghton Mifflin, 1925.

Wolf, Eleanor P. *Trial and Error: The Detroit School Segregation Case.* Detroit: Wayne State University Press, 1981.

Wright, Deil. *Understanding Intergovernmental Relations.* North Scituate, Mass.: Duxbury Press, 1978.

Zimmerman, Joseph F. *The Federated City: Community Control in Large Cities.* New York: St. Martin's Press, 1972.

_____. *Participatory Democracy: Populism Revived.* New York: Praeger, 1986.

_____. *State-Local Relations: A Partnership Approach.* New York: Praeger, 1983.

Zimmermann, Frederick L., and Wendell, Mitchell. *The Law and Use of Interstate Compacts.* Lexington, Ky.: Council of State Governments, 1976.

Public Documents

Air Pollution: Environmental Protection Agency's Inspections of Stationary Sources. Washington, D.C.: U.S. General Accounting Office, 1985.

Air Pollution: EPA's Strategy to Control Emissions of Benzene and Gasoline Vapor. Washington, D.C.: U.S. General Accounting Office, 1985.

Air Pollution: Improvements Needed in Developing and Managing EPA's Air Quality Models. Washington, D.C.: U.S. General Accounting Office, 1986.

Air Pollution: States Assigned a Major Role in EPA's Air Toxics Strategy. Washington, D.C.: U.S. General Accounting Office, 1987.

Air Quality Standards: EPA's Standard Setting Process Should be More Timely and Better Planned. Washington, D.C.: U.S. General Accounting Office, 1986.

All About OSHA. Washington, D.C.: Occupational Safety and Health Administration, U.S. Department of Labor, 1985.

American Federalism: Toward a More Effective Partnership. Washington, D.C.: U.S. Advisory Commission on Intergovernmental Relations, 1975.

Assessment of EPA's Hazardous Waste Enforcement Strategy. Washington, D.C.: U.S. General Accounting Office, 1985.

Awakening the Slumbering Giant: Intergovernmental Relations and Federal Grant Law. Washington, D.C.: U.S. Advisory Commission on Intergovernmental Relations, 1980.

A Block Grant Fact Book. Tallahassee: Florida Advisory Council on Intergovernmental Relations, n.d.

Block Grants Brought Funding Changes and Adjustments to Program Priorities. Washington, D.C.: United States General Accounting Office, 1985.

Block Grants: Federal Data Collection Provisions. Washington, D.C.: U.S. General Accounting Office, 1987.

Burger, Warren E. *Annual Message on the Administration of Justice.* Washington, D.C.: Supreme Court of the United States, 1985.

A Catalog of Federal Grant-in-Aid Programs to State and Local Governments: Grants Funded FY 1978. Washington, D.C.: U.S. Advisory Commission on Intergovernmental Relations, 1979.

A Catalog of Federal Grant-in-Aid Programs to State and Local Governments: Grants Funded FY 1984. Washington, D.C.: U.S. Advisory Commission on Intergovernmental Relations, 1984.

A Catalog of Federal Grant-In-Aid Programs to State and Local Governments: Grants Funded FY 1987. Washington, D.C.: U.S. Advisory Commission on Intergovernmental Relations, 1987.

Categorical Grants: Their Role and Design. The Intergovernmental Grant System: An Assessment and Proposed Policies. Washington, D.C.: U.S. Advisory Commission on Intergovernmental Relations, 1978.

Circular A-128. Washington, D.C.: U.S. Office of Management and Budget, 1985.

Cities—Message from the President. Washington, D.C.: House, 89th Cong. 1st sess.; H. Doc. 99, 1965.

Citizen Participation in the American Federal System. Washington, D.C.: U.S. Advisory Commission on Intergovernmental Relations, 1979.

City Financial Emergencies: The Intergovernmental Dimension. Washington, D.C.: U.S. Advisory Commission on Intergovernmental Relations, 1973.

Civil Rights Act of 1984: Hearing before the Committee on Labor and Human Resources, United States Senate on S. 2568. Washington, D.C.: Government Printing Office, 1985.

Civil Rights Division. Enforcing the Law: January 20, 1981–January 31, 1987. Washington, D.C.: U.S. Department of Justice, 1987.

The Commission on Intergovernmental Relations. *A Report to the President for Transmittal to the Congress.* Washington, D.C.: Government Printing Office, 1955.

The Commission on the Organization of the Executive Branch of the Government. *Overseas Administration, Federal-State Relations, Federal Research.* Washington, D.C.: Government Printing Office, 1949.

Committee on Government Operations. House of Representatives. *Office of Surface Mining: Beyond Reclamation?* Washington, D.C.: Government Printing Office, 1985.

The Community Development Block Grant Program: Discretionary Grant Funds Not Always Given to the Most Promising Small City Programs. Washington, D.C.: U.S. General Accounting Office, 1978.

Community Development Block Grants: Reauthorization Issues. Washington, D.C.: Congressional Budget Office, 1980.

Community Development: HUD's Decision to Restrict Philadelphia's Block Grant Funds. Washington, D.C.: U.S. General Accounting Office, 1986.

Congressional Research Service. *The Clean Air Act in the Courts.* Washington, D.C.: Government Printing Office, 1981.

————. *Federal-State Relations in Transition: Implications for Environmental Policy.* Washington, D.C.: Government Printing Office, 1982.

Constitutional Convention Implementation Act of 1984: Report of the Committee on the Judiciary, United States Senate on S. 119, As Amended. Washington, D.C.: Government Printing Office, 1984.

Constitutional Convention Implementation Act of 1985: Report of the Committee on the Judiciary, United States Senate on S. 40, As Amended. Washington, D.C.: Government Printing Office, 1985.

The Cost of Clean Air and Water Report to Congress: 1984. Washington, D.C.: U.S. General Accounting Office, 1984.

Criteria for Preparation and Evaluation of Radiological Emergency Response Plans and Preparedness in Support of Nuclear Power Plants. Washington, D.C.: U.S. Nuclear Regulatory Commission and Federal Emergency Management Agency, 1987.

Cuciti, Peggy L. *Federal Constraints on State and Local Governments.* Washington, D.C.: Congressional Budget Office, 1979.

Danger on Our Highways: The Critical Problem of Unsafe Large and Heavy Trucks. Albany: New York State Legislative Commission on Critical Transportation Choices, 1988.

Death Penalty Legislation. Hearing before the Committee on the Judiciary, United States Senate, Ninety-Ninth Congress on S. 239. Washington, D.C.: Government Printing Office, 1986.

A Decent Home: The Report of the President's Committee on Urban Housing. Washington, D.C.: Government Printing Office, 1968.

Delays in EPA's Regulation of Hazardous Air Pollutants. Washington, D.C.: U.S. General Accounting Office, 1983.

Department of Environmental Conservation: Division of Water. Albany: New York State Comptroller, 1985.

The Department of Environmental Conservation: A Program and Budget

History. Albany: New York State Assembly Ways and Means Committee, 1985.

The Department of Labor's Enforcement of the Fair Labor Standards Act. Washington, D.C: U.S. General Accounting Office, 1985.

Devolving Federal Program Responsibilities and Revenue Sources to State and Local Governments. Washington, D.C.: U.S. Advisory Commission on Intergovernmental Relations, 1986.

Does New York State Have the Constitutional Power to Mandate "Cigarette" Type Warning Labels on Alcoholic Beverage Containers and Advertisements? Albany: New York State Legislative Commission on Critical Transportation Choices, 1984.

Education Block Grant Alters State Role and Provides Greater Local Discretion. Washington, D.C.: U.S. General Accounting Office, 1984.

The Effect of the President's Tax Plan on State and Local Taxpayers. Hearings before the Joint Economic Committee, Congress of the United States, May 29–30, 1985. Washington, D.C.: Government Printing Office, 1985.

Emergency Planning: Federal Involvement in Preparedness Exercise at Shoreham Nuclear Plant. Washington, D.C.: U.S. General Accounting Office, 1986.

Emerging Issues in American Federalism. Washington, D.C.: U.S. Advisory Commission on Intergovernmental Relations, 1985.

Environmental Quality: The Ninth Annual Report of the Council on Environmental Quality. Washington, D.C.: Government Printing Office, 1978.

EPA-Approved Revisions to State Implementation Plans Allowing Increased Sulfur Dioxide Emissions Were Legal. Washington, D.C.: U.S. General Accounting Office, 1985.

EPA Could Benefit from Comprehensive Management Information on Superfund Enforcement Actions. Washington, D.C.: U.S. General Accounting Office, 1984.

EPA Needs to Improve Its Oversight of Air Pollution Control Grant Expenditures. Washington, D.C.: U.S. General Accounting Office, 1984.

EPA's Asbestos Regulations: Report on a Case Study of OMB Interference in Agency Rulemaking by the Subcommittee on Oversight and Investigations of the Committee on Energy and Commerce, United States House of Representatives. Washington, D.C.: Government Printing Office, 1985.

EPA's Delegation of Responsibilities to Prevent Significant Deterioration of Air Quality: How Is It Working? Washington, D.C.: U.S. General Accounting Office, 1985.

Federal Aid Simplification: White House Status Report. Washington, D.C.: The White House, 1978.

Federal and State Roles in Economic Development: Hearings before a Sub-

committee of the Committee on Government Operations, House of Representatives, December 2, 4, and 5, 1985. Washington, D.C.: Government Printing Office, 1986.

Federal and State Roles in Economic Stabilization: Twenty-Sixth Report by the Commission on Government Operations, United States House of Representatives. Washington, D.C.: Government Printing Office, 1985.

Federal Constraints on State and Local Government Actions. Washington, D.C.: Congressional Budget Office, 1979.

Federal Grants: Their Effects on State-Local Expenditures, Employment Levels, Wage Rates. Washington, D.C.: U.S. Advisory Commission on Intergovernmental Relations, 1977.

Federal Highway Administration. *Guidelines for Applying Criteria to Designate Routes for Transporting Hazardous Materials.* Washington, D.C.: Government Printing Office, 1980.

The Federal Influence on State and Local Roles in the Federal System. Washington, D.C.: U.S. Advisory Commission on Intergovernmental Relations, 1981.

The Federal Role in the Federal System: The Dynamics of Growth. Washington, D.C.: U.S. Advisory Commission on Intergovernmental Relations, 1981.

Final Task Force Report on the Agreement State Program. Washington, D.C.: U.S. Nuclear Regulatory Commission, 1977.

"First Principles" of American Federalism: A Working Paper. Washington, D.C.: U.S. Advisory Commission on Intergovernmental Relations, 1982.

Fiscal Balance in the America Federal System. Washington, D.C.: U.S. Advisory Commission on Intergovernmental Relations, 1967.

The 14th Amendment and School Busing: Hearings before the Subcommittee on the Constitution of the Committee on the Judiciary, United States Senate, May 14 and June 3, 1981. Washington, D.C.: Government Printing Office, 1982.

Freeman, A. Myrick III. *The Benefits of Air and Water Pollution Control: A Review and Synthesis of Recent Estimates.* Washington, D.C.: Council on Environmental Quality, 1979.

The Future of Federalism in the 1980s. Washington, D.C.: U.S. Advisory Commission on Intergovernmental Relations, 1981.

The Gap Between Federal Aid Authorizations and Appropriations: Fiscal Years 1966–1970. Washington, D.C.: U.S. Advisory Commission on Intergovernmental Relations, 1970.

General Revenue Sharing: An ACIR Re-evaluation. Washington, D.C.: U.S. Advisory Commission on Intergovernmental Relations, 1974.

Governor's Task Force on Block Grant Implementation: Final Report. Springfield, Ill.: Office of the Governor, n.d.

Grant Formulas: A Catalog of Federal Aid to States and Localities. Washington, D.C.: U.S. General Accounting Office, 1987.

Groundwater Standards: States Need More Information from EPA. Washington, D.C.: U.S. General Accounting Office, 1988.

Hazardous Waste: Environmental Safeguards Jeopardized When Facilities Cease Operation. Washington, D.C.: U.S. General Accounting Office, 1986.

Hazardous Waste: EPA Has Made Limited Progress in Determining the Wastes to Be Regulated. Washington, D.C.: U.S. General Accounting Office, 1986.

Hazardous Waste: EPA's Superfund Program Improvements Result in Fewer Stopgap Cleanups. Washington, D.C.: U.S. General Accounting Office, 1986.

Hazardous Waste: Federal Civil Agencies Slow to Comply with Regulatory Requirements. Washington, D.C.: U.S. General Accounting Office, 1986.

Hazardous Waste: Status of Private Party Efforts to Clean Up Hazardous Waste Sites. Washington, D.C.: U.S. General Accounting Office, 1985.

The Hazardous Waste System. Washington, D.C.: U.S. Environmental Protection Agency, 1987.

Hearings before the Subcommittee on Air and Water Pollution of the Committee on Public Works, United States Senate, on S. 780. Washington, D.C.: Government Printing Office, 1967.

How Much Power Do New York State & Local Governments Have to Abate Airport Noise? Albany: New York State Legislative Commission on Critical Transportation Choices, 1984.

How Much Tougher Should New York State's Anti–Drunk Driving Laws Be? Albany: New York State Legislative Commission on Critical Transportation Choices, 1984.

Hunter, Lawrence A., and Oakerson, Ronald J. *Reflections on Garcia and Its Implications for Federalism.* Washington, D.C.: U.S. Advisory Commission on Intergovernmental Relations, 1986.

The Impact of the Proposed Elimination of the General Revenue Sharing Program on Local Governments: Hearings before a Subcommittee of the Committee on Government Operations, March 11, 15, 18, 29, and April 3, 1985. Washington, D.C.: Government Printing Office, 1985.

Improvements Needed in Controlling Major Air Pollution Sources. Washington, D.C.: U.S. General Accounting Office, 1979.

Information on Airport and Airway Trust Fund Revenues and Outlays by States and Large Airports. Washington, D.C.: U.S. General Accounting Office, 1985.

The Interaction of Federal and State Aid in New York State: Trends and Patterns, 1969–1975. Washington, D.C.: U.S. General Accounting Office, 1980.

Intergovernmental Regulatory Relief Act of 1985: Hearings before the Subcommittee on Intergovernmental Relations, United States Senate on S.

483, April 2 and May 14, 1985. Washington, D.C.: Government Printing Office, 1986.

Investigation of Civil Rights Enforcement by the Department of Education. Hearings before a Subcommittee of the Committee on Government Operations, House of Representatives, Ninety-Ninth Congress, First Session, July 18 and September 11, 1985. Washington, D.C.: Government Printing Office, 1986.

Investigation of Civil Rights Enforcement by the Office for Civil Rights at the Department of Education. Twenty-Fourth Report by the Committee on Government Operations, United States House of Representatives. Washington, D.C.: Government Printing Office, 1985.

Is Constitutional Reform Necessary to Reinvigorate Federalism? A Round-table Discussion. Washington, D.C.: U.S. Advisory Commission on Intergovernmental Relations, 1987.

Local Governments: Targeting General Fiscal Assistance Reduces Fiscal Disparities. Washington, D.C.: U.S. General Accounting Office, 1986.

Management and Evaluation of the Community Block Grant Program Need to be Strengthened. Washington, D.C.: U.S. General Accounting Office, 1978.

A Market Approach to Air Pollution Control Could Reduce Compliance Costs Without Jeopardizing Clean Air Goals. Washington, D.C.: U.S. General Accounting Office, 1982.

Materials Safety Regulation Review Study Group Report. 51 *Federal Register* 45122–31 (December 17, 1986).

Maternal and Child Health Block Grant: Program Changes Emerging Under State Administration. Washington, D.C.: U.S. General Accounting Office, 1984.

Means for Improving State Participation in the Siting, Licensing, and Development of Federal Nuclear Waste Facilities. Washington, D.C.: Office of State Programs, U.S. Nuclear Regulatory Commission, 1979.

Message from the President of the United States Transmitting Recommendations for City Demonstration Programs. Washington, D.C.: House, 89th Cong. 2d sess., H. Doc. 368, 1966.

Mine Safety: Labor's Progress in Doing Required Inspections. Washington, D.C.: U.S. General Accounting Office, 1986.

Motor Carrier Safety: Transportation of Hazardous and Nuclear Materials: Hearing before the Subcommittee on Telecommunications, Consumer Protection, and Finance of the Committee on Energy and Commerce, House of Representatives, July 19, 1985. Washington, D.C.: Government Printing Office, 1986.

Municipal Antitrust Legislation: Local Government Antitrust Act of 1984. Hearings before the Subcommittee on Monopolies and Commercial Law, United States House of Representatives. Washington, D.C.: Government Printing Office, 1987.

National Air Quality and Emissions Trends Report, 1986. Washington, D.C.:

U.S. Environmental Protection Agency, 1988.
National Commission on Urban Problems. *Building the American City.* Washington, D.C.: Government Printing Office, 1968.
The Nation's Water. Key Unanswered Questions about the Quality of Rivers and Streams. Washington, D.C.: U.S. General Accounting Office, 1986.
New York State Air Quality Implementation Plan: Transportation Element, New York City Metropolitan Area. Albany: New York State Department of Environmental Conservation, 1978.
The 1984 Anniversary of the Constitution: Hearing before the Subcommittee on the Constitution of the Committee on the Judiciary, United States Senate. Washington, D.C.: Government Printing Office, 1985.
1984 Needs Survey Report to Congress. Assessment of Needed Publicly Owned Wastewater Treatment Facilities in the United States. Washington, D.C.: U.S. Environmental Protection Agency, 1985.
NRC Coziness with Industry: An Investigative Report. Washington, D.C.: Subcommittee on General Oversight and Investigations, House, 1987.
Nuclear Regulation: Oversight of Quality Assurance at Nuclear Power Plants Needs Improvement. Washington, D.C.: U.S. General Accounting Office, 1986.
Nuclear Regulation: Public Knowledge of Radiological Emergency Procedures. Washington, D.C.: U.S. General Accounting Office, 1987.
Nuclear Regulation: Unique Features of Shoreham Nuclear Plant Emergency Planning. Washington, D.C.: U.S. General Accounting Office, 1986.
The Nuclear Regulatory Commission Should Report on Progress in Implementing Lessons Learned from the Three Mile Island Accident. Washington, D.C.: U.S. General Accounting Office, 1985.
Nuclear Safety: Safety Analysis Reviews for DOE's Defense Facilities Can Be Improved. Washington, D.C.: U.S. General Accounting Office, 1986.
Nuclear Waste: DOE Should Provide More Information on Monitored Retrievable Storage. Washington, D.C.: Government Printing Office, 1987.
Nuclear Waste: Institutional Relations under the Nuclear Waste Policy Act of 1982. Washington, D.C.: U.S. General Accounting Office, 1987.
The Nuclear Waste Policy Act: 1984 Implementation Status, Progress, and Problems. Washington, D.C.: U.S. General Accounting Office, 1985.
Nuclear Waste: Status of DOE's Implementation of the Nuclear Waste Policy Act. Washington, D.C.: U.S. General Accounting Office, 1987.
Office of Legal Policy. *Original Meaning Jurisprudence: A Sourcebook.* Washington, D.C.: U.S. Department of Justice, 1987.
Office of Policy Development and Research. *CDBG Execution: Problems and Prospects.* Washington, D.C.: U.S. Department of Housing and Urban Development, 1979.
Office of Technology Assessment, Congress of the United States. *Protecting the Nation's Groundwater from Contamination.* Washington, D.C.: Government Printing Office, 1984.

The Partnership for Health Act: Lessons from a Pioneering Block Grant. Washington, D.C.: U.S. Advisory Commission on Intergovernmental Relations, 1977.

Perspectives on Intergovernmental Policy and Fiscal Relations. Washington, D.C.: U.S. General Accounting Office, 1979.

President's Urban and Regional Policy Group. *A New Partnership to Conserve America's Communities: A National Urban Policy.* Washington, D.C.: U.S. Department of Housing and Urban Development, 1978.

Product Liability Act: Report of the Senate Committee on Commerce, Science, and Transportation. Washington, D.C.: Government Printing Office, 1984.

Proposed Changes in Federal Matching and Maintenance of Effort Requirements for State and Local Governments. Washington, D.C.: Government Printing Office, 1980.

Protecting the Environment: Politics, Pollution, and Federal Policy. Washington, D.C.: U.S. Advisory Commission on Intergovernmental Relations, 1981.

Public Involvement in Block Grant Decisions: Multiple Opportunities Provided but Interest Groups Have Mixed Reactions to States' Efforts. Washington, D.C.: U.S. General Accounting Office, 1984.

Public Technology, Incorporated. *Air Quality Regulation and Planning.* Washington, D.C.: U.S. Department of Transportation, 1980.

_____. *Transportation System Management, Air Quality, and Energy Conservation.* Washington, D.C.: U.S. Department of Transportation, 1980.

Quarterly Report on DOE's Nuclear Waste Program as of September 30, 1985. Washington, D.C.: U.S. General Accounting Office, 1985.

Rail Safety: States' Reaction to Proposed Elimination of Inspection Funding. Washington, D.C.: U.S. Accounting Office, 1987.

Reagan Administration Regulatory Achievements. Washington, D.C.: Presidential Task Force on Regulatory Relief, 1983.

Referral of Federal Criminal Cases to Local Law Enforcement Agencies. Washington, D.C.: U.S. General Accounting Office, 1985.

Regulating Hazardous Waste Generation in Massachusetts. Boston: Massachusetts Senate Committee on Post Audit and Oversight, 1985.

Regulation of Naturally Occurring and Accelerator-Produced Radioactive Materials: A Task Force Review. Washington, D.C.: U.S. Nuclear Regulatory Commission, 1977.

Regulation of Naturally Occurring and Accelerator-Produced Radioactive Materials: An Update. Washington, D.C.: U.S. Nuclear Regulatory Commission, 1984.

Regulatory Federalism: Policy, Process, Impact and Reform. Washington, D.C.: U.S. Advisory Commission on Intergovernmental Relations, 1984.

The Role of Equalization in Federal Grants. Washington, D.C.: U.S. Advisory Commission on Intergovernmental Relations, 1964.

School Prayer Constitutional Amendment: Report of the Committee on the Judiciary, United States Senate on S.J. Res. 212. Washington, D.C.: Government Printing Office, 1984.

Secretary of Health, Education and Welfare. *Progress in the Prevention and Control of Air Pollution.* Washington, D.C.: Government Printing Office, 1969.

Staats, Elmer B. "The New Mix of Federal Assistance: Categorical Grants, Block Grants, and General Revenue Sharing." In *American Federalism: Toward a More Effective Partnership.* Washington, D.C.: U.S. Advisory Commission on Intergovernmental Relations, 1975, pp. 57–63.

State Administrators' Opinions on Administrative Change, Federal Aid, Federal Relationships. Washington, D.C.: U.S. Advisory Commission on Intergovernmental Relations, 1980.

State and Local Governments' Views on Technical Assistance. Washington, D.C.: U.S. General Accounting Office, 1978.

State and Local Roles in the Federal System. Washington, D.C.: U.S. Advisory Commission on Intergovernmental Relations, 1982.

State Programs: Background. Washington, D.C.: Occupational Safety and Health Administration, August 1985.

State Rather Than Federal Policies Provided the Framework for Managing Block Grants. Washington, D.C.: U.S. General Accounting Office, 1985.

A State Response to Urban Problems: Recent Experience under the "Buying In" Approach. Washington, D.C.: U.S. Advisory Commission on Intergovernmental Relations, 1970.

States Fund an Expanded Range of Activities under Low-Income Home Energy Assistance Block Grant. Washington, D.C.: U.S. General Accounting Office, 1984.

States Have Made Few Changes in Implementing the Alcohol, Drug Abuse, and Mental Health Services Block Grant. Washington, D.C: U.S. General Accounting Office, 1984.

States Use Added Flexibility Offered by the Preventive Health and Health Services Block Grant. Washington, D.C.: U.S. General Accounting Office, 1984.

States Use Several Strategies to Cope with Funding Reductions under Social Services Block Grant. Washington, D.C.: U.S. General Accounting Office, 1984.

Status of EPA's Air Quality Standards for Carbon Monoxide. Washington, D.C.: U.S. General Accounting Office, 1984.

Status of the Department of Energy's Implementation of the Nuclear Waste Policy Act of 1982 as of June 30, 1985. Washington, D.C.: Government Printing Office, 1985.

Stronger Enforcement Would Help Improve Motor Carrier Safety. Washington, D.C.: U.S. General Accounting Office, 1985.

Subcommittee on the Constitution of the United States Senate Committee on the Judiciary. *Federal Civil Rights Laws: A Sourcebook.* Washington, D.C.: Government Printing Office, 1984.

Summary of the Nuclear Regulatory Commission's Program for Transfer of Regulatory Authority to States. Washington, D.C.: U.S. Nuclear Regulatory Commission, 1986.

Supreme Court Workload: Hearings Before the Subcommittee on Courts, Civil Liberties, and the Administration of Justice of the Committee on the Judiciary, House of Representatives, Ninety-Eighth Congress, First Session on H.R. 1968, April 27, May 18, September 22, and November 10, 1983. Washington, D.C.: Government Printing Office, 1984.

Surface Coal Mining Operations in Two Oklahoma Counties Raise Questions about Prime Farmland Reclamation and Bond Adequacy. Washington, D.C.: U.S. General Accounting Office, 1985.

Surface Mining. Difficulties in Reclaiming Mined Lands in Pennsylvania and West Virginia. Washington, D.C.: Government Printing Office, 1986.

Surface Mining: Information on Coal Mining Citations Issued by Kentucky Inspectors. Washington, D.C.: U.S. General Accounting Office, 1986.

Surface Mining: Interior Department and States Could Improve Inspection Programs. Washington, D.C.: U.S. General Accounting Office, 1986.

Surface Mining: Interior Department Oversight of State Permitting and Bonding Activities. Washington, D.C.: U.S. General Accounting Office, 1985.

Surface Mining: State and Federal Use of Alternative Enforcement Techniques. Washington, D.C.: U.S. General Accounting Office, 1987.

Surface Mining: State Management of Abandoned Mine Land Funds. Washington, D.C.: U.S. General Accounting Office, 1987.

Surface Mining: States Not Assessing and Collecting Monetary Penalties. Washington, D.C.: U.S. General Accounting Office, 1987.

Tandem Truck Safety Act of 1984: Hearing before the Subcommittee on Surface Transportation of the Committee on Commerce, Science, and Transportation, United States Senate. Washington, D.C.: Government Printing Office, 1984.

Toward an Understanding of Johnson. Washington, D.C.: U.S. Commission on Civil Rights, 1987.

The Transformation in American Politics: Implications for Federalism. Washington, D.C.: U.S. Advisory Commission on Intergovernmental Relations, 1986.

Twin Trailer Trucks: Effects on Highways and Highway Safety. Washington, D.C.: Transportation Research Board, 1986.

United States Bureau of the Census. *Expenditures of General Revenue Sharing and Antirecession Fiscal Assistance Funds: 1977–78.* Washington, D.C.: Government Printing Office, 1980.

United States Department of the Treasury. *Federal-State-Local Fiscal Rela-*

tions: Report to the President and the Congress. Washington, D.C.: Government Printing Office, 1985.

United States Department of the Treasury. *Federal-State-Local Fiscal Relations: Technical Papers.* Washington, D.C.: Government Printing Office, 1986. 2 vols.

United States Environmental Protection Agency. *Safe Drinking Water Act Cost Impacts on Selected Water Systems.* Springfield, Va.: National Technical Information Service, 1987.

Urban Mass Transportation Administration's New Formula Grant Program: Operating Flexibility and Process Simplification. Washington, D.C.: U.S. General Accounting Office, 1985.

USDA's Oversight of State Meat and Poultry Inspection Programs Could Be Strengthened. Washington, D.C.: U.S. General Accounting Office, 1983.

Viewpoints and Guidelines on Court-Appointed Citizens Monitoring Commissions in School Desegregation. Washington, D.C.: U.S. Department of Justice, 1978.

Voluntary Silent Prayer Constitutional Amendment: Report of the Committee on the Judiciary, United States Senate on S.J. Res. 2. Washington, D.C.: Government Printing Office, 1985.

Zimmerman, Joseph F. *Federal Preemption of State and Local Authority.* Washington, D.C.: U.S. Advisory Commission on Intergovernmental Relations, 1990.

_____. *Measuring Local Discretionary Authority.* Washington, D.C.: U.S. Advisory Commission on Intergovernmental Relations, 1981.

_____. *Pragmatic Federalism: The Reassignment of Functional Responsibility.* Washington, D.C.: U.S. Advisory Commission on Intergovernmental Relations, 1976.

_____. *State Mandating of Local Expenditures.* Washington, D.C.: U.S. Advisory Commission on Intergovernmental Relations, 1978.

Articles

Abraham, Henry J. "Limiting Federal Court Jurisdiction: A Self-Inflicted Wound?" *Judicature* 65 (October 1981): 178–84.

Anton, Thomas J. "Decay and Reconstruction in the Study of American Intergovernmental Relations." *Publius* 15 (Winter 1985): 65–97.

Apple, R. W., Jr. "Senate Rejects Reagan Plea and Votes 67–33 to Override His Veto of Highway Funds." *The New York Times,* 3 April 1987, 1, A25.

Atiyeh, Victor. "Unreasonable and Inflexible Federal Mandates." *Western Report* (Western Governors' Association), 19 December 1986, 1–2.

Bahl, Roy W. "A Reaction to the National Urban Policy Report." *Government Finance* 11 (September 1982): 29–33.

Bancroft, Bill. "Banking on Deregulation Can Be Hazardous to Your State's Financial Institutions." *Governing* 1 (January 1988): 44–49.

Barry, Harry J., III. "Reclamation of Strip-Mined Federal Land: Preemptive Capability of Federal Standards over State Controls." *Arizona Law Review* 18 (1977): 385–404.

Bator, Paul M. "Congressional Power Over the Jurisdiction of the Federal Courts." *Villanova Law Review* 27 (May 1982): 1030–41.

Beer, Samuel H. "A Political Scientist's View of Fiscal Federalism." In Wallace E. Oates, ed., *The Political Economy of Fiscal Federalism*. Lexington, Mass.: Lexington, 1977, pp. 21–46.

Bezdek, Roger H. "Federal Matching Requiring and State-Local Government Spending." In U.S. Department of the Treasury, *Federal-State-Local Fiscal Relations: Technical Papers*. Washington, D.C.: Government Printing Office, 1986, vol. 3, pp. 855–70.

Blair, George S. "Changing Federal-Local Relations." In Richard H. Leach, ed., *Intergovernmental Relations in the 1980s*. New York: Marcel Dekker, 1983, pp. 33–43.

Block, Beate. "Supreme Court Helps, Hurts Federalism." *State Government News* 28 (September 1985): 20–21.

Bowden, Henry L., Jr. "A Conceptual Refinement of the Doctrine of Federal Preemption." *Journal of Public Law* 22 (Fall 1973): 391–405.

Bowman, Ann O. M. "Hazardous Waste Management: An Emerging Policy Area within an Emerging Federalism." *Publius* 15 (Winter 1985): 131–44.

Bowsher, Charles A. "Federal Cutbacks Strengthen State Role." *State Government News* 29 (February 1986): 18–21.

Briceland, Alan V. "Virginia's Ratification of the U.S. Constitution." *Newsletter* (Institute of Government, University of Virginia) 61 (October 1984): 1–14.

Brown, George D. "The Tenth Amendment Is Dead. Long Live the Eleventh!" *Intergovernmental Perspective* 13 (Winter 1987): 26–30.

Buckley, James L. "The Trouble with Federalism: It Isn't Being Tried." *Commonsense* 1 (Summer 1978): 1–17.

Bullock, Charles S., III. "Role of the Expert in Voting Rights Litigation." *National Civic Review* 74, no. 10 (November 1985): 493–96.

"Busing in Boston." *New Perspectives* 17 (Fall 1985): 36–37.

Byczynski, Lynn. "Judge Raises Taxes to Pay for School Bias Remedy." *The National Law Journal*, 5 October 1987, 25.

Capozzola, John M. "Affirmative Action Alive and Well Under Courts' Strict Scrutiny." *National Civic Review* 75 (November/December 1986): 354–62.

Caraley, Demetrios. "Changing Conceptions of Federalism." *Political Science Quarterly* 101 (1986): 289–306.

Carmody, Robert F. "Attacking the Myth of Uncontrollable Expenditures." In

Richard H. Leach, ed., *Intergovernmental Relations in the 1980s.* New York: Marcel Dekker, 1983, pp. 75–85.

Carnival, Douglas. "Here's How State Anti-takeover Law Survived Constitutional Test." *Minnesota Journal* 2 (12 February 1985): 1, 7.

Carson, Clarence B. "The Meaning of Federalism." *The Freeman* 33 (January 1983): 12–23.

Clark, Charles E. "New Hampshire's First Look at Anti-Ratification Arguments." *The Keene Sentinel,* 18 November 1987, 5.

Collins, Ronald K. L. "New England's Where the Action is As the 'New Federalism' Heads East." *The National Law Journal,* 18 November 1985, 18–20.

Conlan, Timothy J. "Politics and Governance: Conflicting Trends in the 1990s? *The Annals* 509 (May 1990): 128–38.

———. "The Politics of Federal Block Grants: From Nixon to Reagan." *Political Science Quarterly* 99 (Summer 1984): 247–70.

Cooper, Ann. "FTC Suits Spur Congress to Protect Cities from Paying Antitrust Damages." *National Journal* 16 (18 August 1984): 1569–72.

Cooper, Philip J. "Conflict or Constructive Tension: The Changing Relationship of Judges and Administrators." *Public Administration Review* 45 (November 1985): 643–51.

Coyle, Marcia. "Ban OK's on Agency-Review Forum Shopping." *The National Law Review* 10 (January 25, 1988): 9.

Crihfield, Brevard, and Reeves, H. Clyde. "Intergovernmental Relations: A View from the States." *The Annals* 416 (November 1974): 99–107.

Crone, Theodore, and DeFina, Robert H. "Cleaning the Air with the Invisible Hand." *Business Review* (Federal Reserve Bank of Philadelphia) (November/December 1983): 11–19.

Crotty, Patricia M. "Assessing the Role of Federal Administrative Regions: An Exploratory Analysis." *Public Administration Review* 48 (March/April 1988): 642–48.

———. "The New Federalism Game: Primacy Implementation of Environmental Policy." *Publius* 17 (Spring 1987): 53–67.

Derthick, Martha. "American Federalism: Madison's 'Middle Ground' in the 1980s." *Public Administration Review* 47 (January/February 1987): 66–74.

Distasco, John. "NRC Adopts New Nuke Evac Rule." *The Union Leader* (Manchester, N.H.), 30 October 1987, 1, 9.

Downey, Gary L. "Federalism and Nuclear Waste Disposal: The Struggle over Shared Decision Making." *Journal of Policy Analysis and Management* 5 (1985): 73–99.

Durant, Robert F., and Holmes, Michelle D. "Thou Shall Not Covet Thy Neighbor's Water: The Rio Grande Basin Regulatory Experience." *Public Administration Review* 45 (November/December 1985): 821–31.

Durham, G. Homer. "Politics and Administration in Intergovernmental Relations." *The Annals* 207 (January 1940): 1–6.

Dusenbury, Patricia J., and Beyle, Thad L. "The Community Development Block Grant Program: Policy by Formula." *State and Local Government Review* 12 (September 1980): 82–90.

Dye, Thomas R., and Hurley, Thomas L. "Responsiveness of Federal and State Governments to Urban Problems." *Journal of Politics* 40 (February 1978): 196–207.

Elazar, Daniel J. "The Federal Government and Local Government Reform." *National Civic Review* 72 (April 1983): 190–98.

———. "Is Federalism Compatible with Prefectorial Administration?" *Publius* 11 (Spring 1981): 3–22.

———. "Opening the Third Century of American Federalism: Issues and Prospects." *The Annals* 509 (May 1990): 11–21.

———. "States as Polities in the Federal System." *National Civic Review* 70 (February 1981): 72–82.

"Enforcement May Be Weakest Link in States." *Conservation Foundation Letter* (November 1980): 1–8.

"Federal Judge Orders a Panel to Monitor State Schools for Retarded." *The Boston Globe,* 15 March 1986, 16.

Feron, James. "Yonkers Council, in a 4-to-3 Vote, Defies Judge on Integration Plan." *The New York Times,* 2 August 1988, 1, B3.

Fiordalisi, Georgina. "Schools Given Reprieve on Asbestos Date." *City & State* 5 (1 August 1988): 4.

Fix, Michael. "Regulatory Relief: The Real New Federalism?" *State Government News* 28 (January 1985): 7–8, 14.

Foderaro, Lisa W. "U.S. Court Halts Fines for Yonkers on Desegregation." *The New York Times,* 10 August 1988, 1, B2.

Fordham, Jefferson B. "To Foster Disunity." *National Civil Review* 52 (September 1963): 5–8, 20.

Franklin, Ben A. "Nuclear Panel Denies Waiver on New Hampshire Reactor." *The New York Times,* 23 April 1987, A24.

Franklin, James L. "Court Denies License Delay at Seabrook," *The Boston Globe,* 15 March 1990, 1 and 22.

Fried, Robert C. "Prefectorialism in America?" *Publius* 11 (Spring 1981): 23–29.

Friedman, Frank B. "Corporate Environmental Programs and Litigation: The Role of Lawyer-Managers in Environmental Management." *Public Administration Review* 45 (November 1985): 766–69.

Fulton, William. "EPA Sanctions Smoggy Cities." *City & State* 4 (August 1987): 3, 22.

Gemperlein, Joyce. "Coffers Bare, Johnstown Grinds Along." *The Philadelphia Inquirer,* 11 January 1987, B1, B5.

Gosling, James J. "Changing U.S. Transportation Policy and the States." *State and Local Government Review* 20 (Spring 1988): 84–93.

Grainey, Michael W. "Federal Energy Policy and State Solar Incentives Programs, Federalism Stuck in Reverse Gear." *Solar Today* 1 (September/October 1987): 18–20.

Grant, J. A. C. "The Scope and Nature of Concurrent Power." *Columbia Law Review* 34 (June 1934): 995–1040.

Graves, W. Brooke, ed. "Intergovernmental Relations in the United States." *The Annals* 207 (January 1940): 1–218.

Gurwitt, Rob. "The Tap Has Run Dry on EPA Extensions to the Clean Water Act." *Governing* 1 (January 1988): 15–19.

Hamilton, Randy H. "Local Self-Government Through Citizen Legislators: The Bedrock of Liberty." In *Is Constitutional Reform Necessary to Reinvigorate Federalism: A Roundtable Discussion*. Washington, D.C.: U.S. Advisory Commission on Intergovernmental Relations, 1987, pp. 17–25.

Hanks, William E., and Coran, Stephen E. "Federal Preemption of Obscenity Law Applied to Cable Television." *Journalism Quarterly* 63 (Spring 1986): 43–47.

Hanus, Jerome J. "Intergovernmental Authority Costs." In Richard H. Leach, ed., *Intergovernmental Relations in the 1980s*. New York: Marcel Dekker, 1983, pp. 57–73.

Harris, Joseph F. "The Future of Federal Grants-in-Aid." *The Annals* 207 (January 1940): 14–26.

Hart, Henry M., Jr. "The Relations Between State and Federal Law." *Columbia Law Review* 54 (April 1954): 489–542.

Hartman, Paul J., and McCoy, Thomas R. "Garcia: The Latest Retreat on the 'States Rights' Front." *Intergovernmental Perspective* 11 (Spring/Summer 1985): 8–11.

Hawkins, Robert B., Jr. "The Chairman's View." *Intergovernmental Perspective* 11 (Spring/Summer 1985): 22–23.

———. "Conclusion: Administrative versus Political Reform." In Robert B. Hawkins, Jr., ed., *American Federalism: A New Partnership for the Republic*. San Francisco: Institute for Contemporary Studies, 1982, pp. 247–52.

———. "Turnbacks: A Promising Approach." *Intergovernmental Perspective* 12 (Summer 1986): 10–12.

Henderson, James A., Jr., and Pearson, Richard N. "Implementing Federal Environmental Policies: The Limits of Aspirational Commands." *Columbia Law Review* 78 (November 1978): 1429–70.

Hernandez, Peggy. "Garrity Expected to Yield Control of Schools Today." *The Boston Globe,* 3 September 1985, 15.

Herzik, Eric B., and Pelissero, John P. "Decentralization, Redistribution, and Community Development: A Reassessment of the Small Cities CDBG Program." *Public Administration Review* 46 (January/February 1986): 31–36.

Hettinger, Kyle B. "NLRA Preemption of State and Local Plan Relocation

Laws." *Columbia Law Review* 86 (March 1986): 407–26.

Hickok, Eugene W., Jr. "Federalism's Future before the U.S. Supreme Court." *The Annals* 509 (May 1990): 73–82.

Hill, Gladwin. "EPA Head, Conceding Errors, Reports Gain on Water Pollution." *The New York Times,* 10 October 1979, A24.

_____. "E.P.A. Plans a Drive on Sewage Cleanup." *The New York Times,* 11 October 1979, A17.

Holcombe, Arthur N. "The Coercion of States in a Federal System." In Arthur W. MacMahon, *Federalism: Mature and Emergent.* Garden City, N.Y.: Doubleday, 1955, pp. 137–56.

Howard, A.E. Dick. "Garcia and the Values of Federalism: On the Need for a Recurrence to Fundamental Principles." *Georgia Law Review* 19 (Summer 1985): 789–97.

_____. "Garcia: Federalism's Principles Forgotten." *Intergovernmental Perspective* 11 (Spring/Summer 1985): 12–14.

_____. "Judicial Federalism: The States and the Supreme Court." In Robert B. Hawkins, Jr., ed., *American Federalism: A New Partnership for the Republic.* San Francisco: Institute for Contemporary Studies, 1982, pp. 215–37.

_____. "The Roots of American Constitutional Principles." *Newsletter* (Institute of Government, University of Virginia) 60 (January 1984): 25–30.

_____. "The Supreme Court and Federalism." In *The Courts: The Pendulum of Federalism.* Washington, D.C.: The Roscoe Pound–American Trial Lawyers Foundation, 1979, pp. 49–79.

Howard, Jeffrey H., and McCabe, John L. "New Cable TV Law: Opportunity to Improve Service." *Current Municipal Problems* 14 (1987): 106–17.

Howard, S. Kenneth. "A Message from Garcia." *Public Administration Review* 45 (November 1985): 738–41.

Hrezo, M. S., and Hrezo, W. E. "From Antagonistic to Cooperative Federalism on Water Resource Development." *The American Journal of Economics and Sociology* 44 (April 1985): 199–214.

Hudson, Edward. "Accord Allows Westchester to Restrict Airport Activity." *The New York Times,* 5 March 1985, B2.

Johnson, Gerald W., and Heilman, John G. "Metapolicy Transition and Policy Implementation: New Federalism and Privatization." *Public Administration Review* 47 (November/December 1987): 468–78.

Johnson, Stephen J., and Spiegel, Hans B. C. "Helping to Decide Who Gets What: Evaluating Communities in Allocating Block Grant Funds." *National Civic Review* 74 (December 1985): 521–30.

Kaden, Lewis B. "Politics, Money, and State Sovereignty: The Judicial Role." *Columbia Law Review* 79 (June 1979): 847–97.

Kaufman, Irving R. "What Did the Founding Fathers Intend?" *The New York Times Magazine,* 23 February 1986, 42, 59–60, 67–69.

Kay, Kenneth R. "Limited Federal Court Jurisdiction: The Unforeseen Impact on Courts and Congress." *Judicature* 65 (October 1981): 185–89.

Kearney, Richard C., and Garey, Robert B. "American Federalism and the Management of Radioactive Wastes." *Public Administration Review* 42 (January/February 1982), 14–24.

Kearney, Richard C., and Stucker, John J. "Interstate Compacts and the Management of Low Level Radioactive Wastes." *Public Administration Review* 45 (January/February 1985), 210–20.

Kennedy, Jay B. "DOE Mandates: Taking Power Away from the States." *Public Utilities Fortnightly* 106 (November 6, 1980): 11–14.

Kessler, Jeffrey. "The Clean Air Act Amendments of 1970: A Threat to Federalism?" *Columbia Law Review* 76 (October 1976): 990–1028.

Key, V. O., Jr. "State Legislation Facilitative of Federal Action." *The Annals* 207 (January 1940): 7–13.

Kilpatrick, James J. "The Case for States Rights." In Robert A. Goldwin, ed., *A Nation of States: Essays on the American Federal System.* 2d ed. Chicago: Rand McNally, 1974, pp. 91–107.

Kincaid, John. "From Cooperative to Coercive Federalism." *The Annals* 509 (May 1990): 139–52.

Koch, Edward I. "The Mandate Millstone," *The Public Interest* 61 (Fall 1980):42–57.

Laski, Harold J. "The Obsolescence of Federalism." *The New Republic,* 3 May 1939, 362–69.

Leach, Richard H. "Federalism and the Constitution: Whither the American States?" *Newsletter* (Institute of Government, University of Virginia) 61 (December 1984): 21–25.

Lee, Dwight R. "The Political Economy of the U.S. Constitution." *The Freeman* 37 (February 1987): 59–69.

Levine, Charles H., and Posner, Paul L. "The Centralizing Effects of Austerity on the Intergovernmental System." *Political Science Quarterly* 96 (Spring 1981): 67–85.

Lobenz, George. "Lawmakers Pick Nevada to Host Nuke Waste Dump." *The Union Leader* (Manchester, N.H.), 18 December 1987, 16.

"Localities Get Antitrust Cost Relief." *Intergovernmental Perspective* 10 (Fall 1984): 4.

Lovell, Catherine H. " 'Deregulation' of Intergovernmental Programs: Early Results of the Reagan Policies." *Public Affairs Report* 25 (April 1984): 1–11.

_____. "Evolving Local Government Dependency." *Public Administration Review* 41 (January 1981): 189–202.

_____. "Some Thoughts on Hyperintergovernmentalization." In Richard H. Leach, ed., *Intergovernmental Relations in the 1980s.* New York: Marcel Dekker, 1983, pp. 87–97.

Low-Beer, John R. "The Constitutional Imperative of Proportional Representation." *The Yale Law Journal* 94 (November 1984): 163–88.

Lynch, Edward J. "Commerce and the American Character: Constitutional Stability Amid Technological Changes." *Newsletter* (Institute of Government, University of Virginia) 61 (April 1985): 45–50.

MacManus, Susan A. "Financing Federal, State, and Local Governments in the 1990s." *The Annals* 509 (May 1990): 22–35.

_____. "Mixed Electoral Systems: The Newest Reform Structure." *National Civic Review* 74 (November 1985): 482–92.

Marek, Elizabeth A. "Education by Decree." *New Perspectives* 17 (Summer 1985): 36–41.

"Massachusetts Governor Seeks to Stop Nuclear Plant Opening." *The New York Times,* 21 September 1986, 24.

Meese, Edwin, III. "The Attorney General's View of the Supreme Court: Toward a Jurisprudence of Original Intention." *Public Administration Review* 45 (November 1985): 701–4.

_____. "Taking Federalism Seriously." *Intergovernmental Perspective* 13 (Winter 1987): 8–10.

Melnick, R. Shep. "The Politics of Partnership." *Public Administration Review* 45 (November 1985): 653–60.

Menzel, Donald C. "Implementation of the Federal Surface Mining Control and Reclamation Act of 1977." *Public Administration Review* 41 (March/April 1981): 212–19.

Miller, Louise B. "The Burger Court's View of the Relationship Between the States and Their Municipalities." *Publius* 17 (Spring 1987): 85–92.

Moore, W. John. "Mandates Without Money." *National Journal,* 4 October 1986, 2366–70.

Morris, Thomas R. "The Supreme Court and Interstate Commerce." *Newsletter* (Institute of Government, University of Virginia) 61 (March 1985): 39–44.

Mosher, Frederick C. "The Changing Responsibilities and Tactics of the Federal Government." *Public Administration Review* 40 (November/December 1980): 541–48.

Moynihan, Daniel P. "On Court Stripping." *Congressional Record,* 10 December 1985, S17274–76.

Nagel, Robert F. "Federalism as a Fundamental Value: National League of Cities in Perspective," In *1981: The Supreme Court Review.* Chicago: University of Chicago Press, 1982, pp. 81–109.

Nathan, Richard P. "The New Federalism Versus the Emerging New Structuralism." *Publius* 5 (Summer 1975): 111–29.

Nathan, Richard P., and Dommel, Paul R. "Federal-Local Relations under Block Grants." *Political Science Quarterly* 93 (Fall 1978): 421–42.

Nathan, Richard P., and Lago, John R. "Intergovernmental Fiscal Roles and Relations." *The Annals* 509 (May 1990).

Neighbor, Howard D. "The Supreme Court Speaks, Sort of, on the 1982

Voting Rights Act Amendments." *National Civic Review* 75 (November/ December 1986): 346–53.

Neiman, Max, and Lovell, Catherine. "Federal and State Mandating: A First Look at the Mandate Terrain." *Administration & Society* 14 (November 1982): 343–72.

"Nevada's Radioactive Jackpot." *The New York Times,* 5 January 1988, A18.

"New Federal Environmental Mandate Applies to Counties as well as to Industries." *Georgia County Government* 39 (February 1988): 10–17.

Nichol, Gene R., Jr. "The Judicial Protection of Unenumerated Constitutional Rights." *Newsletter* (Institute of Government, University of Virginia) 62 (August 1986): 77–81.

O'Brien, David M. "Opening the Courthouse Doors: The First Amendment as the Key." *Newsletter* (Institute of Government, University of Virginia) 61 (May 1985): 51–56.

"Ohio Told to Meet Clean-Air Deadline." *The New York Times.* 18 October 1979, p. A16.

Ostrom, Vincent. "The Meaning of Federalism in the *Federalist:* A Critical Examination of the Diamond Theses." *Publius* 15 (Winter 1985): 1–21.

Pemberton, Jackson. "On Amendment XVII." *The Freeman* 26 (November 1976): 654–60.

Perlman, Ellen. "EPA Small-City Study Backfires." *City & State* 5 (23 May 1988): 1, 31.

Peterson, Doug. "Failing Grades Given on Deficit, City Issues." *Nation's Cities Weekly* 10 (January 5, 1987): 5–7.

Peterson, Paul. "Federalism at the American Founding: In Defense of the Diamond Theses." *Publius* 15 (Winter 1985): 23–29.

Pols, Cynthia M. "The Fair Labor Standards Act: New Implications for Public Employers." In *The Municipal Year Book 1986.* Washington, D.C.: International City Management Association, 1986, pp. 80–89.

Powell, H. Jefferson. "The Original Understanding of Original Intent." *Harvard Law Review* 98 (March 1985): 885–948.

"Questions and Answers to Guide Local Officials through Fair Labor Compliance." *Georgia County Government* 37 (September 1985): 9, 11–20.

Raffel, Jeffrey A. "The Impact of Metropolitan School Desegregation on Public Opinion: A Longitudinal Analysis." *Urban Affairs Quarterly* 21 (December 1985): 245–65.

Rapaczynski, Andrzej. "From Sovereignty to Process: The Jurisprudence of Federalism after Garcia." In Philip B. Kurland, Gerhard Casper, and Dennis J. Hutchinson, eds., *1985: The Supreme Court Review.* Chicago: University of Chicago Press, 1986.

"The Reagan Record." *The Urban Institute Policy and Research Report* 14 (August 1984), 1–17.

Reagan, Ronald. "America's Agenda for the Future." *Congressional Record,* 6 February 1986, S1137–45.

———. "Federalism: Executive Order 12612, October 26, 1987." *Weekly Compilation of Presidential Documents,* 2 November 1987, 1230–33.

———. "Regulatory Program of the U.S. Government—Message from the President Received During the Adjournment—PM 73." *Congressional Record,* 14 August 1985, S11023–24.

"Redefining the National League of Cities State Sovereignty Doctrine." *University of Pennsylvania Law Review* 129 (June 1980): 1460–84.

Reeves, Mavis Mann. "The States as Politics: Reformed, Reinvigorated, Resourceful." *The Annals* 509 (May 1990): 83–93.

Reischauer, Robert D. "Governmental Diversity: Bane of the Grants Strategy in the United States. "In Wallace E. Oates, ed., *The Political Economy of Fiscal Federalism.* Lexington, Mass.: Lexington, 1977, pp. 115–27.

Rice, Charles E. "Limiting Federal Court Jurisdiction: The Constitutional Basis for the Proposals in Congress Today." *Judicature* 65 (October 1981): 190–97.

Riley, Joseph P., Jr. "Turnbacks: A Misguided Effort." *Intergovernmental Perspective* 12 (Summer 1986): 14–16.

Robbins, William. "Racial Bias Ruling Raises School Taxes." *The New York Times,* 17 September 1987, A20.

Roberts, Robert N. "Municipal Antitrust Immunity and the State-Action Exemption: Developments in the Law." *State Government* 55 (Winter 1986): 164–71.

Ross, Douglas. "Safeguarding 'Our Federalism': Lessons for the States from the Supreme Court." *Public Administration Review* 45 (November 1985): 723–31.

Salmon, David D. "The Federalist Principle: The Interaction of the Commerce Clause and the Tenth Amendment in the Clean Air Act." *Columbia Journal of Environmental Law* 2 (1976): 290–367.

Scheiber, Harry N. "The Condition of American Federalism: An Historian's View." In Frank Smallwood, ed., *The New Federalism.* Hanover, N.H.: The Public Affairs Center, Dartmouth College, 1967, pp. 19–55.

———. "Federalism and Legal Process: Historical and Contemporary Analysis of the American System." *Law & Society Review* 14 (Spring 1980): 633–722.

Schmidhauser, John R., and McAnaw, Richard L. "Calhoun Revisited." *National Civic Review* 52 (September 1963): 17–20.

Scholz, John T., and Wei, Feng Heng. "Regulatory Enforcement in a Federalist System." *The American Political Science Review* 80 (December 1986): 1249–88.

Schultze, Charles L. "Federal Spending: Past, Present, and Future." In Henry Owen and Charles L. Schultze, eds., *Setting National Priorities: The Next Ten Years.* Washington D.C.: Brookings Institution, 1976, pp. 323–69.

Seltzer, E. Manning, and Steinberg, Robert E. "To Succeed, Developers of

Wetlands Must Justify Proposals from Outset." *The National Law Journal,* 8 December 1986, 24–26.

Sentell, R. Perry, Jr. "Gesticulations of Garcia." *Urban Georgia* 35 (October 1985): 33–35.

Shabecoff, Philip. "Most Sewage Plants Meeting Latest Goal of Clean Water Act." *The New York Times,* 28 July 1988, 1, A18.

Smith, Zachary A. "Federal Intervention in the Management of Groundwater Resources: Past Efforts and Future Prospects." *Publius* 15 (Winter 1985): 145–59.

Stark, J. Norman, and Stark, M. C. D. "Court Orders New Standards: OSHA Hazard Communication Standard Mandates Compliance for Employee Safety." *Current Municipal Problems* 14, no. 4 (1988): 476–88.

Stewart, Richard B. "Pyramids of Sacrifice? Problems of Federalism in Mandating State Implementaiton of National Economic Policy." *The Yale Law Journal* 86 (May 1977): 1196–1272.

Sundquist, James L. "In Defense of Pragmatism: A Response to 'Is Federalism Compatible with Prefectorial Administration?' " *Publius,* 11 (Spring 1981): 31–37.

"Supreme Court Okays Seabrook," *The Keene Sentinel* (New Hampshire), 27 April 1990, 1.

Swindler, William F. "Congressional Bypass." *National Civic Review* 52 (September 1963): 9–16.

————. "Our First Constitution: The Articles of Confederation." *American Bar Association Journal* 69 (February 1981): 166–69.

Sylves, Richard T. "Nuclear Power Plants and Emergency Planning: An Intergovernmental Nightmare." *Public Administration Review* 44 (September/October 1984): 393–401.

Taylor, Telford. "Limiting Federal Court Jurisdiction: The Unconstitutionality of Current Legislative Proposals." *Judicature* 65 (October 1981): 199–207.

Temples, James R. "The Nuclear Regulatory Commission and the Politics of Regulatory Reform: Since Three Mile Island." *Public Administration Review* 42 (July/August 1982): 355–62.

Thomas, Robert D. "National-Local Relations and the City's Dilemma." *The Annals* 509 (May 1990): 106–17.

Trevor, Leigh B., and Edwards, John W., II. "CTS Reaffirms State Role in Corporate Affairs." *The National Law Journal,* 8 February 1988, 22, 24.

Tye, Larry, "NRC Approves Licesning of Seabrook," *The Boston Globe,* 2 March 1990, 1 and 12.

"U.S. is Faulted for Role in Water Quality," *The New York Times,* 8 October 1990 A9.

Van Alstyne, William W. "The Second Death of Federalism." *Michigan Law Review* 83 (June 1985): 1709–33.

Vitrres, M. Elliot. " 'New Wave Federalism' and the Dilemma for State Government." *State Government* 59 (September/October 1986): 91–94.

Wald, Matthew L. "Clean Air Deadline is History." *The New York Times* 3 January 1988, E9.

Walker, David B. "Intergovernmental Management and the Federal System: Where Have We Been (1964–1988) and What Have We Learned?" *Assistance Management Journal* 5 (Winter 1989): 19–24.

———. "Intergovernmental Relations and Dysfunctional Federalism." *National Civic Review* 71 (February 1981): 68–76, 82.

———. "Intergovernmental Relations and the Well-Governed City: Cooperation, Confrontation, Clarification." *National Civic Review* 75 (March/April 1986): 65–97.

———. "A Perspective on Intergovernmental Relations." In Richard H. Leach, ed., *Intergovernmental Relations in the 1980s*. New York: Marcel Dekker, 1983, pp. 1–13.

———. "Some Perspectives on the Impact of Reagan Federalism." *Assistance Management Journal* 4 (Spring 1987): 1–12.

Wasby, Stephen L. "Arrogation of Power or Accountability: 'Judicial Imperialism' Revisited." *Judicature* 65 (October 1981): 208–19.

Wechsler, Herbert. "The Political Safeguards of Federalism: The Role of the States in the Composition and Selection of the National Government." In Arthur W. MacMahon, *Federalism: Mature and Emergent*. Garden City, N.Y.: Doubleday, 1955, pp. 97–136.

———. "Toward Neutral Principles of Constitutional Law." *Harvard Law Review* 73 (November 1959): 1–35.

Weissman, Charles I. "United Transportation Union v. Long Island Rail Road: National League of Cities Derailed?" *Rutgers Law Review* 34 (Fall 1981): 189–219.

Williamson, Richard S. "Block Grants—A Federalist Tool." *State Government* 54, no. 4 (1981), 114–17.

———. "Reagan Federalism: Goals and Achievements." In Lewis G. Bender, and James A. Stever, eds. *Administering the New Federalism*. Boulder, Colo.: Westview Press, 1986, pp. 41–73.

———. "A Review of Reagan Federalism." In Robert B. Hawkins, Jr., ed., *American Federalism: A New Partnership for the Republic*. San Francisco: Institute for Contemporary Studies, 1982, pp. 99–110.

———. "The Self-Government Balancing Act: A View from the White House." *National Civic Review* 71 (January 1982): 19–22.

Winkle, John W., III. "Interjudicial Relations." In Richard H. Leach, ed., *Intergovernmental Relations in the 1980s*. New York: Marcel Dekker, 1983, pp. 45–56.

Witt, Elder. "The Civil (Defense) War Between the States and the Federal Government." *Governing* (June 1988): 19–22.

Wright, Deil S. "Intergovernmental Relations: An Analytical Overview." *The Annals* 416 (November 1974): 1–16.

———. "Intergovernmental Relations in the 1980s: A New Phase of IGS." In

Richard H. Leach, ed., *Intergovernmental Relations in the 1980s.* New
York: Marcel Dekker, 1983, pp. 15–32.

_____. "Policy Shifts in the Politics and Administration of Intergovernmen-
tal Relations, 1930s–1990s." *The Annals* 509 (May 1990): 60–72.

Yarbrough, Jean. "Rethinking 'The Federalist's View of Federalism.' " *Publius* 15 (Winter 1985): 31–53.

Yarbrough, Tinsley E. "The Political World of Federal Judges as Managers."
Public Administration Review 45 (November 1985): 660–66.

Ylvisaker, Paul. "Some Criteria for a 'Proper' Areal Division of Governmental Power." In Arthur Maas, ed., *Area and Power.* Glencoe, Ill.: Free
Press, 1959, pp. 27–49.

Zaleski, Alexander V. "A New Authority for Massachusetts: Best Solution for
A Difficult Task." *National Civic Review* 74 (December 1985): 531–37.

Zimmerman, Joseph F. "Alternative Local Electoral Systems." *National Civic
Review* 79 (January/February 1990): 23–36.

_____. "Can Governmental Functions be 'Rationally Reassigned'?" *National
Civic Review* 73 (March 1984): 125–31.

_____. "Cities Versus Atoms." *National Civic Review* 50 (April 1961): 183–
88.

_____. "The Cooperative Approach to Environmental Enhancement." In
U.S. Environmental Protection Agency, *Managing the Environment.*
Washington, D.C.: Government Printing Office, 1974, pp. 367–83.

_____. "Developing State-Local Relations: 1987–1989." In *The Book of the
States: 1990–91 Edition.* Lexington, Ky.: The Council of State Governments, 1990, pp. 533–48.

_____. "A 'Fair' Voting System for Local Governments." *National Civic
Review* 68 (October 1979): 481–87, 507.

_____. "Federal Judicial Remedial Power: The Yonkers Case." *Publius* 20
(Summer 1990): 45–61.

_____. "Federal Preemption: A Recommended ACIR Research Agenda."
Publius 14 (Summer 1984): 175–81.

_____. Federal Preemption of State and Local Government Activities." *Se-
ton Hall Legislative Journal* 13 (1989): 25–51.

_____. "The Federal Voting Rights Act and Alternative Election Systems."
William and Mary Law Review 19 (Summer 1978): 621–60.

_____. "The Federal Voting Rights Act: Its Impact on Annexation." *Na-
tional Civic Review* 66 (June 1977): 278–83.

_____. "Frustrating National Policy: Partial Federal Preemption." In
Jerome J. Hanus, ed., *The Nationalization of State Government.* Lexington, Mass: Lexington Books, 1981, pp. 75–104.

_____. "Local Representation: Designing a Fair System." *National Civic
Review* 69 (June 1980): 307–12.

_____. "Mandating in New York State." In *State Mandating of Local Ex-
penditures.* Washington, D.C.: U.S. Advisory Commission on In-

tergovernmental Relations, 1978, pp. 69–85.

_____. "The Metropolitan Area Problem." *The Annals* 416 (November 1974): 133–47.

_____. "Metropolitan Governance: The Intergovernmental Dimension." In Alan K. Campbell and Roy W. Bahl, eds., *State and Local Government.* New York: Free Press, 1976, pp. 54–64.

_____. "The Metropolitan Governance Maze in the United States." *Urban Law and Policy* 2 (1979): 265–84.

_____. "The Municipal Stake in Environmental Protection." In *Municipal Year Book, 1972.* Washington, D.C.: International City Management Association, 1972, pp. 105–9.

_____. "A National Tax Credit Program: Could It Replace Federal Grants?" *National Civic Review* 71 (October 1982): 459–60, 467.

_____. "Obstacles to Establishment of Interstate Compacts." In Deirdre A. Zimmerman, and Joseph F. Zimmerman, eds., *The Politics of Subnational Governance.* Lanham, Md.: University Press of America, 1983, pp. 66–72.

_____. "The Patchwork Approach: Adaptive Responses to Increasing Urbanization." In Amos H. Hawley and Vincent P. Rock, eds., *Metropolitan America in Contemporary Perspective.* New York: Halsted, 1973, pp. 431–98.

_____. "Political Boundaries and Air Pollution Control." *Journal of Urban Law* 46, no. 2 (1969): 173–97.

_____. "Pollution Abatement by Regional Action." In Steven Carter and Lyle Sumek, eds., *An Anthology of Selected Readings for the National Conference on Managing the Environment.* Washington, D.C.: International City Management Association, 1973, pp. III-44–56.

_____. "Public Finance in a Federal System." In Sanford D. Gordon, ed., *The Economy of New York State.* Cincinnati: South-Western, 1987, pp. 122–26.

_____. "Reforming the Single Member District Electoral System." *Georgia County Government Magazine* 32 (March 1981): 12, 21–24.

_____. "Regulating Atomic Energy in the Federal System." *Publius* 18 (Summer 1988): 51–65.

_____. "Regulating Intergovernmental Relations in the 1990s." *The Annals* 509 (May 1990): 48–59.

_____. "The Role of the State Legislature in Air Pollution Abatement." *Suffolk University Law Review* 5 (Spring 1971): 850–77.

_____. "The Single-Member District System: Can It Be Reformed?" *National Civic Review* 70 (May 1981): 255–59.

_____. "The State Mandate Problem." *State and Local Government Review* 19 (Spring 1987): 78–84.

_____. "Zoning for Atomic Energy Uses." *Zoning Digest* 16 (1964): 161–69.

Unpublished Materials

Addresses

Burns, Arnold I., Associate Attorney General of the United States. Before the American Bar Association Annual Meeting. San Francisco, Calif., August 11, 1987.

_____. Before the Center for Civic Education International Conference on the Constitution. Washington, D.C., April 1, 1986.

Meese, Edwin, III, Attorney General of the United States. Before the American Enterprise Institute, Washington, D.C., September 6, 1985.

_____. Conservative Political Action Conference, Washington, D.C., January 30, 1986.

_____. Before the D.C. Chapter of the Federalist Society Lawyers Division, Washington, D.C., November 15, 1985.

_____. Before the Economic Club of New York, New York City, January 23, 1986.

_____. Before the Federal Bar Association, Detroit, Mich., September 13, 1985.

_____. Before the Palm Beach County Bar Association, West Palm Beach, Fla., February 10, 1986.

_____. Before the St. Louis School of Law, St. Louis, Mo., September 12, 1986.

_____. To Students and Faculty of Dickinson College, Carlisle, Pa., September 17, 1985.

Kennedy, Edward M. Conference on Federalism, Center for National Policy, Boston, Mass., May 8, 1982.

Reynolds, William Bradford, Assistant Attorney General, Civil Rights Division. Before the Wilmington Rotary Club, Wilmington, Del., October 31, 1985.

Stevens, Justice John Paul. Luncheon Meeting of the Federal Bar Association, Chicago, Ill., October 23, 1985.

Annual Message on the Administration of Justice from Warren E. Burger, Chief Justice of the United States. Presented at the Midyear Meeting of the American Bar Association, Detroit, Mich., February 17, 1985.

Barilleaux, Ryan J., and Bath, C. Richard. "The Coming Nationalization of Southwestern Water: A Cautionary Tale." A paper presented at a meeting of the Southwestern Political Science Association, San Antonio, Tex., March 20, 1986.

Beam, David R., Conlan, Timothy J., and Walker, David B. "Government in Three Dimensions: Implications of a Changing Federalism for Political Science." A paper presented at the 1982 annual meeting of the American Political Science Association, Denver, Colo., September 2–5, 1982.

Biden, Joseph R., Jr. "The Role of Advice and Consent in Constitutional

Interpretation." A paper presented at the Georgetown University Law Center, November 6, 1985.

Bork, Robert H. "The Constitution, Original Intent, and Economic Rights." A paper presented at the first Sharon Siegan Memorial Lecture, University of San Diego Law School, San Diego, Calif., November 18, 1985.

Bowers, James R. "The Supreme Court and Intergovernmental Relations: Searching for Voting Patterns." A paper presented at the annual meeting of the American Political Science Association, Washington, D.C., August 28–31, 1986.

Brennan, William J., Jr. "The Bill of Rights and the States: The Revival of State Constitutions as Guardians of Individual Rights." The James Madison Lecture, New York University, November 18, 1986.

———. "The Constitution of the United States: Contemporary Ratification." A paper presented at a text and teaching symposium, Georgetown University, Washington, D.C., October 12, 1985.

Caswell, Julie A. "Federal Preemption, State Regulation, and Food Safety and Quality: Major Research Issues." A paper presented at Resources for the Future Conference on Consumer Demands in the Marketplace, Airlie, Va., October 27–29, 1986.

Conlan, Timothy J. "Transformations in Party Politics and Their Implications for American Federalism." A paper presented at the 1985 annual meeting of the American Political Science Association, New Orleans, La., August 29–September 1, 1985.

Crotty, Patricia M. "The New Federalism Game: Options for the States." A paper presented at the annual meeting of the Northeastern Political Science Association, Philadelphia, Pa., November 14–16, 1985.

Fino, Susan P. "Unconstitutional Inequality: Judicial Review under State Equal Protection." A paper presented at the 1985 annual meeting of the American Political Science Association, New Orleans, La., August 29–September 1, 1985.

Garrity, W. Arthur, Jr. *Memorandum Regarding Final Orders.* Boston: U.S. District Court, D. Mass., November 1, 1985; memorandum filed in civil action no. 72-911-G, *Tallulah Morgan v. John A. Nucci.*

Gates, John B. "The Invalidation of State Statutes and Constitutional Provisions by the U.S. Supreme Court, 1837–1964: Judicial Review, Partisanship, and Critical Elections." A paper presented at the 1985 annual meeting of the American Political Science Association, New Orleans, La., August 29–September 1, 1985.

Gruhl, John. "Federalism and Contrasting Patterns of Compliance with U.S. Supreme Court Rulings." A paper presented at the 1979 annual meeting of the American Political Science Association, Washington, D.C., August 31-September 3, 1979.

Hyde, Albert C. "The Politics of Environmental Decision Making: The Non-Decision Issue." Ph.D. diss., State University of New York at Albany, 1980.

Kaufman, Irving R. "The Impossible Dream: The Improbable Genesis of the Constitution and the Contemporary Debate Over Its Meaning." A keynote address at the Student Conference on United States Affairs, U.S. Military Academy, West Point, N.Y., November 19, 1986.

Knapp, James I. K. "Intergovernmental Cooperation in Criminal Prosecutions under the Reagan Administration." A paper presented at the annual meeting of the Pennsylvania District Attorneys Association, Pittsburgh, Pa., February 6, 1986.

Koch, Edward I. "The Mandate Millstone." A statement made at the midwinter meeting of the U.S. Conference of Mayors, Washington, D.C., January 24, 1980.

Kraft, Michael E., Clary, Bruce B., and Tobin, Richard J. "The Impact of New Federalism on State Environmental Policy: The Midwestern Great Lakes States." A paper presented at a meeting of the Southwestern Political Science Association, San Antonio, Tex., March 19–22, 1985.

Letter to Chairman Strom Thurmond of the U.S. Senate Committee on the Judiciary, dated September 19, 1984, from Assistant Attorney General Robert A. McConnell, relative to interstate compacts formed in pursuance of the Low-Level Radioactive Waste Policy Act of 1980.

Light, Alfred R. "Federal Preemption, Federal Conscription under the New Superfund Act." A paper delivered at the annual meeting of the American Political Science Association, Washington, D.C., August 28–31, 1986.

Markham, Walter G. "Impact of Federal Initiatives on Local School Board Governance." A paper presented at the annual meeting of the Northeastern Political Science Association, Philadelphia, Pa., November 14–16, 1985.

Meese, Edwin, III. "The Law of the Constitution." A lecture presented at the Tulane University Citizen's Forum on the Bicentennial of the Constitution, New Orleans, La., October 21, 1986.

Merrifield, John. "The Federal Interest in Flexible Interstate Water Allocations in the Southwest." A paper presented at a meeting of the Southwestern Political Science Association, San Antonio, Tex., March 19–22, 1986.

Morris, Thomas R. "The Burger Court and Federalism: The Representation of State Interests before the U.S. Supreme Court." A paper presented at the 1985 annual meeting of the American Political Science Association, New Orleans, La., August 29–September 1, 1985.

Nagel, Robert F. "Federalism as a Subject of Interpretation." A paper presented at the 1986 annual meeting of the American Political Science Association, Washington, D.C., August 28, 1986.

Nathan, Richard P. "The Role of the States in American Federalism." A paper presented at the annual meeting of the American Political Science Association, Chicago, Ill., September 4, 1987.

Ostrom, Vincent. *"Garcia,* Constitutional Rule, and the Central Government Trap." A paper presented at the annual meeting of the American Political Science Association, Washington, D.C., August 28–31, 1986.

Quigley, John M., and Rubinfeld, Daniel L. "Budget Reform and the Theory of Fiscal Federalism." A paper prepared for the 1985 annual meeting of the American Economic Association, New York, N.Y., December 1985.

Remarks

Meese, Edwin, III, Attorney General of the United States. At the University of Richmond, Richmond, Va., September 17, 1986.

Reynolds, William Bradford, Assistant Attorney General, Civil Rights Division. At the American Jewish Committee Learned Hand Award Dinner, Los Angeles, Calif., January 23, 1985.

————. Before the Committee on Employment and Labor Relations Law of the Litigation Section and the Equal Employment Opportunity Committee of the Labor and Employment Law Section of the American Bar Association, New York, N.Y., August 12, 1986.

————. Before the Florida Bar Continuing Legal Education Committee and the Labor and Employment Law Section, Equal Employment Opportunity Practice Seminar, Miami, Fla., February 8, 1985.

————. Before the National Construction Industry Council, Washington, D.C., September 18, 1985.

————. Before the University of Chicago's Chapter of the Federalist Society, Chicago, Ill., January 10, 1986.

Reynolds, William B. "The Bicentennial: A Constitutional Restoration." Presented at the Lyndon Baines Johnson Library, The University of Texas, February 19, 1987.

————. "Civil Rights: Beyond the Conventional Agenda." Presented before the Stanford University Law School, San Francisco, Calif., February 17, 1987.

————. "Individual Rights: The Principle Matters." A speech delivered before The Whig-Cliosophic Society, Princeton University, Princeton, N.J., October 8, 1985.

————. "Securing Equal Liberty in an Egalitarian Age." A paper presented at the University of Missouri School of Law, Columbia, Mo., September 12, 1986.

Rockefeller, Nelson A. Remarks of the Vice President at the National Governors' Conference, Statler Hilton Hotel, Washington, D.C., Office of the Vice President, February 24, 1976 (mimeographed).

Rule, Charles F. "Deregulating Antitrust: The Quiet Revolution." A paper presented at the nineteenth New England Antitrust Conference, Antitrust at the Crossroads, Harvard University Law School, Cambridge, Mass., November 8, 1985.

Schram, Sanford F. "The Intergovenmental Structure of AFDC: The Consequences for the Poor in an Age of Social Cutbacks." A paper presented
at the annual conference of the New York State Political Science Associa-
tion, Albany, N.Y., April 5, 1986.
Shannon, John. "Fend-for-Yourself Federalism – The Reagan Contribution."
A paper presented at the annual meeting of the American Political
Science Association, Chicago, Ill., September 5, 1987.
Smith, Chesterfield. "Strong State Constitutions as the Key to a Viable Fed-
eral System." A paper delivered at the seventy-ninth National Con-
ference on Government, Dallas, Tex., November 15, 1973.
Smith, Zachary A. "Interstate Competition and Federal Intervention in
Groundwater Management." A paper presented at a meeting of the
Southwestern Political Science Association, San Antonio, Tex., March
19–22, 1986.

Statements
Fultz, Keith O., Associate Director, Resources, Community, and Economic
Development Division. Before the Subcommittee on Energy Research
and Production, House Committee on Science and Technology on Prog-
ress and Problems in Implementing the Nuclear Waste Policy Act of
1982, November 6, 1985 (Available from the U.S. General Accounting
Office, Washington, D.C. 20458).
Habicht, F. Henry, Assistant Attorney General, Land and Natural Resources
Division. Before the Subcommittee on Oversight and Investigations,
Committee on Energy and Commerce, U.S. House of Representatives
Concerning Federal Facility Compliance with Environmental Laws on
April 28, 1987.
_____. Before the Subcommittee on Water Resources, Committee on Public
Works and Transportation, House of Representatives, Concerning Su-
perfund Reauthorization on March 28, 1985.
Keeney, John C., Deputy Assistant Attorney General, Criminal Division.
Before the Subcommittee on Civil and Constitutional Rights, Committee
on the Judiciary, House of Representatives Concerning Election Fraud
on September 26, 1985.
Reynolds, William Bradford, Assistant Attorney General Civil Rights Divi-
sion. Before the Committee on Commerce and Human Resources, Sub-
committee on Labor, U.S. Senate, Concerning Impact of *Garcia v. San
Antonio Metropolitan Transit Authority* on September 10, 1985.
Stephens, Jay B., Associate Deputy Attorney General, U.S. Department of
Justice. Before the Subcommittee on Administrative Practice and Proce-
dure of the Senate Judiciary Committee Concerning S.1562 on Septem-
ber 17, 1985.
Trott, Stephen S., Assistant Attorney General, Criminal Division. Before the
Subcommittee on Criminal Justice, Committee on the Judiciary, U.S.

House of Representatives, Concerning Death Penalty Legislation on November 7, 1985.

———. Before the Committee on the Judiciary, U.S. Senate, Concerning Death Penalty Legislation—S.239—on September 24, 1985.

Stenberg, Carl W. "Federal-Local Relations in a Cutback Environment: Issues and Future Directions." A paper presented at the annual conference of the American Politics Group of the United Kingdom Political Studies Association, Manchester, England, January 4, 1980.

Tramontozzi, Paul N. "Opportunities for Reforming the Clean Water Act." Center for the Study of American Business, Washington University, St. Louis, Missouri, 1985.

Walker, David B. "The Changing Dynamics of Federal Aid to Cities." A paper presented at the annual meeting of the American Political Science Association, New York, N.Y., September 4, 1981.

———. "The Federal Role in Today's Intergovernmental Relations and the Emergence of Dysfunctional Federalism." A paper presented at the 86th National Conference on Government, Houston, Tex., November 15, 1980.

The Working Group on Federalism. "The Status of Federalism in America." Washington, D.C.: The Domestic Council, November 1986 (multilithed).

Zech, Lando W., Jr. Remarks at the National State Liaison Officer's Meeting, Washington, D.C., September 9, 1987 (available from the U.S. Nuclear Regulatory Commission).

Zimmerman, Joseph F. "The Dynamics of Intergovernmental Relations." A paper presented at a meeting of the New York State Assembly Graduate Scholars, Albany, N.Y., May 6, 1982.

———. "Electoral Systems and Direct Citizen Law-Making." A paper presented at the University of Würzburg, Federal Republic of Germany, July 1, 1987.

———. "Federalism and the Urban Fiscal System." A paper presented at a conference on The Challenge of the Eighties: Reforming the Urban Fiscal System, Cologne, Federal Republic of Germany, November 14, 1984.

———. "Federalism in the United States of America." A paper presented at Moscow State University, Moscow, U.S.S.R., June 4, 1990.

———. "Federalism in the United States: The Preemption Revolution." A paper presented at the Maxwell Graduate School, Syracuse University, Syracuse, New York, October 25, 1990.

———. "Federalism Theory in the Post Reagan Era." A paper presented at Die Geschwister-Scholl-Institut für Politische Wissenschaft, Der Universität München, July 3, 1989.

———. "Federal Preemption and the Erosion of Local Discretionary Authority." A paper presented at the Congress of Cities, Atlanta, Ga., December 1, 1980.

_____. "Federal Preemption under Reagan's New Federalism." A paper presented at the annual meeting of the American Political Science Association, Atlanta, Ga., September 1, 1989.

_____. "Fiscal Implications of Federal Mandates." A paper presented at the annual meeting of the American Political Science Association, Chicago, Ill., September 5, 1987.

_____. "A General Theory of American Federalism." A paper presented at Temple University, Philadelphia, Pa., March 28, 1990.

_____. "The Impact of Federal Preemption on the American Governance System." A paper presented at the annual conference of the American Politics Group of the United Kingdom Political Studies Association, Manchester, England, January 4, 1980.

_____. "Partial Federal Preemption and Changing Intergovernmental Relations." A paper presented at the 1979 annual meeting of the American Political Science Association, Washington, D.C., August 31–September 3, 1979.

_____. "Preemption, Federal Mandates, and Goal Achievement." A paper presented at the annual conference of the Council of University Institutes of Urban Affairs, Washington, D.C., March 20, 1980.

_____. "President Reagan's New Federalism." A paper presented at the University of Hamburg, Federal Republic of Germany, July 5, 1988.

_____. "Reforming the Single Member District System." A paper presented at the 86th annual National Conference on Government, Houston, Tex., November 17, 1980.

_____. "Representational Equity in Local Governments." A paper presented at the annual meeting of the American Political Science Association, San Francisco, Calif., August 31, 1990.

_____. "Representational Equity in Local Governments." A paper presented at the annual meeting of the American Political Science Association, San Francisco, Calif., August 31, 1990.

_____. "The Silent Revolution: Federal Preemption." A paper presented at the annual meeting of the American Political Science Association, Washington, D.C., September 4, 1988.

Index